ZANZIBAR
In Contemporary Times

Published in 2001 by
The Gallery Publications
P.O. Box 3181, Zanzibar
email: gallery@swahilicoast.com
http: www.galleryzanzibar.com

London office:
32 Deanscroft Avenue
London NW9 8EN
email: zjafferji@aol.com

© The Gallery Publications for modern and edited translation
Text by Robert Nunez Lyne
Edited by Mark Wilson
Designed by The Swahili Coast Publishers

ISBN 9987 667 08 2

All rights reserved. No part of this publication may be reproduced, stored in a retrieval system or transmitted, in any form or by any means, electronic, mechanical, photocopying, recording or otherwise, without the prior written permission of the publishers and the copyright holders

Cover picture: Biggest ivory tusks found in Zanzibar
Back cover: Zanzibar seafront before 1896
Previous page: Water-front of Zanzibar

ZANZIBAR
In Contemporary Times

A SHORT HISTORY OF THE SOUTHERN EAST
AFRICA IN THE NINETEENTH CENTURY

BY
ROBERT NUNEZ LYNE

GALLERY PUBLICATIONS

Dedicated to the memory of

SIR LLOYD WILLIAM MATHEWS, K.C.M. . G.,

First Minister of the Zanzibar Government,
and other Englishmen,
Pioneers of Progress and, Freedom,
who sacrificed their lives in the cause of
the Arab and the Slave,
and helped to bring to the Coast-Lands of East Africa

THE PAX BRITANNICA.

Go, stranger! track the deep, Free, free the white sail spread!
Wave may not foam, nor wild wind sweep, Where rest not England's dead.
England's Dead.
MRS. HEMANS.

PREFACE

IT has been my endeavour in the following chapters to describe briefly the most interesting persons and events that are connected with the history of the Rulers of Zanzibar and their Dominions on the East Coast of Africa during the nineteenth century, and to give some account of this Island of the Southern East, its people and industries. The story is that of an Arab potentate from the Persian Gulf founding a nation in a land which from time immemorial had been colonized by his countrymen; of a small and unnoticed, almost unknown island, advancing to wealth and fame, enslaving half a continent and afterwards at death grips with the Powers of Christendom; of those Powers, like vultures upon the prey, dividing the spoils of their exhausted victim; and of an island, still perhaps to some extent in the trough, yet buoyant and of fair promise.

Zanzibar is looked upon as an obscure corner of the earth. Few people know where it is; fewer still what it is. Yet it has a history, and a tragic one. This history has been moulded by our countrymen, whose achievements are recorded in the archives of the Foreign Office, the India Office, and the Admiralty. For facilities of research in those archives I am indebted to the kindness of Sir Clement Hill, K.C.M.G., C.B., and to other officials of those Departments, whose help and whose courtesy I here most gratefully acknowledge. I am also indebted to Sir John Kirk, K.C.M.G., K.C.B., F.R.S., etc., England's greatest pro-consul in East Africa, for many corrections and much assistance in the work; to Mr. Frank Adams, M.A., who kindly read through the manuscript - to Dr. A. H. Spurrier, His Honour Judge Lindsey Smith of Zanzibar and the Rev. Dr. Palmer, of Kirton Vicarage, Lincolnshire; to Mrs. George Cave and Mrs. Laurence for the record of circumstances connected with the life of their brother the late Sir Lloyd Mathews;

and to many friends, in the old country and in Zanzibar, for advice and sympathy, as well as for actual help.

But though my object has been to describe rather than criticise, I do not on that account expect to escape criticism myself. I would only ask indulgence of my readers for the story; for the manner of telling it I must plead guilty to many imperfections. Still it has been a labour of love, for I will confess to being among those upon whom the spell of Africa has fallen.

R.N. LYNE.

Zanzibar
   March 1905.

CONTENTS

Chap. Page

I. - First Appearance of the English - Ancient Records - The Portuguese - The Imamus of Oman...11
II. - Seyyid Said Bin Sultan..21
III. - Seyyid Said - Subjugation of Mombasa..27
IV. - Seyyid Said - Rise of Zanzibar - The Slave Traffic Across the Western Ocean..37
V. - Seyyid Majid - Rebellion in Zanzibar - Separation from Oman...........47
VI. - Seyyid Majid - The Slave Trade of Zanzibar and Arabia....................59
VII. - Zanzibar under Seyyid Majid...65
VIII. - Seyyid Barghash - Frere's Mission..69
IX. - Seyyid Barghash - Visit to England - Revival of the Slave Trade - Lieutenant Mathews..83
X. - Seyyid Barghash - The Death of Captain Brownrigg and its Results..97
XI. - Seyyid Barghash - The German Surprise of 1885.............................113
XII. - Seyyid Barghash - Delimitation - Portuguese Aggression.................119
XIII. - Seyyid Khalifa - Risings in the German Sphere - The Blockade.......129
XIV. - Witu and the British Coast - Mbaruk Rebellions.............................141
XV. - The End of Slavery..153
XVI. - Organisation of Zanzibar Government...165
XVII. - The Bombardment...171
XVIII. - Missions...181
XIX. - The People..187
XX. -The Plantation...209
XXI. - The Climate..231

CONTENTS

Chap.   Page

Appendix I.- Rulers of Zanzibar..243
      ,,   II.- Meteorology..244
      ,,   III.- Finance..255
      ,,   IV.- Commerce...257
      ,,   V.- Customs Duties...259
      ,,   VI.- Shipping..260
      ,,   VII.- Soils...262

Bibliography..264

CHAPTER I

FIRST APPEARANCE OF THE ENGLISH-ANCIENT RECORDS
THE PORTUGUESE-THE IMAMS OF OMAN

TOWARDS the close of the eighteenth century a British Squadron, under Commodore Blanket, was despatched to the Red Sea "to counteract the operations of Bonaparte, who, it was supposed, would attempt to get to India by way of the Red Sea or Persian Gulf." The squadron worked round the Cape of Good Hope, and in December, 1798, it was threshing up the east coast of Africa against the north-east monsoon and a strong current; but making no headway it was ultimately obliged to turn and bear up for the Island of Zanzibar to look for "refreshments." On December 24, it put in at "Rogues River or Juba Town" to water, and Lieutenant Mears of the Commodore's ship, the *Leopard*, 50 guns, was sent ashore to interview the natives. He and his men were lured from the boat, stripped of their clothes and then set upon by the natives with spears. Mears and his whole boat's crew, with the exception of two, who were rescued on the return of the ship, being killed.

Lieutenant Bissel of the *Daedalus* was transferred to the *Leopard*, in the place of Mears, and the *Daedalus* being sent back to the Cape, the *Leopard* and the *Orestes*, sloop-of-war, trimmed their course for Zanzibar.

On February 17, 1799, they saw three remarkable hummocks on the land, which turned out to be the town of "Mombaze," and the next morning they observed "Moorish Colours" on the Fort. "The Town was obscured by trees but we saw the Entrance to the Harbour plain." In the course of that day they made Pemba, "a low Island, about 14 leagues long, having many openings, like small Bays, for Boats to go in. This Island is everywhere very woody." On the 18th they sighted the Island of Zanzibar and a small island to the northward of it, off which they anchored till the next day, when they made sail and ran down along the island in gradual soundings from 29 to 10 fathoms, anchoring that night somewhere off Mtoni in 10 fathoms, mud.

This is the first record of English ships having visited Zanzibar, and in his account of what took place there, Lieutenant Bissel, who kept the journal of the voyage, has revealed to us something of the condition of Zanzibar at the close of the eighteenth century. His journal is freely adorned with italics and capitals: in the following extracts the italics have not been retained.

"At 2 P.M.," he wrote, "I was sent by the Commodore with 2 boats, well-armed (having an Interpreter), to endeavour to form an intercourse with the inhabitants. Half past 3 landed the Interpreter, close to the Town, among the immense crowd on the Beach, keeping the boats at (anchor). The Interpreter soon returned to the Boat with the chief of the Island, and informed us we could obtain all kinds of Refreshments at this Place. I went to look at the Watering Place, and then returned on board: when I found that some Country Boats had been alongside, with Presents for the Commodore, and inviting him to come on shore. We got a Pilot the next morning, and ran close into the Inner Harbour at low Water, through a very narrow channel, scarce $3/4$ mile wide and (anchored) about $3/4$ or 1 mile from the Town. The Fort saluted us with 3 guns, as did a ship lying there under Moorish colours and bound to Muscat. Several of the Natives came on board with Refreshments for the people. The Commodore went on shore, two days after, to return the visit of the Chief of this Place, whom we saluted at this coming on board, and going on shore. Here we got wood, water, bullocks and every kind of Refreshment."

While they were lying here, they received information by a vessel that had come from Patta, that some Englishmen were still living at the Juba, whom they took to be some of their men "who had escaped the fury of the savages on the 24th December last."

The people of Zanzibar made every profession of serving the visitors, but they were so slow and indolent that they gave but little assistance by boats and the sailors were compelled to use the ships' boats to water. "You roll your casks some distance from the Beach, and bale out of the stream; but at High Water it is rather brackish; it is therefore advisable to fill with the falling Tide, and take them off on the Flood." There were several wells in and about the town, but "they would not allow the water to be taken from some of the Wells from Religious Motives."

Provisions were plentiful: "Here you can obtain many kinds of Refreshments but as the Governor or chief made a monopoly of the sale of all kinds of articles, we paid exorbitantly dear for them. The inhabitants sell their things much cheaper. We got very fine Bullocks, Goats, Poultry, Rice, Dholl, Coco Nut Oil, etc. Their Fruits are very delicious, and they are of all kinds."

At that time apparently there was little trade with the south: "The small Trading Vessels, from Muscat, and the Red Sea, after discharging their Cargoes, which is chiefly dates, always dismantle, and move into the Inner Harbour, at the back of the Town, and wait the return of the monsoon. The Island is tributary to the Imam of Muscat, and the Governor or Chief is appointed by him. They have a great deal of trade with the French for Slaves and Coffee; and many of them talk that language in consequence. The *Orestes* captured a small French Lugger off the N.W. Point of the Island; but (on) the account he gave of himself, of his having come from the Isle of Mahe, one of the Seychelles, in search of some of his countrymen, who were supposed to be wrecked off the coast of Mozambique, the Commodore suffered him to depart. This Island has a most beautiful appearance in sailing along it, and everywhere very woody. The Town is composed of some few houses, and the rest are Huts of Straw mat, which are very neat."

The visitors were at Zanzibar during the month of Ramadan when "they eat nothing from Sunrise to Sunset, when they begin to feast and pass the Night in Dancing, Shouting and all kinds of revelling till Day-break." The inhabitants always went about armed and were expert with the matchlock. "In their Modes of Traffic, they are singular. A Guinea is of no value; but an Anchor Button, or a Button of any kind, is a Gem in the Eyes of their Lower Class of People. An instance occurred on board the *Leopard* where they refused a Guinea, which was offered in change for some Fowls; and a marine's button put an end to the bargain. Some of the higher Order of the Inhabitants chose their favourites among the Officers; to whom they were very kind, taking them near their houses (for they never admit them inside), and seating them in a little recess, entertained them with fruits, and every nicety possible, while some of their slaves were employed in loading a boat with coco nuts, poultry, eggs, and everything that was to be had; this was repeated by many of them, and they would not receive a remuneration for it. The natives are very timid in themselves, but when they are in throngs they appear not so; most of them, even the peasantry, carry side arms; but it is an invariable rule among them, when one friend visits another, he lays down his arms outside the door, and then goes in; otherwise it is considered a

Women in veil

signal of hostility."

During their stay they had light variable winds and calms, with at first a land breeze at night and a sea breeze in the day. The thermometer stood at 81° to 83°. "There had not been an English ship in Zanzibar within the memory of the oldest inhabitant."

On Tuesday, March 5, 1799, "The chief came on board and received the payment for our supplies at this place, being about 2,500 dollars." The Commodore then made the signal to prepare to sail and at daylight the next morning they got under weigh with a fresh south-west wind, passing the north end of Zanzibar at noon, Pemba on the 6th, Mombasa on the 7th, being " favoured with a northerly current of 30 miles a day."

The ubiquitous interpreter had made his appearance even in those early days. It is interesting to observe that, after the tragedy at the Juba, they took the precaution of first unloading the interpreter among the "immense crowd" on the beach, keeping the boats meanwhile anchored off at a safe distance.

Lieutenant Bissel's description of the town, in which he states that "the rest are *huts* or *straw mat*, which are very neat," seems to show that the wattle and daub style of architecture, now common, had not then been introduced into Zanzibar.

We next hear of Zanzibar from Captain Smee, of the Honourable East India Company's ship *Ternato* who, with Lieutenant Hardy of H.C. *Sylph*, visited the island in February, 1811, and in some observations he made gives us an idea of its condition at that time. The Hakim or Governor was one Yakuti, a eunuch, and a slave of Seyyid Said, ruler of Muscat, whose representative he was. Yakuti was an extortioner and a tyrant though he served his master well. He built part of the fort and, in the absence of regular troops, maintained a garrison of 400 or 500 armed slaves, and sent to Seyyid Said the revenue of the island, which amounted to 60,000 crowns, derived principally from a 5 per cent. *ad valorem* import duty, and a land tax, imposed when occasion required. Slaves and ivory were the principal items of trade, the French taking large numbers of slaves for Mauritius and paying a premium of 10 dollars for each slave. Pemba in those days supplied her sister island with nearly all the rice and cattle she consumed; the old inhabitants still recall the time when the valleys of Pemba, now alas! almost empty, pastured fat herds of cattle which were subsequently killed off by the "sickness." Some seasons "upwards of 100 large dhows, etc., have been known to arrive at this

Zanzibar Stone Town

port (Zanzibar) from Arabia and India." Captain Smee observed two ships, presumably French. "Previous to our arrival," he wrote, "only one English vessel had touched at the island since Admiral Blankett's squadron was there in 1799, on his passage up the coast to the Red Sea."

The Island of Zanzibar is very much like the Isle of Man in shape, though nearly three times the size. It is approximately 54 miles long, 23 broad, at the widest part, and has an area of 625 square miles. It lies across the 6th degree of south latitude. The longitude of the town is about 39° 11' E. of Greenwich, and the island is separated from the mainland by a channel $22^1/_2$ miles across at its narrowest part. To the north-east, at a distance of $27^1/_2$ miles from land to land, across what is known as the Pemba Channel, lies the Island of Pemba, in 5° S. latitude. Pemba is much smaller than Zanzibar, being but 43 miles long, with an extreme width of 14 miles and an area of 369 square miles. The dimensions given, especially the areas, are only approximate. On its western side Pemba is cut up by a multitude of small bays and inlets protected from the open sea by a fringe of islands, behind which, in the old days, the slave traders concealed themselves from our boats' crews till, under the shelter of night, they were able to steal into the remote and shallow recesses of the mangrove creeks. Pemba is about 35 miles from the mainland. Its two principal towns are Wete and Chake Chake, both on the west side. It was known to the Arabs as Jezira El Khathra, or the Green Island. The writer of the Periplus describes how, in his run down from Guardafui, he coasted along Azania, and it is supposed by some that from this word we obtained Zanguebar and subsequently Zanzibar; land of the Zans or Zangs, meaning blacks. Bar is the Swahili word *bara* signifying coast; it is used to indicate the continental coast opposite Zanzibar Island.

Marco Polo, who flourished about A.D. 1260, wrote: "Zanghibar is a great and noble Island with a compass of 2,000 miles. The people are all idolators and have a King and a language of their own and pay tribute to nobody. They are both tall and stout, but not tall in proportion to their stoutness, for if they were, being so stout and brawny they would be absolutely like giants; and they are so strong they will carry for four men and eat for five.

"They are all black and go stark naked, with only a little covering for decency. Their hair is as black as pepper, and so frizzly that even with water you can scarcely straighten it. And their mouths are so large, their noses so turned up, their lips so thick, their eyes so big and bloodshot, that they look like very devils; they are, in fact, so hideously ugly that the world has nothing to show more horrible ....

"The people live on rice and flesh and milk and dates, and they make wine of dates and of rice and of good spices and sugar. There is a good deal of trade, and many merchants and vessels go thither. But the staple trade of the Island is in elephant's teeth, which are very abundant; and they also have much ambergris, as whales are plentiful."

Yule, translator and editor of Marco Polo's writings, from whom I have quoted, remarks that Zanghibar, the Region of the Blacks, was known to the ancients as Zingis and Zingium. That, according to Albulfeda, the King of the Zingis dwelt at Mombasa. Referring to the confusion of the old writers about India, with their greater and lesser India, and India Tertia, Yule says: "and the three-fold division, with its inclination to place one of the Indies in Africa, I think may have originated with the Arab Hind, Sind and Zinj . . . . The Japanese Encyclopedia states that In the country of the *Tsengu*, in the S.W ocean, there, is a bird called *Pheng,* which, in its flight eclipses the sun. It can swallow a camel, and its quills are used for water casks. This was probably got from the Arabs, *Tsengu* seems to be *Zinj* or *Zanjibar* ..... The name as pronounced seems to have been *Zangibar* (hard g), which polite Arabic turned into *Zangibar*, whence the Portuguese *Zanzibar.*"

Yule points out that Marco Polio's "Island" was an error simply, his information being certainly secondhand, though no doubt he had seen the negroes he describes with so much disgust. Unless we are to conclude that they have undergone considerable modification since his day, they must have been natives of some other part of Africa, as his description of them, save in the matter of appetite, does not correspond to the type now found in East Africa. The Azania of Ptolemy and the author of the Periplus, the Zinj of the ancient Arabs, Zanjibar of the more modern Arabs, Zanghibar of Marco Polo, and Tsengu of the Japanese, all refer to the East Africa Coast. The Portuguese seem to have been the first to have applied the name to the island, and to have called it Zanzibar. The English adopted this word, but the French and Germans called it Sansibar.

Natives in East Africa call Zanzibar Island *Unguja*, and the town *mgine* or *mjine*; *mji* meaning town or village: *mjini*, in the town. In Pemba the town of Chake Chake is *mgine* to those in the south of that island, Wete *mgine* to those in the north.

The old capital of Zanzibar Island was Unguja Ukuu (ukuu - great), about 15 miles to the south of the present capital, at the mouth of Kiwani Bay. The site of the modern town was much too exposed and accessible to suit the ideas of the early inhabitants. Unguja Ukuu is protected by a flat foreshore which at low tide is half a mile or more wide, while the mangrove swamps behind Uzi Island provided the people with a secure retreat from the raids and attacks to which they were continually exposed, especially during the period of Portuguese ascendency.

The Portuguese, known to the people of Zanzibar as *Wareno*, first made those regions known to Europe in A.D. 1498. In that year Vasco da Gama doubled the Cape of Good Hope, and, sailing up the East coast of Africa, visited Mozambique, Mombasa and Malindi. The Portuguese, after several expeditions and reverses, established a dominion over the east coast, and in 1509 appointed Duarte da Lemos Governor of the Provinces of Aethiopia and Arabia. Their rule, which was one of tyranny, oppression and extortion, continued down to 1698. In that year Seif bin Sultan, Imam of Muscat, at the invitation of the inhabitants, sent a naval force, one of the ships of which carried 80 guns, "each gun measuring three spans at the breach," to deliver Mombasa from the hands of their tyrants. This he succeeded in doing, capturing from the Portuguese not only Mombasa, but Zanzibar, Pemba and Kilwa. These reverses caused the Portuguese to abandon the whole coast north of Cape Delgado, though in the year 1727 they succeeded, after many attempts, in temporarily restoring their power in Mombasa and some of the coast towns.

The sovereignty of the Portuguese was succeeded by that of Imams of Oman whose dominion extended from Mogadishu to Cape Delgado, about 250 miles South of Zanzibar. But this sovereignty became merely nominal, and in 1746, during the reign of the Imam Ahmed bin Said, Mombasa, under Ali bin Athman, chief of the Mazrui, the hereditary ruling tribe of Mombasa, declared its independence of Muscat, an independence which it maintained till 1837, when it finally submitted to Seyyid Said. Zanzibar was subdued in 1784 during the, Regency of Harried bin Said, grandson of Ahmed bin Said, and thereafter remained in the possession of the rulers of Muscat.

The Imam Ahmed bin Said, referred to above, was the 47th Imam of Oman, though the first of the tribe of Albusaidi to ascend the throne at Muscat. A man of no pedigree, he hewed his way to power after the approved manner of the times, through deeds of treachery and murder, and was elected Imam in 1741. At his death he left his sons and other claimants to quarrel for the succession to the throne, which at first falling to his indolent and tyrannical son, Said, who was superseded by his son Ahmed as Regent, subsequently passed to Ahmed's son, Sultan, who proved to be the craftiest among them. He died in 1804, and the accession of his famous successor, Seyyid Said, gives us an insight into Oriental ethics and practices.

CHAPTER II

SEYYID SAID BIN SULTAN

IN the succession to the throne of Muscat the law of primogeniture carried no weight unless the heir could support his cause by cunning or the sword, as well as the suffrages of the people. The tools were to him who could use them, and this is why, in Zanzibar, till quite recently, the succession could never pass without a struggle and an outbreak of lawlessness among the people.

On the death of Sultan bin Ahmed, in 1804, his two sons, Salim and Said, jointly ascended the throne, the former being a weak and gentle prince who soon sank into obscurity. During their minority the management of affairs was entrusted to Bedr bin Seif, their first cousin. Bedr was a man of ability and enterprise, and rendered the young rulers valuable aid against their uncle, Kais, who disputed the succession with them. Indeed, Bedr performed his part so well that he excited the suspicion of Said, who, encouraged, it is said, by his mother, resolved to compass his cousin's destruction.

With this object he invited Bedr to join him in an attack upon his uncle at El Khaburah. The tribes selected for the enterprise assembled at Huaman, and the two cousins, with several chiefs, entered the fort presumably to discuss the plan of attack. The conversation was led round to the subject of swords and daggers, whereupon one of those present drew the dagger of Bedr from its sheath. This was done for the purpose of disarming him. Seyyid Said immediately drew his sword and struck Bedr in the arm, breaking it. Bedr leapt, howling, from the window, and fled on horseback. Overcome by loss of blood he soon fell from his horse and was despatched by Said and his horsemen, who had followed in pursuit. This treacherous Murder by the youth, only fifteen years of age, was considered by his uncle, Kais, to be so meritorious a deed that a reconciliation forthwith took place between them.

In 1820 a British expedition was despatched from Bombay to punish the Beni

Bu Ali Arabs, a fierce and piratical tribe of Jaalin, a province belonging to Seyyid Said, whose authority they had lately thrown off. It consisted of six companies of Sepoys, with eight pieces of artillery. On arriving at Muscat it was joined by 2,000 men belonging to the Seyyid, and the combined forces proceeded to Bulad Beni Bu Ali, the residence of the hostile tribe, and attacked them in their entrenchments. From some unexplained cause the Sepoys, at the moment of the charge, turned about and threw themselves upon their allies in the rear. Nearly the whole of the British detachment was cut up, and the Seyyid, who had displayed great courage and coolness throughout the action, was shot through the hand in endeavouring to save an artilleryman, for which act of gallantry he received the thanks of the Indian Government.

In the year 1828 his wars, of which he had a fuller measure than falls to most warriors, cost him another wound. His troops were in flight from the Utubees and he himself forced to swim out towards his fleet in the harbour of Munamana. But ere he could be rescued by the boats he was struck in the sole of the foot by a spear. On another occasion he received a ball in the hip from the effects of which he always afterwards limped a little.

The young ruler, as revealed to us, is one of the most interesting personalities of the nineteenth century, whether we regard him as soldier, sailor, merchant, statesman, prince, or conqueror. Captain Hart, in some notes on a visit he paid to Zanzibar in February, 1834, in H.M.S. *Imogene*, described him as a tall, stout, noble-looking man, with a benevolent countenance, clever, intelligent, sharp eyes, and remarkably pleasant and agreeable manner. He was at that time forty-three years old, having been born in A.D. 1791 (A.H. 1206).

He was a very powerful man, especially in the arms, and he used to entertain his country with the exhibition of feats of strength. A book called the "Full Moon," written by the eloquent Fakih, Ali bin Razik, and entitled, "A Ray from the Resplendent Life of the Seyyid Said, the Son of Sultan, Son of the Imam Ahmed-bin-Said, with a Narrative of some of his Glorious and Renowned Achievements," * is a record of the wars he waged against, and the victories he gained over, rebellious subjects, and turbulent petty powers in alliance with Muscat, one of the most renowned of the achievements recorded by the eloquent Fakih being the murder of his cousin Bedr, when he was fifteen years old.

Few rulers have entered upon their career with less promising prospects than

* Imâms and Seyyids of Omân. Badger.

Seyyid Said; few have closed them with records of greater achievement. Not only had he to cope at the outset with his uncle Kais, as we have described, while keeping a vigilant eye on the too-capable administration of his cousin Bedr, but disturbances with the allied chiefs, who had been kept more or less under control by his father, at once began to increase. During his reign of forty-two years his intervals of peace in Oman were of but short duration, yet he found time during those intervals to obtain possession of a vast African dominion, and to found in Zanzibar a new nation with new industries.

Before we pass to this interesting career we may pause to explain that Seyyid Said, although in official documents alluded to as the Imam of Muscat and Sultan of Zanzibar, and popularly so called by Europeans, had, in reality, no claim to either title.

The Imamate was originally a priestly office, but for 1,000 years-that is to say, from 751-the Imams had combined supreme civil power with their high religious functions. They were elected by the people, who sought out the fittest person; but in 1624 the principle was set up that the Imaumate belonged by right to the eldest son.

The last of the Imaums to succeed to the temporal power was Said, second son of Ahmed, who was elected over his elder brother Hilal's head, as the latter was physically infirm, but he only reigned four years, and in 1779 was superseded by his son Hamed, whose chief qualifications appear to have been deceit and treachery. This proved to be the divorce of Church and State, as the father, Said, after having been betrayed by his son into surrendering the administration, still retained the title of Imam, and continued to retain it till his death in the second decade of the nineteenth century. It also led to the disappearance of the Imamate, as, after the death of the Imam Said bin Ahmed, no successor was elected to the office.

Nor was Seyyid Said ever officially styled Sultan, which was a title given to him by foreigners, and by foreigners applied also to his successors, Majid and Barghash, neither of whom ever used it. The title Sultan had in the eyes of an East African potentate no value, being applied to every petty chief of a coast village.

Said, although the most renowned of the rulers of Muscat, and the greatest of those of Zanzibar, was, therefore, neither Imam of Muscat nor Sultan of Zanzibar, but "Seyyid" merely. This title, which means lord, was first applied to the sons of the Imam Ahmed, their daughters being styled Seyydah, and their descendants have retained the titles ever since.

Arabs in Zanzibar seldom speak of His Highness as Sultan, but as Seyyid, or more rarely, Bwana. Other members of the reigning house also bear the title Seyyid prefixed to their names but in referring to the Sultan the title is generally used by itself. "Es-Seyyid" is the Sultan, just as "The Duke" was the Duke of Wellington, and is now the Duke of Devonshire. Bwana means "master," bwana mkubwa "great master." The latter is a vulgarised complimentary distinction used in respect of the head of every household where there will also generally be a bwana mdogo, "little master," perhaps the eldest son, or principle relative. A native will salute a fellow native as bwana mkubwa if he wants a favour from him. The Bwana Mkubwa is the First Minister of the Government. The late Sir Lloyd Mathews was known almost solely by this name; there were thousands of natives in remote parts of the islands who knew him by no other, and had probably never heard his real name.

On one occasion all Arabs who had met Livingstone in the interior of the Continent, spoke to me of the great explorer, Doctari Mkubwa Sana, the very Great Doctor, the only instance I remember of the superlative "sana" being used in this connection. But the Sultan is seldom called Bwana Mkubwa but simply Bwana or The Master.

We return from this digression on Said's title to catch a glimpse of him as sailor and a diplomatist.

He had a squadron of one line-of-battle ship, three frigates, two corvettes and a brig. Captain Hart tells us: "When on board he conducts everything himself; gets her under weigh, shifts her berth, or brings her to anchor, by giving every word of command."

He had about three hundred men only to man these ships, which were kept in harbour till the squadron was wanted for service, when Arab and Lascar crews were sent for from Muscat.

The ships lay off Mtoni, the Seyyid's principal residence in Zanzibar, now an old ruin, about three miles north of the town. This anchorage was specially reserved for the squadron. In Captain Hart's account of his reception we get a glimpse of the Seyyid at his court, exhibiting the same hospitality and consideration towards his guests, the same charm of manner and conversation for which the Arabs of Zanzibar, and especially the Sultan, are renowned.

In the incident of the *Liverpool*, we can observe him as a diplomatist. Captain

Hart wrote: " "We came to an anchor off the Imam's palace, alongside of the *Liverpool*, seventy-four guns, His Highness' flagship, carrying a red flag at the main. . . . We found at this anchorage besides the *Liverpool*, two frigates, two corvettes, and a brig . . . . . At the anchorage off the town of Zanzibar, which is about five miles from this, there were lying one English merchant brig, one American merchant ship and two brings, with several small craft of the country. Before we anchored, His Highness had sent off a Captain of one of his frigates to welcome us on our arrival, and to express His Highness' great pleasure on seeing an English man-of-war. I thanked him for his attention and said I was sorry it was after sunset, as I could not salute His Highness until early the next morning, when I would do so with twenty one guns. He said they knew our customs very well, and that the flagship was ready to return our salute whenever we began. . . . The next morning, at daylight, we fired a royal salute, which was taken up by the flag-ship immediately after our last gun, and in the same time, so that it appeared a continuation of the same salute; and this exactness of returning a salute they observed in all subsequent firing, taking it up at our last gun." The next morning Captain Hart went ashore: "His Highness, with his officers, received me at the steps of the Verandah in the most courteous and kind manner, coming up to shake hands, and, pointing out the way I was to go, followed me to a long room, at the head of which he placed me on his right. We conversed through his interpreter, Captain Hassan, of His Highness' Navy." The Seyyid expressed himself as delighted to see an English man-of-war, as he considered the English his best friends and was always glad to see them. "The next day I went to introduce the Officers to His Highness, who was happy to see them, receiving us at the door; and we were shown into the same room as yesterday, and served with coffee and sherbet. His Highness and the young princes (his two sons) shaking hands in the most good-humoured manner with all who offered to do so. . . . *The Imogene*, in compliment to His Highness, had been dressed in colours since eight in the morning, and at the appointed time all the boats attended to escort His Highness on board, he coming off in the barge which hoisted his red flag, the other boats attending and forming in two lines. He was received with a royal salute, and the officers in full uniform, and was attended on board by two of his sons, the governor (who is his uncle) and several officers. From the quarter-deck we went to the cabin, when they all took seats, and sat for some time. Refreshments were offered, but it being their great fast of Ramadan none were accepted. His

Highness began by thanking me for my great kindness and attention-that he could not sufficiently express all he felt, but that it came from his inside, and from the bottom of his heart.' As the *Liverpool* was lying close under our stern, our attention was called to her. I admired her very much and repeated that I was struck with her great likeness to the *Melville*. He said she was a very fine ship and built by the English, and that nothing would please him so much as for the English to have her-that if they would accept of her he should be very happy. I thanked him, and told him I would faithfully report his munificent offer to my Admiral. He said That is what I wish; and to the Admiralty, and to the King. She is in very good condition, but is too large for the service of Muscat, and if the King of England would accept of her it will make me very happy. I will send her to Bombay, or, if you like, give her to you here.' We then went round the ship, and returned to the cabin for a short time, when he took his leave, apparently highly pleased, and left with every expression of thanks and gratitude. He proceeded to the shore under a royal salute, the boats attending in the same manner as they brought him off."

The *Liverpool* was subsequently sent as a present to King William IV. She was attached to the British Navy, and as a compliment to Seyyid Said her name was changed to the *Imam*.

Seyyid Said, it is obvious, possessed in a high degree the qualities of generosity and hospitality for which his race is justly famed, and it need not detract from our admiration of these qualities, invaluable for a statesman and a diplomatist, to discover that he had favours to ask of the British Government, whose aid he was at that time sorely in need of.

CHAPTER III

SEYYID SAID-SUBJUGATION OF MOMBASA

TWELVE years before Captain Hart's visit, Captain Vidal, with H.M.S. Barracouta and Albatross, anchored in Mombasa Harbour. These vessels formed part of an expedition which, under Captain Owen, in H.M.S. Leven, had, in 1822, been despatched by the Lords of the Admiralty to carry out a survey of the east coast of Africa. The Mombassians were at that time in arms against Seyyid Said, and as we are told that while Zanzibar, groaning under its tribute of more than 60,000 crowns a year, was suffering in its trade, Mombasa and Lamu, under independent Arab chiefs, were prosperous, we can sympathise with them in their endeavours to defend their liberties. Now, "oppressed by numbers, their resources cut off and resistance hopeless, they had unanimously resolved to give up their country to the English, who, although differing so widely in religion and customs, yet ever protected the oppressed, and respected the Shrines of Liberty."

Thus, on his arrival at Mombasa, Vidal was hailed as a deliverer, and he was urged forthwith to hoist the English flag. It was an opportunity they had long hoped for, and they had even gone the length of providing themselves with a British ensign of their own manufacture, to hoist, if not with the consent of the British Government, then without it; "for," they said, "beneath its protecting shade we may defy our enemies; as the lamb trembles at the lion's roar, so will the Imam shrink from that which is the terror of the World."

The chief's name was Mbaruk. His predecessor, Abdullah bin Ahmed, had taken a bold line with Seyyid Said, and on his accession in 1814, in place of the usual annual present, had sent the Seyyid "a little powder and shot with a shirt of mail, and a kebaba, or small measure for corn," the kebaba presumably being empty. Seyyid Said "understood what was meant, but made no comment," while Abdullah, to provide against that day of reckoning which he knew must come, endeavoured to enlist the support of the Indian Government.

Captain Vidal, not being sure of that support, asked for time to consider Mbaruk's request, and next day sent Lieutenant Boteler ashore with his reply. The following extracts are taken from Lieutenant Boteler's account of his experiences:

"On landing I was completely hemmed in by a number of men and boys, who seemed determined to set no bounds to their curiosity. My sword, hat, and every article of apparel, underwent as strict an examination as the short time I had to wait for the Sheikh's nephew would admit. He soon arrived with several more Arabs to escort me to the castle, to which we at once ascended by means of a log of wood over a deep and apparently natural rent in the ground leading to the moat, over which, opposite to the entrance of the fortress, lay a huge mass of rock that had always remained unhewn as a natural bridge."

Boteler describes the fort used as the residence of the reigning family, and be sets forth the contents of an inscription on a tablet over the door, recording the achievements of the Portuguese Governor who had built the fort, and had subdued, chastised and oppressed the inhabitants of the region.

Lieutenant Boteler was conducted to a low building inside the fort. "The Arabs sat on huge stone benches projecting from the walls, while as a mark of attention two old-fashioned three-cornered chairs were brought for the accommodation of myself and companion. The appearance of the hovels around, the ragged set that curiosity had collected at the windows, and their general look of poverty and wretchedness, could not fail, in spite of the ostentatious decoration of their arms, to excite surprise and commiseration; for these were the people who had successfully opposed the Portuguese, when, in the plenitude of their power, they sought boundless dominion upon these shores; and in later days, in fact up to the present moment, these Arabs had firmly resisted the whole force of the Imam of Muscat."

Shortly after they were seated the Sheikh entered, a tall, thin, venerable man, in whose anxious countenance "there still remained a mild and pleasing expression, perhaps the effect of Mohammedan education, which teaches to speak little, and always first to examine the words before they are uttered."

On the appearance of the Swahili chief, "the hereditary Prince of Maleenda," a man with a silvery-white moustache, of short stature, slight and well made", dressed in a large turban and a green joho, the assembly adjourned to a more private room where the subject of delivering up Mombasa to Great Britain was discussed, and Lieutenant Boteler was requested to hoist the British flag. The assembly plied him with so many arguments and entreaties that he began to think they intended to make him hoist the flag either with or without his consent; but acting on instructions from Captain Vidal, be persisted in his refusal, and three days afterwards the *Barracouta,* to the intense disappointment of the Mombassians, sailed away to Pemba.

Pending the arrival of Captain Owen, who was shortly to come and fulfil the longing hopes of the Mombassians, we may follow the *Barracouta* for a glimpse at Pemba. No more placid and picturesque spot could be conceived than Pemba; it is the coral island of romance, and, like those beautiful islands described for us by writers of fiction, it has a tragic history. "It is strange," wrote Captain Owen, the following year, "that we should have been so long in ignorance of this fine port, called Muscat ul Chak Chak (the port of Chake Chake, Pemba), and which Captain Moresby describes as having no anchorage but numerous reefs; while, on the contrary, we could see no reefs, but found a good and secure anchorage. It is, besides, one of the most fertile islands in the world, luxurious vegetation springing spontaneously from the soil, and abounding in excellent ship-timber." Pemba had been subject to Mombasa, but about the year 1822 Mohammed bin Nassur, Governor of Zanzibar, captured it from Mbaruk, the Mazrui Chief, and the island came under the rule of Seyyid Said. We have evidence to show that the people of Pemba preferred the yoke of Mombasa to that of Muscat, for their chief and defender, Mbaruk, became their popular hero and his wars the subject of patriotic songs. Nevertheless, Mbaruk, though a clever and courageous soldier, could not resist Mohammed bin Nassur's superior forces; so the island succumbed.

Meanwhile a squadron of dhows was on its way from Muscat to chastise the Mombassians. This was Seyyid Said's answer to the pound of shot of the impudent Abdullah, on which, at the time, "he had made no comment." On its way down the squadron put in at Mogadishu, abducted two of the chiefs of that place, and took them off to Zanzibar to be held against a ransom of two thousand dollars.

When the dhows arrived they found 25,000 Mombassians standing to arms under their home-made Jack, which they had hoisted on the departure of Captain Vidal. The appearance of the flag and the fighting men had the desired effect upon Abdullah bin Saleum, the commander of the dhow squadron, who contented himself with blockading the port. But during the blockade Captain Owen in the *Leven* turned up, and decided to accede to the request of the people and place Mombasa and its dependencies, including Pemba Island and the coast between Malindi and Pangani River, under British protection.

The convention was drawn up by Captain Owen and Suliman bin Ali, the ruling chief of Mombasa, on February 8, 1824, the day following the arrival of the *Leven*, and consisted of six conditions providing:

    1. That Great Britain should reinstate the Chief of Mombasa in his former possessions.

    2. That the sovereignty of the State should continue to be exercised by the Chief of the Mazrui Tribe and be hereditary in his family.

    3. That an Agent of the protecting Government should reside with the Chief.

    4. That the Customs revenue should, be equally divided between the two contracting parties.

    5. That trade with the interior be permitted to British subjects.

    6. That the slave trade be abolished at Mombasa.

The commander of the blockading squadron readily accepted this arrangement, no doubt hailing it as a happy release from an arduous task. He anchored his ships off the town, and he and his were soon fast friends with their whilom opponents.

Lieutenant John James Reitz, third lieutenant of the *Leven*, was made commandant of Mombasa, Mr. George Phillips, midshipman, a corporal of marines, and three seamen remaining with him for the time. It was a peculiar arrangement, such as only Englishmen could have made, a lieutenant of twenty-one and a midshipman with a guard of four men coolly and confidently committing themselves to a warlike and turbulent tribe; secure in the great name of their country, in the high principles and ideals in which they had been trained, but utterly ignorant of the character of the people they had come to protect and watch, and, what was far more serious, of the dangers of the climate to which they were exposed. Within six months three of the six were dead. The inhabitants, after the manner of natives of East Africa, in whom there is no gratitude, having found relief from the power of the Seyyid, began to tire of their newly-found friends, and Reitz discovered they were not the virtuous people he had at first taken them to be.

On first receiving possession of Mombasa Island the English representatives were given a plantation on the mainland, opposite the town. This plantation, now known as English Point, was presented to them by the hereditary Chief of Malindi. On the death of Lieutenant Reitz, Mr. Midshipman Phillips became acting-commandant of Mombasa, and established at English Point a colony of freed slaves- the first of the kind we read of in East Africa. The slaves were rescued from a dhow which Mr. Phillips had captured and confiscated for being engaged in the contraband traffic, much to the consternation of the Arabs, who strove, but in vain, to recover it by promises of future good conduct. "This little negro establishment," we are told, "presented a picture of perfect content; each individual had a portion of ground to cultivate, the proceeds of which, together with other supplies, supported them in a manner far superior to that which they had been accustomed to."

The East African career of Lieutenant Reitz is of interest since he was but the first of many who, equally hopeful and vigorous, have had similar experience, and have met a similar fate. "Wave may not foam, nor wild winds sweep, where rest not England's dead," is the inscription over the gateway of the Naval burial ground at Grave Island, Zanzibar Harbour; a plot of ground now, alas! only too full.

Lieutenant Reitz, having been instructed by Captain Owen to make himself acquainted with the history and topograhpy of the country, resolved to visit Pangani Falls, and to see something of the country intervening. The big rains usually begin at the close of March or beginning of April in Zanzibar, and set in with the month of May at Mombasa. But at both places, and along the coast generally, there is a false monsoon, a short period of heavy rain, followed by an interval of fine weather, before the real masika, as the big rains are called, really begins.

These facts lead to misapprehensions every year as to what is taking place, though they never deceive Arabs, who are excellent weather prophets, and understand their climate thoroughly; and it was ignorance of these facts that cost Reitz his life. After a month of partial showers, fine weather set in at Mombasa on April 26, and Reitz, concluding that the rains were over, though in reality they had not begun, set out, on May 4, against the advice of the Arabs, whose remonstrances he considered as not worthy of attention. Torrents of rain fell on the day after the departure of Reitz and his party, which consisted of seventy followers. The night of the 6th they spent in the miserable shelter of rock cavities. They passed through Wassein and proceeded to Mkumbi, but not finding their boats, which had gone on to Tanga by mistake, and their donkeys being tired out, Reitz and a few of his followers decided upon making Tanga in native canoes. They were overtaken by deluges of rain during which they drifted out to sea, only with difficulty discerning the land when it cleared again.

Reitz no sooner escaped from one dilemma than he got into another. We witness a brave young Englishman scorning exposure and hardship, which, in a temperate climate, would but have added excitement to the expedition, plunging forward to his destruction. After a few days stay at Tanga the party proceeded to Tongoni. Next Morning Reitz, once more against the advice of the Arabs, started off in an open boat to pull to Pangani. The sea was rough, the rain came down in floods, the strong ebb tide swept back all but the boat in which Reitz was travelling. After a nine hours' pull they reached the mouth of the river, but it was too dark and too stormy to see anything or to hear anything until they were finally startled by the sound of breakers. They dropped anchor and rode out the night; and in the morning entered the river, putting in at the village of Mbweni. Here on May 14, the day after his arrival, Reitz went down with fever, and on the 29th, just as they came in sight of Mombasa, whither his followers had deemed it expedient to convey him, he died "in a most awful state of delirium." He was buried at Mombasa in the ancient Portuguese Cathedral, near the place where the altar had once stood. Port Reitz, one of the reaches of Kilindini Harbour, is called after him.

The intervention of the British at Mombasa took Said by surprise, but he showed himself equal to the occasion. He was not the man to sit down and resign himself to the will of Allah, till he had satisfied himself beyond doubt as to what the will of Allah might be. He was as ready to meet his adversaries with the weapons of diplomacy as with the weapons of war. From the beginning of the century the Honourable Company had, by a treaty concluded January 18, 1800, kept an Agent in the Persian Gulf to represent the interests of Great Britain and, without interfering with the internal administration of the country, we held the Rulers of Oman to their responsibilities in keeping the peace in the gulf, and generally supported them in their efforts to control rebellious tribes. Seyyid Said had always been loyal to Great Britain; his love for the English was one of his most striking characteristics, being shrewd enough to appreciate the value of the friendship, he lost no opportunity of proclaiming it. When he discovered what had taken place at Mombasa be made a strong remonstrance, intimating to the Bombay Government that he considered his connection with Great Britain as being in the nature of an offensive and defensive alliance. To this the Government, acknowledging not alliance but strict friendship, replied that His Majesty's Ministers had decided to drop all further proceedings with regard to Mombasa and to disavow the action of Captain Owen.

Great Britain has been censured for giving up Mombasa, although it is difficult to see what other course she could have adopted. Her interests in the Persian Gulf were paramount, and those interests were best served by maintaining her influence with the Seyyid, which she could only do by keeping faith with him. Arabs know how to submit and endure in silence, but they remember an injury and know how to wait. We find evidence of this when, fifty years later, Barghash recalled to Sir Bartle Frere the attitude of the British Government towards his father. What should we have thought of Seyyid Said if, while professing friendship towards us in the Persian Gulf, and finding himself by a happy accident in a position of advantage in the Straits, he had endeavoured to wrest from us Singapore, which we were at that time acquiring? We should have denounced the attempt as a mean act of treachery.

The British Establishment was removed from Mombasa in 1826 by Commodore Christian, the officer commanding the Naval force on the Cape of Good Hope station, acting under the orders of the Governor of Bombay in Council. The Commodore in his report remarked that he did not consider the inhabitants of Mombasa entitled to British protection, an opinion no doubt based on the persistent endeavours of the inhabitants to evade their obligations under the convention, especially with regard to the abolition of the slave trade. The British Agent in the Persian Gulf was instructed to intercede with the Seyyid on behalf of Mombasa, but in 1829 the rebellious state of the island called for another effort on the Seyyid's part to subdue it, and accordingly, in December of that year, he set out with an expedition of nine vessels, taking command himself, with the *Liverpool* as his flagship. This was the first occasion on which a Ruler of Muscat had visited the continental African dominions, and this fact alone is sufficient to show that Said was a man of energetic and commanding character. In the light of his subsequent career we may also credit him with a shrewd appreciation of the latent wealth of those dominions, though whether he had at that time any definite plans respecting them we can only conjecture. On proceeding to Mombasa in 1829 be left his nephew Seyyid Salim, a man with no judgment or decision, to act with full powers as his Wakil, or Agent, at Muscat. Previous to his departure be had treacherously seized and imprisoned his cousin Seyyid Hillal,

Governor of Soweik, a young man much beloved by the Arab tribes on the coast of Oman for his gallant behaviour and liberal disposition, but dreaded by the Seyyid as a dangerous and ambitious character. In consequence of this short-sighted and unjust act, the coast towns of the Gulf were soon in a flame of rebellion, Muscat itself being only saved from attack by the presence of a British warship, specially despatched by the Political Agent to assist in the defence of that place. On his return to Zanzibar in 1832 he confided the care of his Arabian possessions to two boys, his son Seyyid Hillal, and his nephew Mohammed bin Salim. He had no sooner sailed than the two youthful cousins were entrapped and imprisoned by the equally youthful Said bin Ali, Chief of Burka, who declared that be had been left by the Seyyid in control of the Government. The British Government, their policy being to preserve the integrity of the Seyyid's dominions, again despatched warships to quell the disturbances that arose. It was British influence alone, and the prestige our support gave to him, that at this time prevented Seyyid Said's downfall.

In 1832, on his second failure to reduce Mombasa, Seyyid Said conceived the idea of forming an alliance with Madagascar. His own troops consisted largely of Baluchis, who succumbed to fever. When he appeared with his ships, his rebellious subjects ran away, and he had not sufficient troops either to pursue them or bold the place against them when they returned. So he sent an Envoy to the Court of Antananarivo with an offer of marriage to the Queen of Madagascar, and a request for 2,000 troops. The Envoy returned in December, 1833, with the Queen's reply, and met the Seyyid at Lamu. The story of the delivery of this reply is so amusingly told by Captain Hart that we reproduce his account.

"His Highness," we are told, "had long been expecting these tender documents, and, cruel as love letters always are, he found, contrary to all expectations, that they were written in English-not only the letter from the Queen, but also those from her Ministers. His Highness had no one who could translate these letters, for although his Ambassador could speak English, yet he could not read it, and His Highness was obliged to have recourse to an English brig lying in the roads, the master of which, as good luck would have it, was able to read. This master was therefore employed to read the Queen's letter to the Ambassador, whilst he translated it to the anxious ear of his royal master, and thus it was that His Highness became acquainted with the reply to his royal love from the Madagascar Queen. . . .

. . . The Queen said she had been made happy by hearing from one who had long been in friendship with her father, and she hoped always to hear of his welfare, and wished be could pay a visit to Tananarivo; in case he did not do so she would be much obliged if he would have the kindness to send her a coral necklace of a thousand dollars, and she would order the money to be paid whenever it was landed. She hoped their friendship would increase, and that opportunities would offer for their becoming better acquainted.

"The Ministers were also glad to hear of His Highness, and wished much that he would come and show himself, or send some of his men-of-war, which should have every attention paid them. They could not offer the Queen, because by their law it was contrary for her to marry, but there was a young princess he might have. As for the men, he might have as many as he pleased, and he had only to give them a musket. This was the substance of the two letters. His Highness was disappointed that there was not more said about love in the Queen's letter, but the master of the brig consoled him by saying, she had said as much as she could in a first letter.'"

The imagination depicts the Seyyid seated on a low divan of cushions at one end of a long narrow room, two or three of his chief councillors on either hand; the interpreter with hands clasped in front, standing upright before his master, gravely delivering himself of each sentence as it was read and expounded to him by the bewildered skipper. Arabs have little sense of humour and rarely understand a joke, or if by chance they do, they never betray the fact, and we may be quite sure that no suspicion of a smile crossed the face of His Highness or of any of those present, saving perhaps the skipper, who was probably too hot and uncomfortable to see a joke of any sort.

The Malagasy troops do not seem to have been employed, and Mombasa continued to defy the Arab power till 1837, when for the third time Seyyid Said set out from Muscat with an expedition to subdue the town. He put in with his fleet and his troops at Kilindini Harbour to the south of Mombasa Island, where he was welcomed by a section of the people who had become tired of the tyranny of the Mazrui. The Seyyid and his advisers, more skilful in diplomacy than in arms, made such good use of their opportunities that the Mazrui were soon brought to terms. The terrors of previous years had taught him that his possession would never be secure as long as this warlike tribe remained in power, so he determined to remove the principal representatives of the Mazrui, and with this object he dispatched his son Seyyid Khaled, Governor of Zanzibar, in a war vessel to Mombasa with instructions to seize the leading chiefs. This, through gross treachery, was successfully accomplished, twenty-five of the Mazrui, including the chief Rashid bin Salim bin Ahmed, being betrayed and carried off first to Zanzibar and then to Oman, where they disappeared; the remainder fled to Takaungu and Gazi. As a reward for their meritorious services the, betrayers were given pensions and made elders of Mombasa. These circumstances are commemorated in a native song.

The fall of Mombasa consolidated the Seyyid's power from Mogadishu to Cape Delgado, restored his prestige in Muscat, and left him free to develop his schemes for the opening up of trade and the settlement of Zanzibar.

CHAPTER IV

SEYYID SAID-RISE OF ZANZIBAR-THE SLAVE TRAFFIC ACROSS THE WESTERN OCEAN

MANY Kings and Rulers have subdued foreign countries, but Said was one of the few who have established their people in the conquered lands. He was the first to perceive the superiority of the islands of Zanzibar and Pemba over the coast towns. The Portuguese and his Arab predecessors had fought for Mombasa, Zanzibar counting only as a pawn in the game, but Said saw that the coast towns in themselves were worth very little; their chief value being as gates to the interior, while Zanzibar was in reality the Land of Promise. That his Arab subjects thought so is evident from the flood of emigration which followed their Ruler's early visits to the island, and the manner in which they occupied and planted up the soil. The spirit in which they entered upon their new inheritance is expressed by one of their number who, in a poem setting forth the riches of Zanzibar, wrote:-

> "We ate the fruits that they had grown;
> And others after us will eat
> The fruits that we have grown."

It was probably at the time of his second visit to the island in 1832 that Said first conceived the idea of making Zanzibar his principal place of residence. He built himself a palace at Mtoni and another in the town; and in the year 1840, he transferred his court to Zanzibar, residing there till 1850, when he returned to Muscat to support his son Seyyid Thuwaini, "a man of temperament singularly weak and vacillating-one totally unfit and unable to uphold the dignity of his father, or to command the obedience of his subjects."

Seyyid Said made Bet el Mtoni his head-quarters in Zanzibar, holding his barazas there, and maintaining a household of a thousand souls. His revenues in 1834 had increased to 150,000 dollars from Zanzibar, to which must be added 100,000 dollars from Muscat. But this was in addition to the money he made from his own private trade, and the property he inherited from the Bet el Mali. According to the law of Islam the property of persons dying without heirs goes to the Bet el Mali (Bet = house, Mali = property or riches) or the Public Purse; but as all public expenditure was borne by the Sultans personally, they were accustomed to appropriate all public revenues, including those from the Bet el Mali.

The revenue was largely derived from foreign ships, chiefly American, only four English traders having touched at Zanzibar in 1833, against nine American, and none of any other nationality. These vessels were generally brigs and they had often great difficulty in collecting cargo. "Their plan is to touch upon different parts of the coast, and leave one or two of their crew behind, with an interpreter, whilst they visit some other parts, or come to Zanzibar which is the great mart and rendezvous." They brought out goods and dollars and took back gum copal and ivory. With a view to further opening up the trade Seyyid Said in 1833 sent a letter by one of the American brig-masters to be published in the United States, but the owners said, "No, Mr. Waters, if we allow this to be published, everybody will hear of the place and we shall lose our trade."

Fortunately for posterity, Seyyid Said did not permit his schemes to perish in the waste-paper basket of these Yankee traders. On September 21, 1833, a Treaty of Amity and Commerce was concluded between the United States of America and Seyyid Said, not only safe-guarding the rights and liberties of American subjects but also providing for Consular jurisdiction, and, in 1835, Mr. Richard P. Waters was appointed American Consul at Zanzibar.

Great Britain entered into a Treaty of Commerce dated May 31, 1839, drawn up and signed by Captain Robert Cogan, of the East India Company's Naval service and of the firm of Messrs. Cogan, Zanzibar. This treaty was ratified at Muscat on behalf of Her Britannic Majesty by Captain Rennel, Resident in the Persian Gulf, on July 22, 1848. In August 1841, Captain Atkins Hamerton arrived in Zanzibar in the capacity of agent of the East India Company, and on December 9, of that year, he was in addition appointed British Consul there.

The appointment of the British Consul, following close upon the transference by Seyyid Said of his court from Muscat to Zanzibar, marks the beginning of Zanzibar's prosperous career of trade. The presence of the British Consul, carrying with it the assurance that justice could be obtained, induced a large number of British Indian subjects to settle and trade in the island. Where Indians go trade follows.

To fill up the measure of his ambition Seyyid Said had now to conclude a treaty with France, the only remaining Great Power having interests in those regions. The manner in which that country signified her readiness to meet the Seyyid's wishes is in amusing contrast with the methods adopted by the two Anglo-Saxon nations. "A French squadron," we read, "commanded by Captain Fosse, arrived at Zanzibar armed with full powers to enter into a Treaty with His Highness." We have, however, to bear in mind the mutual jealousy between England and France in those days, and the preponderating influence of Great Britain in the Persian Gulf, and in the affairs of the Ruler of Muscat. Seyyid Said had already communicated with the British Government, "in order to obtain their sentiments on the proposed measure," and having been informed through Captain Hamerton, "that no objections existed to his entering into relations with the French," a Treaty of Commerce and Consular jurisdiction was concluded between His Highness and the King of the French. It bore date November 17, 1844, and was ratified February 4, 1846. Treaties of Consular jurisdiction, etc., between Zanzibar and other European countries were contracted as follows: with Portugal, October 23, 1879, Italy, May 28, 1885, Belgium, May 30, 1885, Germany, December 20 1885, Austria-Hungary, August 11 1887.

French trade with Zanzibar, which at the beginning of the century exceeded that of all other foreign countries put together, was afterwards surpassed by American. In 1859, of a total of 23,340 tons entered, 3066 only were French, the United States having 10890, and the British 493 tons. From what we know of the participation of the French in the Slave Traffic we must to some extent attribute the decline of their trade to the effect of the treaty of 1822, which prohibited the export of slaves from the dominions of the Imam of Muscat, and the treaty of 1845, which forbade the export of slaves from his African dominions. The first time a trading vessel from the United States visited Zanzibar was in 1830, when Americans first introduced their cotton cloth known as Merikana, which became the medium of exchange among the natives in the interior of Africa. There was no direct trade between Great Britain and Zanzibar in Said's reign, the foreign mercantile houses being three of Hamburg, three American and two French.

There are no trustworthy figures to show the increase of the trade in Zanzibar during Seyyid Said's reign. Smee, in 1811, calculated from the amount of the customs collected that the value of the imports could not be less than £300,000- How much of this total was made up by the import of slaves we can only conjecture. The export of slaves to Muscat, India and Mauritius was estimated at that time to be from 6,000 to 10,000 per annum, but we can safely conclude that the imports of Zanzibar considerably exceeded the exports. Slaves from 7 to 10 years of age were worth 7 to 15 dollars; from 10 to 20 years, 15 to 20 dollars; full-grown men 17 to 20 dollars; a good stout female 35 to 40 dollars. Taking the number imported at 15,000, at the average price at 20 dollars, we have an annual value of 300,000 dollars, equal at that time to nearly £70,000 ($4^1/_2$ dollars to £). Roughly the slave trade constituted, in the second decade of the century, a quarter of the total trade of Zanzibar.

Captain Cogan stated that the resources of the Seyyid amounted in 1839 to £80,000 a year, of which £20,000 arose from the sale of slaves, of whom 40,000 to 45,000 were annually sold at Zanzibar, 20,000 of these being exported to Egypt, Arabia, Persia and the coast of Makran. Captain Hamerton in 1855 estimated the value of the Seyyid's gross annual revenue to be £100,000 one year with another, a third of this being derived from Muscat.

Turning from these figures, we will endeavour to show the steps taken in Said's time for the suppression of the slave trade in East Africa.

It has taken eighty years to kill slavery and the slave trade in East Africa. The task has been England's unaided-at times hindered-by the Powers of Europe; and amid the world-turmoil in which she was the leading figure, with great patience, yet with perseverance unrelaxed for eighty years she has pressed towards the mark, till "the open sore of the world" is at length healed. "By slow degrees we reach the steep acclivities of time." Fire and murder no longer stalk the interior; the caravan is cut off; the slave-dhow disappears from the sea; and slavery is dead.

On September 7, 1822, an engagement, proposed by Captain Fairfax Moresby, commanding H.B.M ship *Menai*, for the prevention of the slave trade, was signed by Seyyid Said. This engagement provided for the prohibition throughout Said's dominions of the sale of slaves to Christians, and the transport of slaves to Christian countries. It also granted permission for British Agents to reside in his Zanzibar dominions. Another requisition concluded a few days later made all Arab ships with slaves on board found to the eastward of a line drawn from Cape Delgado, passing sixty miles east of Socotra, on to Diu Head, the western point of the Gulf of Cambay, liable to seizure by H.M. cruisers. In July, 1839, and following years Captain Hennel, British Agent at Muscat, succeeded in persuading four of the maritime Arab Chiefs to attach their signatures to a new engagement, in which Seyyid Said joined, moving the line westwards to Pussem on the Makran coast, thus excluding the trade from the whole of the Indian coast.

But the slave traffic was still in full career in the Portuguese Possessions in East Africa. The blockade on the Atlantic sea-board, making it dangerous for slavers to attempt the west coast ports, the traffic was deflected to Quilimane and Mozambique. Lieut. Bosanquet, of H.M.S. *Leveret*, stated that in 1836 upwards of 12,000 slaves must have left those ports for Brazil and Cuba. In December 1836 a Spanish brig obtained 500 slaves at Mombasa, but the following year Mombasa was taken by Seyyid Said, so that the foreign slave trade of that port ceased. Nevertheless a coasting trade, in many cases under the Muscat flag, was to a great extent carried on to supply the two Portuguese ports. In April, 1838, Lieutenant Bosanquet wrote: "The exportation of slaves from the two ports of Mozambique and Quilimane to the Brazils and Cuba is annually from 7,000 to 14,000. All the vessels, with one exception, during the last two years, have sailed under the Portuguese flag, having arrived at Mozambique under various flags." In September of that year thirteen Portuguese slavers, which would take 500 slaves each, were awaiting cargoes at Quilimane.

The Government of Portuguese East Africa maintained itself by the traffic, a duty of 7 dollars being levied on each slave exported. The junta or Council was composed of the chief slave merchants. But the vigilance of the British cruisers hampered though they were in those days of sail by the strength of the current and violence of the monsoon in the Mozambique Channel was effecting much. By 1843 they had so far succeeded in checking the traffic that the slave market was glutted, and the price of slaves in Quilimane fell from 40 dollars to 10 dollars. On September 4, 1843, H.M.S. *Lily* chased a slaver which the crew ran ashore and abandoned off Quilimane. She was recognised as the *Esperance*, which had sailed from St. Catherine's, Brazil, at the end of 1842, with money to buy slaves at Pemba for herself and the *Desangano*, a vessel which had been already captured by the *Lily*. A brigantine captured in 1843 by H.M.S. *Cleopatra*, had 447 slaves on board. During her voyage to the Cape in rough weather, such was the over-crowded state of the vessel, that 177 slaves died on board; and at the Cape

63 more succumbed. What must have been the condition of those vessels on the long and weary way to Brazil, or the still more terrible journey through the tropics to Cuba?

The British Government, meanwhile, was urging upon Seyyid Said another step in the direction of the restriction of the slave trade: assisting him, as they put it, with his enlightened views. It was at first proposed that he should prohibit and abolish the traffic in slaves altogether, but this was more than he had bargained for. The proposal alarmed him. To the many distinctions which Seyyid Said possessed, one more must be added: he was the greatest slave-trader in the world. He derived the greater part of his revenue from the sale of slaves, on whom both import and export duties were charged, from 10,000 to 15,000 being annually sold from his African dominions, and as many more imported into Zanzibar. Consequently when in 1842 Captain Hamerton came with Great Britain's proposal, he was distressed. "All is over now," he said. "This letter and the orders of Azrael, the Angel of Death, are to the Arabs one and the same thing: nothing but to submit. This letter is enough for me. I will now place myself and all I possess under the English."

The relations between Hamerton and the Seyyid do not seem to have been of the best. He states that at this interview, in consequence of the Seyyid's manner, which he describes as "insolent," he "assumed a high tone with him," and we find the Seyyid writing to Lord Aberdeen stating that he wished British functionaries in his dominions to be good-tempered men, and to treat him properly. Though be may have been wanting in tact, Hamerton was hampered in his work by the presence of Captain Cogan, who seems to have acquired considerable influence in the councils of Said; to have been, in fact, his chief adviser at that time in the negotiations which finally led up to the conclusion of the treaty in 1845. There is no doubt, too, that the India Board, in whose employ Hamerton was, did not manifest much consideration for the difficulties of their Arab ally.

Seyyid Said was said to have sustained through the Moresby Treaty of 1822 a diminution in revenue to the extent of 100,000 crowns; and the British Government well understood that the stoppage of the slave trade would result in a still further reduction of his revenues. They had under consideration the expediency of pecuniary aid, but certain arguments, urged at the time, showed the inutility of the measure. It was feared that prohibition would only have the effect of throwing the traffic into the hands of the subjects of the Ottoman Porte and the

Persian Government; and that, were the inhabitants of the gulf to relinquish the traffic in slaves, the place of their vessels would immediately be taken by others from the Red Sea, the coast of Makran, Sind and other maritime provinces in the Arabian Sea. The British Government decided therefore to modify its demands.

The alarm of Seyyid Said at the prohibition which he believed to be impending was so great that, in 1842, he sent his envoy Ali bin Nasur to England in the *Sultanah*, a barque of 300 tons, and 50 guns, with letters to the Queen, Lord Aberdeen, and Lord Palmerston, stating that he would be ruined, requesting consideration for his case, and begging that his means of subsistence might remain. He sent to the Queen two pearl necklaces, two emeralds, an ornament made like a crown, ten cashmere shawls, one box with four bottles of otto of roses and four horses. In reply, Lord Aberdeen, in a letter dated July 12, 1842, expressed to His Highness the anxious desire of her Majesty's Government that no slaves should be taken from Africa to Arabia, Persia or the Red Sea.

Seyyid Said, no doubt relieved at the moderation of this new demand, declared himself ready to do all in his power to give effect to the wishes of the Queen of England, though he should thereby incur the enmity of his subjects and suffer loss in revenue. He imprudently sent through Cogan a present of some horses to the Chairman of the East India Company, an impropriety for which he was rebuked, in not too courteous terms, by the Bombay Government. In a letter which he at the same time sent to Lord Aberdeen through Cogan he requested that in the agreement the free sale and transit of slaves between Lamu and Kilwa, including Zanzibar, Pemba and Mafia, should be confirmed as a right to his heirs and successors. But the British Government were not to be led into this trap. Candour and good faith, as well as forbearance and courtesy marked their dealings with the Seyyid throughout his reign; they therefore told him frankly that the right stipulated for was granted, but that it was to be treated rather as a reservation to himself than a concession by Her Majesty's Government. In reply to a second request that, as a set off against loss of revenue, Great Britain should assist him in recovering and retaining when recovered the island of Bahrain which had belonged to his ancestors, but which had seceded from his Muscat dominions, he was informed that the British Government could not do this, but were willing to help him in meeting the first deficiency in revenue that might arise from the agreement.

The Agreement was signed at Zanzibar by Seyyid Said and Captain Hamerton on October 2, 1845.

It provided for the suppression from and after January 1, 1847, of the exportation of slaves from His Highness's African dominions, and the prohibition of the import of slaves from any part of Africa into his possessions in Asia.

The Persian Government, and several Arab Chiefs in the Persian Gulf, followed in 1848 and 1849 with engagements to prohibit the importation of slaves by sea. Presumably to give effect to the provisions of this agreement, two squadrons patrolled the coast: the Cape of Good Hope and East Coast of Africa squadron cruised as far as the fourth parallel of south latitude, which just included Mombasa; a squadron of the Indian Navy to the north of this. The vessels of the Indian Navy made few if any captures, in consequence of the difficulties placed in their way by the Indian Government, and the legal proceedings in which officers became involved after having made a capture. It was even said that upon sighting a dhow the officers put the helm the other way to get away from her, rather than risk their Commissions in the Bombay Courts of Justice.

H.M.S. *Castor*, Captain Wyvil, Commodore of the Cape Squadron, and four other cruisers, policed the waters of the Mozambique Channel and Zanzibar. Much of the work was done in pinnaces and cutters and has been recorded by Captain Sulivan*, then a midshipman in the *Castor*. The following amusing incident throws a sidelight upon the difficulties of the chase in those days. "Our pinnace," wrote Captain Sulivan, "was now under the command of Mr. Jones, second master of the *Dee*, whose cheery disposition and good temper made him well suited to take the place of Campbell, who, with a similarly cheerful spirit, had succeeded in rendering every one happy in the boats, and in making the service a most agreeable one."

Starting from Ibo one morning in February 1850, in company with the *Dee's* cutter, they steered a northward course, inside the islands, anchoring at noon under the lee of Maheto Island. "From the top of a ruin on this island, we observed what appeared to be a large vessel steering north, and immediately proceeded in chase of her. We had received some information relative to an armed American vessel in the neighbourhood waiting for an opportunity to escape with a cargo of slaves, and as we neared the chase, it was soon pronounced to be a barque. For two hours with a light wind and oars did we pull to the northward and westward after her, now apparently gaining, now losing. 'It's a barque,' said

* **"Dhow Chasing."**

Jones; 'she has just set her royals, and hauled up more.'

"Well, she's inside, out of the current, and we are in the heart of it, and that's how she's gaining.'

"'If it's the Yankee she'll fight for it.'

"'Mount the gun.'

"This done, we gave way again with the oars. The cutter was not far astern of us now. 'It's the Yankee,' said the coxswain, looking at her through the glass I'd swear to it by her sails.'

"'She's bore up to run for it,' said another, and various were the opinions of those who were not pulling. The gun was loaded, and pointed with extreme elevation, with a view of 'letting her have it when near enough;' but a breeze sprang up, and cleared the haze away. The goddess was turned into a laurel, that she might be saved from Apollo:- It was a tree!"

On April 29, 1850, the *Castor* put in at Zanzibar to provision. Seyyid Said was there and entertained the commodore and officers at a dinner, but sat aloof from the table himself, it being against the religion of a Mohammedan to eat with a Christian; a religious scruple which has undergone some modification since then. Having loaded up her decks with live stock, including an Arab horse, a present from the Seyyid to the Commodore, which, by the time it reached the Cape, in nine months, "could do everything but smoke a pipe," the *Castor* put to sea and continued to cruise on the coast till February 1851, leaving it only once during that time, namely in October, when she put in at Mauritius to refit. Never did British man-of-war, since the blockading days of the French war, enter a port needing repair more from truck to keelson. "We-the midshipmen's mess-were reduced to coconut shells to eat out of, coconut shells to drink out of, and one of my messmates, I remember, was reduced to a coconut shell for washing in." Towards the close of the cruise, in December or January, out of a complement of 320 men on the *Castor* and her tender the *Dart*, they had 113 men on the sick-list, many of whom died. We refer to these details, not for any special historic interest they possess, but because they help us to understand what hardships our men worked under in those days before condensers and propellers, and what sacrifices Great Britain has made in her self-imposed task of crushing the slave trade. Great Britain sent forth her sons not to the glory and glamour of battle, but to a monotonous, wearing life, under conditions to which this age can offer no parallel.

The vigilance of our cruisers succeeded in almost exterminating the ocean-borne slave traffic to the west coast, but about the year 1854, entering as we then were upon the Crimea War, this vigilance was relaxed and we hear of no more captures for six years. During this time the export of slaves from Portuguese territory round the Cape of Good Hope underwent a temporary revival, and ships from the Atlantic began to penetrate further up the coast. An American merchant actually published his opinion in a United States journal that the slave traffic on the East Coast of Africa might be carried on with safety. We read of slaves being collected at Kilwa for Reunion; of a Spanish brig from Havana arriving at Zanzibar; of a French ship lurking under the lee of the island and carrying off 600 slaves; of another French ship fully equipped as a slaver, having on board besides provisions, a supply of irons, chains, tin-plates, etc., appearing off the east coast of Zanzibar; but these birds of prey, examples no doubt of not a few never recorded were, like the vanishing spectres of a haunting nightmare, now to disappear, not again to return. For British cruisers were once more upon the trail. In July, 1860, H.M.S. *Brisk* captured a Spanish ship in the Mozambique Channel with 864 slaves on board, and two months later the *Lyra* captured, off Mafia, another Spanish ship, fitted out as a slaver. With these two captures the slave traffic to the Western Ocean came to an end.

CHAPTER V

SEYYID MAJID-REBELLION IN ZANZIBAR-SEPARATION FROM OMAN

TROUBLES in Muscat, which never ceased throughout his long reign, summoned Seyyid Said once more to Oman in 1854. The Persians had forcibly resumed their supremacy over Bunder Abbas, a port on the eastern side of the Persian Gulf, held in feof by the rulers of Oman at an annual rental of 6,000 tomans. His son Thuwaini, a weak and vacillating Prince, was his Governor at Muscat, and he despatched him on an expedition to expel the Persians. But the expedition was unsuccessful, for though Bunder Abbas was saved to Oman for a period of twenty years, it was only upon humiliating terms.

Disappointed and tired out, the weary monarch, in 1856, turned his face for the last time towards his island home which he was never again to see. He embarked on the *Victoria*, a frigate of 32 guns with auxiliary steam; the frigate *Piedmontese* 36, and the corvette *Artemise* 22, acting as escort. The Seyyid was ill with dysentery; his constitution shattered by excessive self-indulgence and the use of stimulating drugs. On October 19 at half past seven in the morning, he died on board the *Victoria* when off Seychelles. He was sixty-five years old and had reigned fifty-two years, seventeen conjointly with his elder brother Salim, thirty-five alone. He married thrice: in 1827 Azze binti Seif, a sister of the Prince of Shirazi, a woman of very strong will, feared and disliked by the whole of her husband's household, over which she ruled; in 1847 Shesade, grand-daughter of Fath Ali Shah, Shah of Persia, a princess of surpassing beauty, who nearly ruined the Seyyid by her extravagance and shocked his people by her assumption of liberty and wild disregard of Arab custom; and subsequently he married a daughter of Seif bin Ali. At his death he had seventy concubines and thirty-six children living. Fifteen of the surviving children were sons, six of whom were to reign, namely: Thuwaini and Turki in Muscat; Majid, Barghash, Khalifa and Ali in Zanzibar.

Another son, Mohammed, a pious and upright prince, became the father of Hamoud, late Sultan of Zanzibar. Seyyid Said is credited with one hundred and twelve children in all, twenty-one being sons.

Honoured in his friendship with Great Britain, respected by his subjects, Seyyid Said was beloved of his family and household. At Zanzibar he kept up two huge establishments, one at Mtoni, and one in the town, each containing about a thousand people-Arabs, Persians, Turks, Circassians, Abyssinians, Nubians, Swahilis, and natives from central Africa, over whom he extended a patriarchal protection. Though he was strict with his children, permitting no familiarity and imposing upon them an exacting etiquette, he was nevertheless very fond of them. His son Majid was subject to epileptic fits, and precautions were taken against leaving him alone, especially in his bath room. On one occasion he was found in convulsion on his bed. A messenger was at once despatched to the Seyyid who was at Mtoni, Majid's house being in the town. There was no boat afloat at the Mtoni palace, so the Seyyid, seizing his weapons, hailed a passing fisherman and turning him out of his canoe jumped in and paddled himself to the town. Tears ran down his venerable white beard as he stood by his son's sick bed, calling upon God to preserve his life. Generous as a Prince should be, he was not a spendthrift, and never exceeded the resources of his treasury, though at the same time, those resources being large, he maintained in Zanzibar a display of luxury and state far exceeding anything he or his forefathers had been accustomed to in Oman.

But to return to the *Victoria* with her tragic cargo bearing down upon Zanzibar like an exploding thunder cloud that was to make the little island reel with rebellion and shake the foundations of Oman. Seyyid Barghash was on board; a youth in his teens, yet a true chip of the old block. Contrary to Mohammedan custom which ordains that the bodies of those who die at sea shall be committed to the deep, he embalmed his father's body, put it into a coffin, and to conceal it from view placed the coffin in one of the boats swung out on the davits. Seven days later Barghash arrived at Zanzibar; but it did not suit his plans to part at once with his dismal charge, so he anchored the *Victoria* off Chumbe Island, to the south of Zanzibar Harbour, and kept the red flag flying at the main. It will be remembered that Seyyid Majid was Governor of Zanzibar, but that fact, though it gave him a potential advantage, did not secure to him the succession. "Might, coupled with the election of the tribes" was "the, only right." The support of the tribes he had secured, he had to show himself worthy of that support. When he saw the *Victoria* and the *Artemise*, Majid put off in a boat to greet his father; but the sea being rough he could not make the ship, so ran in at Chukwani. Upon stepping ashore across a plank suspended from the nose of the boat he was seized with a fit and fell. His attendants carried him to a native house and kept him there till next morning At midnight Barghash lowered the boat containing the body of the deceased monarch, and with two other boats proceeded stealthily to the town and interred the remains in the cemetery known as Bunder Abbas, behind the palace, the place where the Sultans have subsequently been buried. He then tried to obtain possession of the fort, but the Baluchi jemadar in command refused to admit him. Secretly procuring arms and ammunition, he surrounded the palace at Mtoni, but his attempts to collect a following proved unavailing. The next morning Majid, who, upon discovering that the ships had left Chumbe, had made all haste to the town, was hailed by the people as their ruler.

The el Harth tribe of Arabs who had always shown signs of disaffection towards the Seyyid's family, proceeded with their chief, Abdullah bin Salim, to the British Consulate demanding to know of Hamerton what they should do, since the country was without a ruler. Hamerton left them in no doubt about what to do. He told the chief that if he attempted to disturb the peace his head would fall in twenty-four hours, and thereupon turned him out of the Consulate.

Majid assembled his younger brothers who were residing on the island, his family and the chiefs on the continental coast, "in order that they might recognise me. To this they all agreed, and they accordingly elected me to be ruler over them and entrusted me with the direction of their affairs." He despatched his frigate, the *Taj*, with the news of Seyyid Said's death to his brothers, Thuwaini, Governor of Muscat, Turki, Governor of Lohar, and Mohammed. When the sad intelligence was proclaimed, it caused "such a wailing throughout the town that the hills were almost shaken by it." The people went into mourning for three days, praying God for resignation, "in accordance with the words of the Most High: 'Proclaim good tidings unto the patient, who, when a misfortune befalls them, say: We are God's, and to him we shall surely return.'"

In some respects the condition of affairs was unique. Seyyid Said, a ruler of what practically amounted to two states, separated by 3,000 miles of ocean, had died, leaving his second but eldest surviving son, Thuwaini, Governor of the parent state Muscat, and his fourth but second surviving son, Majid, Governor of

Zanzibar. Who was to succeed him? Was there to be one ruler, supreme, as he had been over the whole of the dominions, or was each state now to have its own independent ruler? Who was to decide the point? The case was further complicated by the fact that the parent state was poor while Zanzibar was rich and that Arab law and custom provided for no stability in succession.

In 1844 Seyyid Said had informed Lord Aberdeen that he had appointed his eldest son, Khaled, to succeed him in Africa and Thuwaini in Asia, and he desired to know whether the British Government would guarantee the succession, but the British Government did not see their way to do this. Said's eldest son, Hilal, a favourite with the Arabs, but a man completely abandoned to the use of intoxicating liquors, had been disinherited, but died before his father. Khaled, neither esteemed nor respected, also died before his father, in 1854.

It appeared at first as if the brothers intended to abide by their father's wishes. Thuwaini sent his first cousin, Mohammed bin Salim, one of the executors of Seyyid Said's will, to his brother Majid in Zanzibar, to "declare everything" unto him "by word of mouth." What it was that the crafty Mohammed was instructed to declare, and what it was that he did actually declare, must ever remain a mystery. One thing only is clear about his declarations: that no one thereafter could understand them; that Thuwaini said they were one thing, Majid another; that Mohammed himself never explained them, and that in a very short time the brothers were at each other's throats.

Mohammed, however, succeeded in extracting from Majid a promise to pay Thuwaini annually 40,000 crowns. This payment Majid stopped after the first year, alleging as the reason that one of the conditions of his promise was that Thuwaini should not stir up strife against Seyyid Turki, Governor of Lohar, who was to receive 10,000 crowns to enable him to pay the tribute to the Wahabees, which condition had been violated. The real reason, however, was that though his revenue was large, amounting to 206,000 crowns, about 443,000- rupees a year, his treasury was empty and he wished to be freed from his promise. The chiefs of the warlike northern Arabs, of whom he stood in constant dread, he subsidised to the extent of 10,000 crowns per annum; he owed the customs master 327,000 crowns; and he had borrowed seven lacs of crowns from his orphan brothers. With the exception of the customs master, an Indian named Luddah, who farmed the customs, and on whom he was entirely dependent for money, Majid had not a single honest person about him on whose oath he could rely; and though not of extravagant habits he was surrounded by a horde of greedy mercenaries who preyed upon the State.

Majid had assumed the custody of the six young children of his father in Zanzibar, but not only did he appropriate their inheritance, he neglected their comfort, and drove them to appeal to Thuwaini against his treatment.

So when, in 1859, for the second year the 40,000 crowns was not forthcoming, Seyyid Thuwaini prepared an expedition against Zanzibar to compel the recognition of his rights. To forward the success of his plans which, bearing in mind the cautious and deliberate character of the Arabs and their habit of intrigue, we may be certain he had been contemplating almost from the time of his father's death, he had despatched one, Nasur bin Ali, to receive the second instalment of the first payment of the 40,000 crowns. Having duly received the instalment, Nasur "then went in among the people, secretly corrupting their minds, and promising them all sorts of things from Thuwaini. As reported to us, moreover, he said, 'Barghash will act for Thuwaini, for he is on his side, and do whatever he bids you.' "Nasur then left. But in intrigue Majid was as accomplished as his brother. He succeeded in winning over Seyyid Turki of Lohar, who sat like a watchdog on Thuwaini's flank, awaiting his opportunity. Majid supplied him with arms and ammunition, and so successful was his strategy that had Thuwaini carried out his projected invasion he would in all probability have lost Oman. But all this was *sub rosa*. Majid proclaimed his deliverance in quite other terms. "With the aid of God," he wrote, "I prepared to meet and resist him with all the men and materials of war at my disposal, and I myself went on board one of my frigates for the same purpose, confident that God would cause me to triumph over one who had violated his treaty and sought to do me injury, knowing full well that the wicked cannot prosper; and God did, indeed thwart his evil designs, and made the (British) Government the instrument of his salvation."

The whole of the Swahilis of the coast rose in support of Majid, many of the tribes under their own chiefs crossing to Zanzibar to his assistance. The Swahilis of the island and the Wangazija (natives of the Comoro islands) armed themselves in readiness to help in repelling the invasion. The dhows with Thuwaini's troops that first began to arrive at the northern ports of the coast found them all occupied by Majid's friendly tribes and ships of war, and being unable to land or to procure wood and water were obliged to surrender.

But the time had come for Great Britain to interfere. Thuwaini was upon the sea; Oman was in a ferment Majid and the Arabs of Zanzibar and the African coast were under arms.

The maritime interests of Great Britain were too great to permit the highway to India to be disturbed by two petulant princes. The British Government persuaded the contending parties to submit their claims to the arbitration of Lord Canning, Governor-General of India. Thuwaini returned to Muscat, abandoning his expedition to Zanzibar; Majid contentedly laid down his arms and resigned himself to wait for information from Bombay; "and it is believed that none will come for five years."

Apparently Thuwaini also thought that deliberations of the Governor-General would be of a protracted character, for in the meanwhile he prepared another little diversion. He still had, or thought he had, another card to play. There were the el Harth Arabs of Zanzibar and there was Barghash, a "lackbrain," as he afterwards termed him, when his plans had failed; "Think you that I would correspond with a lackbrain ; such he is?" He bethought him of another esteemed "brother," Hamed bin Salem; no lackbrain, at least in Thuwaini's view. Him he sent to Majid. The story is like one from the Old Testament. "Wherefore are you come?" said Majid to Hamed. And Hamed answered, "To effect a reconciliation between you and your brother Thuwaini." Whereat Majid was much surprised, as well he might be, seeing that he and Thuwaini had both agreed that their reconciliation should be left to the Governor General, and he was more surprised still when he came to understand Hamed's methods and his ideas of how this reconciliation was to be brought about. Hamed brought with him Nasur bin Ali; they "went in and out" among the el Harth Arabs for a little time; succeeded in rousing them to revolt, and then returned to Muscat.

Barghash's opportunity had now come. The el Harth Arabs looked to him to lead them against Majid; he looked to the assistance of the el Harth Arabs to enable him to usurp the throne. But the disaffected Arabs, while welcoming the leadership of Barghash, had no intention of being made a convenience of, their object being to get rid of the whole of the reigning family of the Albusaidi and set up a Government of their own.

The French Consul in Zanzibar at that time was a Russianpole, named Cochet, believed by Seyyid Majid and the British Consul, Colonel Rigby, to be carrying on secret negotiations with Thuwaini and Barghash on the understanding that if the rebellion were successful the Port of Mombasa would be ceded to France. But though it is doubtful if any collusion existed between the French Consul and Thuwaini, there is no doubt that Barghash courted, and would have welcomed, French support had it been forthcoming. "What is your opinion," he wrote to Cochet, "if, in coming to the town to attack Majid, we meet with any English or other Christians on the road, shall we kill them or not? Give me your reply on this point." And again he wrote to Cochet, "My brother Majid's wish is to give the country to the English and he has spoken thereof openly, not once, nor twice, but often. We, however, will not give our country to the English, or to the French, or to the Americans, or to anyone else; but if we sell it we shall do so only at the cost of our blood and of war to the death. As to yourself, be fully confident; if you are buying or selling in the plantations be not afraid, your transactions will be safe."

Unlike his father, who always remained the staunch friend of Great Britain, Barghash from his youth hated Europeans though he preferred the French to the English. Seyyid Said possessed several estates and clove plantations. One of the largest of these is situated at Machui, and on this Khaled, Seyyid Said's second son and Governor in Zanzibar before Majid, built a palace, calling it Marseilles, after the French Mediterranean port; another plantation he called Bourbon. These plantations still bear these names, and they are evidence of French influence in the island at that time.

The struggle between Majid and Barghash was now approaching its crisis. The probabilities seemed all against Barghash; yet Seyyid Said had achieved the mastery by sheer force of character and Barghash inherited his father's qualities of courage, resource and perseverance. He was an able man, conscious of his ability. Majid was no fool, but he loved ease and repose; always preferred bribing his opponents to fighting them, and, but for one circumstance, his power would have been wrested from him by Barghash and he himself destroyed. He was defended from this assault by the intervention of the British Consul, a man who, fortunately for Majid, was not afraid of responsibility.

Majid, as soon as he discovered what was afoot, ordered Barghash to quit the island, and upon his refusing to do so confined him to his house in the town. The next day Barghash sent word that he would -go but required money for the voyage, whereupon Majid sent him 10,000 crowns. Barghash's house was situated close to the -shore, almost beneath the shadow of the palace of the Seyyid. Here he lived with his sister Mji, and here he now found himself in a state of siege, his provisions and water cut off. At the back of his house, and separated from it by but a narrow street, across which two people could shake hands, lived two of his sisters, Khole and Salme.*

Forced by the angry discord which always divided the families of the Seyyids in these bitter feuds, the two sisters had espoused the cause of Barghash and in the straits to which he was now reduced became his only hope. The conspirators had for some time been collecting supplies and warlike stores at the palace on Marseilles plantation which Barghash had decided to make his stronghold, and it now devolved upon Khole and Salme to deliver him from his prison. Encompassed by spies, the adjacent streets thronged with troops, it was a desperate task that lay before the two pampered Princesses, but they proved equal to it. Shrouded in their masks and trusting to their wily feminine graces, the sisters, followed by a picked retinue, left their house at midnight and boldly confronted the officers of the watch that had been set at their brother's door. The soldiers, astounded at the apparition of guileless innocence before them, were struck speechless, and the next moment, uttering prayers and excuses, opened the doors of the house and passed the two women in. A few minutes afterwards they emerged with Barghash and his young brother, Abdul Aziz, both armed to the teeth and wrapped in women's clothes. Barghash was recognized by a Baluchi soldier, but out of veneration for the family he held his peace. Once out of the town the fugitives rushed across country like hunted hares till they reached the rendezvous. Here Barghash, divesting himself of his disguise and taking Abdul Aziz by the hand, sped away through the darkness with his escort to the plantation; while the exhausted sisters, trembling at the horror of the situation, crept stealthily back to their house to await the consequences of their deeds.

Marseilles plantation, as we have already mentioned, belonged to Seyyid Khaled bin Said, and after his death it became the property of his two daughters, Chembua and Fachu.

*Khole, favourite daughter of Seyyid Said, was a woman of rare beauty and form. The eyes of Arabs are, as a rule, large and lustrous, but Khole's eyes were so fine that she was given the nickname of the Morning Star. It is related that a young Arab, taking part in some games before the palace, was observed staring up at one of the windows, all unconscious of the blood which gushed from his wounded foot. He had caught sight of Khole, and, overcome with the vision he beheld, had not noticed that he had pierced his foot with his lance. Salme was younger than Khole. In the year 1866, seven years after the events we are now relating, Salme took the desperate step of running away and marrying a young German, the employee of a German commercial house in Zanzibar, with whom, aided by those narrow and treacherous streets, so familiar a feature in the architecture of the town, she had been able, under the very nose of her brother, Majid, who sat upon the throne, to form a friendship which, but for the presence of a British warship, the

The palace was well suited for a rebel stronghold as the Machui range on which it stood is flanked on the west by the marshy river Mwera, which served as a moat against a hostile advance from the town. Here then, Barghash with the el Harth Arabs and their slaves, fortified himself.

Majid prepared to follow him with his forces, endeavouring meanwhile to persuade his brother to desist; but for answer Barghash told him that if he did not come out and attack he would march with his men against him: a clever retort intended to lure Majid from the town; a trap into which the unsuspecting monarch speedily fell. Majid mustered his troops at Bet el Ras and in the morning, reinforced by nine men and a gun from H.M.S. *Assaye*, he marched to Machui. It was the month of October, 1859, and it was raining hard, the northeast monsoon having apparently set in early. Majid, nevertheless, at 3 P.M. opened the assault and bombarded the palace at Marseilles, but was unable to make much impression upon the wall. The rebels issuing from their fortifications, engaged their assailants on the western slope of the hill, and succeeded in keeping them off till sunset. Majid then retired to the Mwera and bivouacked his troops at the sugar factory at Kinuni Moshi. At night he slept, and it is presumed his whole army slept too, for Barghash and his rebel forces, all unknown to the Seyyid, moved upon the town. In the morning Majid, advancing to renew the attack, found the palace abandoned, and having procured a heavier gun from the *Assaye*, he pounded it to a ruin, and then returned to the town to find the rebellion at an end.

Barghash had found the town in possession of Colonel Rigby and was forced to seek shelter again in his house. He had, in the British Consul, a less forbearing adversary than his brother. The shore in Zanzibar harbour being steep and shelving, Rigby moved the Assaye close in and anchored her off Barghash's house. Landing a guard of marines he proceeded to attack the house with rifle-ball till the people from the inside began to shout out their submission. Rigby then went up to the house and, rapping with his walking-stick at the door, called upon Barghash to surrender. He then seized him, put him on board the *Assaye*, and in three days' time sent him off with his little brother, Abdul Aziz, to Bombay. Barghash was kept in Bombay till the end of 1861, when he was permitted to return to Zanzibar with Captain Lewis Pelly, who had been appointed to relieve Lieutenant-Colonel Rigby as British Consul and Political Agent of the East India Company. Abdul Aziz is still in Bombay.

To investigate the claims of Thuwaini and Majid with respect to the succession to the sovereignty over Muscat and Zanzibar, Lord Canning appointed a Commission with Brigadier Coghlan, Political Resident at Aden, in charge. Associated with Coghlan were the Rev. P. Badger and Dr. Welsh. The Commission, in June 1860, proceeded to Muscat to hear the arguments of Seyyid Thuwaini, and to Zanzibar in September, 1861.

One of the most interesting questions the Commission had to determine was the right of the ruler of Muscat to dispose of the succession by will and the laws which regulated the succession of Oman. The investigation of this point was entrusted to Dr. Badger, one of the most learned Arabic scholars of his day. After careful inquiries into the customs that had for centuries prevailed, Dr. Badger wrote: "Among all the sovereigns not one occurs who is recorded to have assumed or exercised the right of nominating a successor, or of disposing of his territories by will or otherwise. On the death of a ruler the member of his family who happened to exercise the greatest influence at the time, either put himself forward, or was put forward by the people, to succeed to the sovereignty. The claim was frequently disputed by other relations of the deceased, and intestine family wars followed, the strongest ultimately gaining the ascendency; but even in such cases the right to the sovereignty does not appear to have been regarded as valid without the concurrence of the principal tribes."

On these grounds, and the altered circumstances and condition of the dependencies during half a century, the Commission reported that they considered the people of Zanzibar fully entitled to elect Seyyid Majid as their ruler, and justified in resisting any attempt made by Seyyid Thuwaini to coerce them into submission. They therefore concluded that Seyyid Majid's claims to sovereignty over Zanzibar and its dependencies was superior to any that could be adduced in favour of the ruler of the parent State.

Lord Canning accordingly awarded as follows: 1st That his Highness, Seyyid Majid be declared ruler of Zanzibar and the African dominions of his late Highness Seyyid Said.

2nd.-That the ruler of Zanzibar pay annually to the ruler of Muscat a subsidy of 40,000 crowns.

3rd.-That His Highness Seyyid Majid pay to His Highness Seyyid Thuwaini the arrears of subsidy for two years, of 80,000 crowns.

<small>Highflyer, in which she escaped to Aden, would have involved her in the fatal vengeance of her family,</small>

The Award bore date April 2, 1861, and was entitled: Award of the Governor-General of India for the Settlement of differences between the Sultan of Muscat and the Sultan of Zanzibar. Recognition of the Independence of their respective States.-The Award was accepted by Seyyid Thuwaini on May 15 and by Seyyid Majid on June 25, 1861.

Lord Canning added that the annual payment of 40,000 crowns was not to be understood as the recognition of the dependence of Zanzibar upon Muscat, nor as merely personal between the two brothers, but was to extend to their respective successors, as compensating the ruler of Muscat for the abandonment of all claims upon Zanzibar, and adjusting the inequality between the two inheritances derived from their father, "the venerated friend of the British Government." On March 10, 1862, a Declaration was made between Great Britain and France, engaging reciprocally to respect the independence of the Sultans of Muscat and Zanzibar; the adhesion of Germany to this Declaration was signed October 29, 1886.

Seyyid Thuwaini reigned ten years in Muscat. On February 11, 1866, he was murdered, while asleep, by his own son, Salim, who succeeded him. The payment of the 40,000 crowns was then discontinued by Barghash on the ground that Salim was a usurper.

View of Zanzibar stone town from the sea.

CHAPTER VI

SEYYID MAJID-THE SLAVE TRADE OF ZANZIBAR AND ARABIA

THE cruelties of the slave trade have been described by many writers, but in order to understand our subject rightly, we must, at the risk of repeating what may be familiar to many of our readers, follow the slave dealer for a little into the interior of Africa, and the slave dhow upon the sea.

During the early part of the century the country behind Quilimane and Mozambique provided the slaves destined for the markets of Brazil and Cuba, but as this traffic was gradually exterminated the caravans were diverted to more northern ports, chiefly Kilwa (Kilwa Kisiwani), and subsequently Bagamoyo; while, owing to the depopulation of the country between Nyasa and the coast, the slave hunters were compelled to go further and further into the interior till in the fifties they penetrated to the western side of Lake Nyasa, whence the bulk of the slaves were drawn. The hunters were sometimes Portuguese subjects, but more often half-caste Arabs. Livingstone has described the method they adopted to procure their supplies. It consisted in stirring up strife between tribes, setting one against the other in warfare, and carrying off or purchasing from the victors for a few yards of cloth, the prisoners that had been made. It must be remembered, however, that kidnapping and the slave trade had been going on in the interior of Africa for hundreds of years; that many of the people were born slaves; and that in times of scarcity and famine a chief would sell his people; natives, their own relations or even their own children. Depopulation again was often due to marauding tribes like the Masai who swept over the country carrying war and desolation wherever they went. Dr. Steere, when in the Zambezi region in 1862, observed that the direction of the slave trade was into the interior and not down to the coast.

But although it is undoubtedly true that the Arabs did not create the slave trade of East Africa and were perhaps responsible for only a portion of it, the slaves that had the misfortune to fall into their hands underwent unspeakable sufferings in the march to the coast and in transit to Zanzibar and Arabia. Livingstone's description of the horrors of the journey to the coast is well known. He believed, and the Rev. H. Waller of the Universities' Mission to Central Africa, who was in the Zambezi country with Livingstone in 1861, was of the same opinion, that probably not much more than one-fifth of the slaves in a caravan reached the coast alive, and that for every slave that came to the coast ten lives were lost in the interior. The slaves were tied together in long strings, the men being yoked in forked sticks, which were fastened round their necks, and kept there day and night till the caravan reached the coast and the tale was delivered to the shipper. The sick were left behind; insubordination was punished with immediate death. Having reached the coast the slaves were embarked in dhows and conveyed to Zanzibar to be sold in the open market or disposed of privately to dealers. The weary toil of the track was replaced by hideous confinement in the hold of a dhow. Sometimes the slaves were closely packed in open boats, their naked bodies exposed day and night to the sun and rain. To the tortures of sea-sickness (for natives not accustomed to the sea are bad sailors) and confinement were added those of hunger and sometimes thirst, for the slaves were purposely kept in low condition and under-fed lest they should gain strength and rise against the dhow master. Those who upon reaching their destination were considered too weak to live were left on board to die, the owners thereby avoiding the customs duty.

The dhows averaged about 80 tons burden-though some were 200 tons and more-and carried usually about 200 slaves; some of the larger dhows would have 300 and even 400 on board. To escape identification and capture the dhow master, if chased by a cruiser would sometimes throw the slaves overboard. An instance is recorded of a dhow that lost a third of her slaves between Kilwa and Zanzibar, to being thrown overboard, dead or in a dying condition.

Although Zanzibar was the great mart and distributing centre, cargoes were, in the south-west monsoon, sometimes carried direct to Muscat, a voyage occupying 40 days from Kilwa. A slave bought in the Zanzibar market for 20 dollars would realise 60 or 100 dollars at Muscat.

To elude our cruisers the dhows would creep up along the shallow waters of the coast or pass outside Pemba. In 1872 a dhow laden with slaves from East

Africa was captured in the Persian Gulf by H.M.S. *Vulture*. The following description of the dhow and its freight is taken from the *Times of India*, of October of that year:

"The number of slaves it was impossible at the time to estimate; so crowded on deck, and in the hold below was the dhow, that it seemed, but for the aspect of misery, a very nest of ants. The hold, from which an intolerable stench proceeded, was several inches deep in the foulest bilge-water and refuse. Down below, there were numbers of children and wretched beings in the most loathsome stages of small-pox and scrofula of every description. A more disgusting and degrading spectacle of humanity could hardly be seen, whilst the foulness of the dhow was such that the sailors could hardly endure it. When the slaves were transferred to the *Vulture* the poor wretched creatures were so dreadfully emaciated and weak, that many had to be carried on board, and lifted for every movement. How it was that so many survived such hardships was a source of wonder to all that belonged to the *Vulture*. On examination by the surgeon, it was found that there were no less than 35 cases of small-pox in various stages; and from the time of the first taking of the dhow to their landing at Butcher's Island, Bombay, 15 died out of the whole number of 169, and since then there have been more deaths amongst them. But perhaps the most atrocious piece of cruelty of the Arabs was heard afterwards from the slaves themselves; viz., that at the first discovery of small-pox amongst them by the Arabs, all the infected slaves were at once thrown overboard, and this was continued day by day, until, they said, forty had perished in this manner. When they found the disease could not be checked, they simply left them to take their chance, and to die. Many of the children were of the tenderest years, scarcely more than three years old, and most of them bearing marks of the brutality of the Arabs in half-healed scars, and bruises inflicted from the lash and stick."

Such are the pictures drawn for us by those who were witnesses of these events; by the Admirals of the squadrons, the British Consuls and Missionaries. They represent to us the extreme sufferings undergone by the poor helpless creatures who fell into the clutches of the slave trader. There were captured slaves, however, who did not undergo the hideous sufferings here described. The dhows were not all crammed full, nor in all cases were the slaves confined completely in the hold. We read of cargoes arriving at Zanzibar, the slaves fat and merry; sunning themselves on the deck. Unlike the French and Portuguese traders the

Arabs, though hot tempered and passionate, were not tyrannical; they shared with their captives such provisions as they carried and shared their privations likewise. Still the sufferings of the slaves, even if shared by their masters, were cruel enough, and were increased by the operations of our cruisers.

In the early years of Seyyid Majid's reign a considerable trade was carried on by the French. The French had agents up and down the coast and in Zanzibar. In Zanzibar the slaves were collected on the east coast of the island, which was, and is, difficult of access, and only sparsely inhabited, and shipped off secretly to Reunion and Mayotte. Majid deriving no profit from this traffic, as the French paid no duty on their slaves, endeavoured to stop it, but when he remonstrated with the French Consul, that functionary threatened him with the intervention of his Government. French warships, stationed on the coast, protected the French slavers from molestation.

The northern traffic was carried on by Arabs from the Arabian coast. These northern Arabs took delivery of the slaves as they were brought to the coast by the half-caste traders, and distributed them to the markets of Zanzibar, Arabia and Persia. Not being subjects of the Ruler of Zanzibar they defied his authority and became the terror of the peaceful Arabs of Zanzibar. Kidnapping went on up and down the coast; in the season the people of Zanzibar were afraid to stir out of their houses after dark, and all who could do so sent their children and young slaves into the interior of the island for safety. Armed bands paraded the town, and such was their wild lawless character that to prevent collisions with them the bluejackets of the squadron were not allowed ashore at Zanzibar, but were taken off to the Seychelles and given their leave there. It was with these Arabs, who were in fact pirates, that our cruisers had to cope.

The trade, it will be remembered, was legal within the limits of Kilwa to the south of Zanzibar and Lamu to the north, a distance of some 430 miles. During the five years 1862-67, 97,203 slaves were exported from Kilwa, 76,703 going to Zanzibar, 20,500 elsewhere. This represents an average export from Kilwa alone of 20,000 slaves. It was estimated that from 1,700 to 3,000 were sufficient to maintain the slave labour of Zanzibar and Pemba, and that at least 17,000 of those who left Kilwa were destined for the foreign market. To this extent were the Treaty stipulations with Great Britain ignored or set at defiance.

An export tax of two dollars was levied upon all slaves shipped from Kilwa for Zanzibar, four dollars upon those for Lamu, and a further export tax of two dollars upon all slaves shipped from Zanzibar. The proceeds of these, as of all other taxes, belonged to the Sultan of Zanzibar and must have represented an annual revenue of over 15,000 pounds sterling.

At the time of which we write the ships of the East India squadron patrolled the coast as far as latitude 23° south. In 1867 this squadron, consisting of seven ships, was under the command of Sir Leopold Heath, who succeeded Rear-Admiral Hillyar, and during the season, that is to say during the south-west monsoon, which blows from May till October, the squadron maintained a blockade of the Arabian coast, Ras el Hadd being the point at which the slave dhows eventually concentrated, the town of Sur, just beyond the Ras, being the principal dhow building centre.

During the three years 1867-69 the squadron of Admiral Heath captured 116 dhows, containing 2,645 slaves, but it was estimated that in the same period dhows carrying 37,000 slaves must have evaded capture. The proportion of captures was then about 7 per cent. In the year 1868 400 dhows were boarded, but 11 only of these were found to be slavers. The mystery of how the slavers evaded our cruisers was never cleared up. The cruisers, not being provided with steam launches, and being entirely dependent upon boats, could not intercept the dhows as they hugged the shore, and the officers, often new to their work, were entirely dependent upon their interpreters, at that time a class of men by no means to be relied upon.

The fact was that Great Britain after twenty-five years, that is to say from the signing of the Treaty of 1845, had been able to accomplish nothing in the direction of putting down the slave trade with Arabia; that the Treaty rather played into the hands of the slavers because, within the legalised limits, and when provided with a licence from the Custom House at Zanzibar, they could defy our cruisers and they not only defied them but jeered at them. Thus the *prestige* of the English suffered, as it was said that while they talked and bullied they could not or would not stop the trade.

Captured dhows when not destroyed at sea were taken to Aden or Zanzibar, where the Political Agent and Consul held the office of judge of the Vice-Admiralty Court. The captors were allowed a bounty of one pound ten shillings a ton. Numbers of the freed slaves were sent to the Seychelles, others were located in Zanzibar. During the time that he held office in Zanzibar, Colonel Rigby freed 6,000 slaves belonging to British Indian subjects, and these were either placed out with their former masters to work four days a week in return for their houses and cultivating rights, or were left to find work as they could. It was a very doubtful privilege for a slave, after having endured the privations of the journey from Nyasaland to Arabia, to be rescued by a British cruiser just as his sufferings were about to terminate. It is well known that Arabs are kind and lenient to their slaves, and a slave having survived the terrible hardships of the voyage would probably be more comfortable with an Arab master than turned adrift in a new country to shift for himself.

It became obvious that the methods upon which we were at that time working were wrong, and that we were beginning at the wrong end. There was but one way, namely, to abolish the traffic altogether. When the Treaty of 1845 was under discussion, Lord Palmerston had instructed Captain Hamerton to inform Seyyid Said "that the traffic in slaves carried on by his subjects was doomed to destruction; that Great Britain was the chief instrument in the hands of Providence for the accomplishment of this object; that it is useless for these Arabs to oppose what is written in the Book of Fate; that if they persisted in the continuance of this traffic it would involve them in trouble and losses; that they had better therefore submit to the will of Providence, and abandon this traffic, cultivate their soil, and engage in lawful commerce."

This view of the great Minister Great Britain had, after 25 years, come to recognise as the true one. She now set herself the task of imposing it upon the Arabs. On July 6, 1871, a Select Committee of the House of Commons was appointed to enquire into the whole question of the slave trade on the east coast of Africa. One important sequel to the enquiry was the mission of Sir Bartle Frere in 1873 and the treaty that followed; another the commissioning of H.M.S. *London* in the same year.

CHAPTER VII

ZANZIBAR UNDER SEYYID MAJID

IN the second year of Seyyid Majid's reign, that is to say in 1857, Captain Hamerton died in Zanzibar, presumably from fever. The symptoms that preceded his death are well known symptoms in Zanzibar, though they are not so frequent now as they were in those days. In December, 1856, Burton landed in Zanzibar, and describing Hamerton as he then found him wrote: "I can even now distinctly see my poor friend sitting before me, a tall, broad-shouldered, and powerful figure, with square features, dark fixed eyes, hair and beard prematurely snow-white, and a complexion once fair and ruddy, but long ago bleached ghastly pale by ennui and sickness. Such had been the effect of the burning heats of Muscat and the Gulf, and the deadly damp of Zanzibar Island and Coast. The worst symptom in his case-one which I have rarely found other than fatal -was his unwillingness to quit the place which was slowly killing him. At night he would chat merrily about a remove, about a return to Ireland; he loathed the subject in the morning. To escape seemed a physical impossibility, when he had only to order a few boxes to be packed and to board the first home-returning ship. In this state the invalid requires the assistance of a friend, of a man who will order him away, and who will, if he refuses, carry him off by main force."

Every resident on the East African coast will recognize the inertia of which Burton speaks, especially with men who have been many years in the country, and have lost touch with their old connections at home.

As British Consul and Political Agent for the Indian Government, Hamerton was in 1858 succeeded by Lieutenant-Colonel Rigby. An interval of eighteen months elapsed between the death of Hamerton and the arrival of Rigby, and during that time the British Consulate was closed. It was in that interval that the slave traffic across the Atlantic showed signs of renewed activity, as described in Chapter IV., and that the Spanish slaver *Venus* had the temerity to anchor in

Zanzibar harbour.

Rigby was at first the only Englishman in Zanzibar. To him we owe much of the information that we possess of Zanzibar during Seyyid Majid's reign, especially with regard to its trade. The imports in 1859 amounted to £905,911, the total annual trade being valued at £1,664,598, Including slaves.

The average annual crop of cloves amounted to 200,000 frasilas, about 7,000,000 pounds, valued at about £85,000 The price of cloves at that time was three pence a pound, though owing to the large quantity grown it had declined 75 per cent. from the figure at which it had stood some years previously. In 1861-62 the imports in legitimate trade were valued at £245,981, and in 1867-68, according to the figures of Dr. Kirk, they had increased to £433,693. More than half the trade was in the hands of Indians.

The customs in 1867 were farmed by an Indian named Jairam Sewji, who paid to the Seyyid 310,000 dollars a year, for which he collected an *ad valorem* duty on all imports and some of the exports. There were at that time about 4,000 British Indian subjects and protected subjects of Cutch.

Dr. Kirk was at that time medical attendant at the Agency. Rigby had in 1861 been succeeded at the Agency by Colonel Pelly, who was in turn succeeded by Colonel Playfair in 1867, and in the same year by Mr. Churchill, the first officer representing British interests in Zanzibar who was not an officer of the Indian Government and had not been trained in the Indian school of diplomacy. The hidebound officialdom of the Government of India and the India Office was the means whereby Great Britain was very nearly deprived of the services of her greatest representative in those regions. It was decided by them that medical officers should not fill the appointment of Political Agents in Zanzibar, and on this ground they rejected the name of Dr. Kirk when it was first recommended to them by Mr. Churchill. Fortunately for Great Britain, for Zanzibar, and for the harassed tribes of East Africa, this objection was reconsidered, and Dr. Kirk was appointed Consul-General and Political Agent in 1873.

Seyyid Majid died on October 7, 1870. He was a voluptuous, easy-going prince of an amiable and generous disposition, fond of the English and well-beloved of his people.

Burton found him "a young man, whose pleasing features and very light complexion generally resembled those of his father." His face was slightly pock-marked. About the year 1867 he built himself a palace at Dar es Salaam, with the object of being able to get away from the worry and strife of Zanzibar to a place where Consuls ceased from troubling. By the side of his palace he built a guests' house, and was in the habit of inviting the British Consul and others to go and stop with him.

Bishop Tozer, writing to his sister in 1864, described Seyyid Majid as "a very pleasing young man." "Every Arab," he wrote, "is a 'perfect gentleman,' and so you may be sure that the Sultan's manner and behaviour were perfect. There was a grace and an ease which I never saw equalled, only to Western taste the humility was rather overdone."

When Majid was dying Dr. Kirk went to see him and found him, just conscious, dressed in his ordinary clothes, lying on the floor. Dr. Kirk began to inquire about the succession, and Majid in reply slowly moved his hand and grasped the hilt of his sword. When he died, Barghash went to see the body, and, as he stooped over it, his dagger fell out of its sheath. His brother, Khalifa, who stood behind, picked up the dagger and handed it to Barghash, to the disappointment of the Arabs with whom he was popular. "What," they asked, "is the use of a man who neglects an opportunity like this?"

The British Consul, Mr. Churchill, called Barghash to the Consulate and received from him a promise that, if he succeeded to the throne, he would support the British policy and accept the treaty respecting the slave trade which had been pressed upon Majid. Thereupon his succession was secure, and he came to power without opposition.

With the death of Majid, what may be called the Middle Ages of Zanzibar's brief history came to an end. In 1869 the Suez Canal was opened, and in 1872 the British India Steam Navigation Company, under contract with the British Government, established a monthly mail service with Aden to connect with Great Britain, the first steamer arriving in Zanzibar on December 15 of that year. Seven years later, on Christmas Day, the Eastern Telegraph Company completed their cable from Aden to Zanzibar, telegraphic communication with Europe being established on December 27, 1879.

Through these channels the surge of Christendom was to flow with increasing volume; to eat away the foundations of the little State and all but devour its inheritance. Nature herself seemed against it for, as it were to warn her people that the old order had passed away, in 1872 she struck Zanzibar with a hurricane and cut off every tree on the island. To enable her to retrieve her losses and to cope with her opponents the country called for a strong man, and, as in the dispensation of Providence it often happens that the necessity of the hour brings the man forth, so in this case Zanzibar did not call out in vain. Seyyid Barghash stepped into the breach, as if specially raised up by Providence for the occasion. To his enterprise Zanzibar owes much of the material wealth she now possesses; to his tenacity the survival of her institutions; to his wisdom the conciliation of the European Powers, whose lust for territory he succeeded in gratifying while saving for his people the rich remnant of the islands.

CHAPTER VIII

SEYYID BARGHASH-FRERE'S MISSION

ON January 12, 1873, H.M.S. *Enchantress*, a paddle-wheel steamship, arrived in Zanzibar with Sir Bartle Frere, Her Majesty's special Envoy, who came to invite His Highness the Sultan to join with the Queen and her Government in framing measures which should have for their object the complete suppression of the "cruel and destructive" slave traffic. Practically the mission was sent to request Barghash to sign a Treaty, prohibiting entirely the export of slaves from the coast, even when destined for transport from one part of the Sultan's dominions to another, which, at certain seasons of the year, had hitherto been permitted. The members of the staff included the Rev. G. P. Badger, Colonel Pelly, H.M.'s Political Resident in the Persian Gulf, Major Euan-Smith, Captain Fairfax, R.N., Mr. (now Sir) Clement Hill, of the Foreign Office, and Mr. Grey, of the Foreign Office. In the afternoon of the day after the arrival of the ship, the Envoy called on the Sultan, who received him with marked respect, meeting him some distance from the door of the palace, a most unusual procedure; and throughout the interview he showed great good humour and gratification at the honour that was being conferred upon him, in enabling him to receive so distinguished a servant of the British Crown as Sir Bartle Frere. But he had not yet seen the terms of the Treaty. These were explained to him in two interviews by Dr. Badger, when it soon became apparent that Barghash and his Arab advisers-for at that time the Seyyid of Zanzibar had not acquired the absolute authority which was one of the indirect results of the suppression of the slave trade-did not see things in the same light as the British Government, and had prepared a very good case in defence.

The mission was badly timed. In August, 1872, the plantations and houses of the island and the coast over against it were blown down by a hurricane, an epidemic of cholera had before this decimated the population, reducing many Arabs to poverty, and in January of the following year the British Government came with this demand, which appeared to Barghash and his advisers like an order to commit suicide. "It will require years to recover the losses," he said, "and now the prospect of being obliged to give up the supply of slave-labour will absolutely ruin us."

"Again," he said, "you import coolies from India into the Seychelles and Mauritius: what would be the consequence to those islands if such supplies were stopped at once? And is it just, I appeal to you as a God-fearing man, to impose such hard conditions upon us under our actual circumstances?" Dr. Badger was forced to admit the hardship. "But let me ask you," he replied, "by what right you impose tenfold greater hardships on the wretched slaves who are torn from their homes-wives from husbands, and children from parents-to alleviate your distress?"

But Barghash could not be persuaded. He was moved almost to tears when he spoke of the consequences which he felt sure would result from the proposed treaty.

He followed up his refusal the next day with a letter, which he evidently hoped would prove the conclusion of the matter. "All our people have become as a sick man," he said, "full of pains, and requiring a skilful physician to treat him with gentle medicines until his disease is cured. But this which the (British) Government requires of us is a grave matter, which we are unable to bear, for we are poor, and we have nothing but agriculture to depend upon, and this agriculture cannot be carried on except by slaves, and their importation to us keeps up the islands. Had your demand been light, we should have been delighted to consent to it at once, out of respect for the (British) Government. This is the exposition of our state. Salaam."

Seyyid Barghash was informed that whether he signed the Treaty or not, the objects which Her Majesty's Government had in view would none the less be pursued, and that Great Britain was determined that the slave traffic should cease. Twenty years ago 60,000 to 70,000 slaves a year had been exported from the West Coast, but now not a single slave ever left that coast, and this result had been brought about by the British Government and a powerful British Squadron.

Barghash stuck to his own view of the case. He declared himself in danger of his life if he yielded, and pleaded for mitigation of the demand, but Dr. Badger continued to ply his shafts. "What would you think if a Foreign Power," he said, "occupying an island contiguous to your own, were to come over here and kidnap not your slaves, but your wives and children to cultivate their land as slaves?"

A treaty ought to benefit both the contracting parties, and Earl Granville had informed Barghash that, should he sign the Treaty, he might count on the friendship and support of the Governments of Great Britain and of India, and authorised Sir Bartle Frere to give the Sultan such assurances as might satisfy him that the payment of the Muscat subsidy of 40,000 dollars would not be enforced against him. As, however, this subsidy had not been paid for several years, the argument had little weight.

The chief Arabs throughout the negotiations exercised such pressure upon the Sultan, that the latter complained," A spear is held at each of my eyes, with which shall I choose to be pierced? Either way is fatal to me." They would not listen to this arrangement. "That is Barghash's affair, not ours," they said; "he pays it, not we Arabs, and no one will be richer or poorer if it be paid or withheld, except the Seyyid." The Envoy rightly refused, before the Treaty was signed, to commit himself to any promise of definite financial relief that might be interpreted as a bribe; he invited the Sultan to indicate in what way he could lighten the burdens of his people, and assured him and his Arabs they might confidently trust to the generosity of the British Government, but the treaty must first be signed. The Arabs, however, preferred something more tangible than promises, and complained that they were being led like blind beasts; "it may be to corn, it may be to chaff."

On February 3, after a third interview between Barghash and Frere, at which the former began to show temper and impatience at the failure of all his arguments, Sir Bartle, with Rear-Admiral Cumming, who was in command of the British Squadron in Zanzibar waters, proceeded in the *Enchantress* to Mkokotoni on a visit to Captain Fraser's shamba. Captain Fraser, formerly of the Indian navy, and at that time the only English merchant in Zanzibar, had a large sugar plantation at Mkokotoni, and oil and soap works in the town. He was the only man who worked plantations with paid labour; hence he exercised great influence over Barghash, and was also much trusted by him for his outspoken frankness.

Sir Bartle Frere drew up a memorandum for Lord Granville on what he saw, from which, since it is too lengthy for reproduction in *extenso* here, we take the more important points.

The estate, about 2,500 acres, was situated at the north end of Zanzibar

Island, on Mkokotoni Channel, which, with its bays and inlets, was a favourite haunt of slave-runners. About eight years before, when no better than a rice swamp, it had been purchased by Captain Fraser in association with certain members of a well-known London and Bombay merchant firm. After large sums had been spent on drainage, road-making, planting and machinery, it was sold to a Hindu-British subject, from whom it was leased by Captain Fraser; and at the time of Sir Bartle Frere's visit it was a well-arranged, well-cultivated estate, on which were grown sugar-cane, coconut trees, screw palms, palm-oil trees, and a variety of tropical fruits, such as oranges, limes, and mangoes. The estate had a stream running through it, and consisted mostly of dark alluvial soil and clay, lying on a flat shore with a background of low hills, one of which was of coral-rag or limestone about 250 feet above the plain. The whole was under the supervision of a European assistant (who found the locality quite healthy), but the work was done by natives, and it is this feature of the work which is of interest here, for the native labour was entirely that of free men. Not only all the field labour and road-making, but all the masonry, carpenters', smiths', and coopers' work; cart-making and mending, the transport and putting together of a large quantity of heavy machinery; its repair and daily starting, feeding, and stopping- all were worked and managed by free natives working for regular wages.

Over the different departments there were headmen of various tribes, and from various parts of the coast and interior. With only one exception all had been slaves; and a sort of leadership was voluntarily attributed to a man whose parents in his own country had belonged to a ruling clan.

One of the most pleasing and noteworthy facts was the presence of troops of healthy-looking, well-fed children, numbering altogether eighty-five, of all ages under eight or nine years old, the total population on the estate being about 500.

Slaves in Zanzibar had few children except under specially favourable circumstances, and, taken as a body, would soon have died out, if no fresh slaves had been brought into the island. The natives, as first collected on the estate, were slaves who naturally retained all the characteristics and vices of slavery. Among other peculiarities observable was that of infertility. Marriage as a permanent tie, or as any restraint on almost promiscuous intercourse, was hardly recognised. Children generally were looked upon simply as a restraint and an encumbrance, and neither shame nor blame was attached, in the opinion of slaves, to any means for preventing or terminating the existence of children before or after their birth.

The change for the better was very gradual and attributable to a great variety of causes, but all resulted more or less directly from the status of freedom. General habits of order, good medical attendance when ill, and many such causes worked towards improvement, but the most efficient agency, no doubt, was the sense of property-that what they had was their own. This cause acted most effectually in raising the freed men from the more degrading vices of slavery.

The first signs of an anxiety to have children about them had been remarked among the men. In the earlier annals of the primitive court for the adjustment of matrimonial, as of all other disputes, it was the husband who had generally appeared the more anxious to see his children grow up around him, but the wife soon learned to look upon her offspring as desirable additions to domestic comfort and respectability.

An important feature in the economy of Mkokotoni was the extent to which extra labour could be got from other shambas. The slaves in Zanzibar had, by long custom, two days in the week to themselves-Thursday and Friday. These days they generally spent in idleness; but in the neighbourhood of Mkokotoni Captain Fraser's practice of paying regular money-wages had induced a habit in the slaves on neighbouring estates of going to work at Mkokotoni on their holidays; and he had at times had as many as six hundred candidates for work on the same day. There was extremely little crime, beyond that of small thefts, which were said to be rarely committed by people resident on the estate.

Captain Fraser's success had an important bearing on the question of slavery, and Sir Bartle Frere maintained that the Arabs had but to follow his example to reach the same result. The Sultan held that it was impossible for the Arabs to do so, and even Captain Fraser saw the difficulties of a change of system, difficulties of which Sir Bartle Frere made too little. The Arabs seem incapable of profiting by regularly paid labour, chiefly because they will not devote enough attention to detail and exercise active supervision over their employees. The natives will not-it would be more correct to say they cannot-work unless they are sharply looked after. If a man be a slave he naturally thinks nothing of sleeping away his time in the shade of a clove tree, but if he is in receipt of regular wages, it is quite otherwise.

Mr. Sunley, in Johanna, "that wonderfully fertile and beautiful spot," one of the Comoro Islands, was carrying on the same sort of work as Fraser at

Mkokotoni. A memorandum on his sugar plantation was drawn up by Mr. Clement Hill, who wrote: "Mr. Sunley has been resident on the island for more than twenty years. Coming to it alone, and with but little capital at his command, he fixed on the land in the vicinity of the little Harbour of Pomony as best suited for his purpose, obtained from the reigning Prince a concession of 6,000 acres of wholly uncultivated land at a rent of 200 dollars per annum, and at once set to work to form an estate, now fully equal in its products to the majority of those in Mauritius." On this estate (about 700 acres of which were devoted to sugar cultivation) Mr. Sunley employed 800 native labourers, male and female, slave and free. His free labourers he paid their full wages, but to the slaves, all of whom were hired, he gave only two-fifths of their earnings, their owners receiving the remainder.

Dr. Kirk was left in charge of the negotiations during Sir Bartle Frere's absence, but being limited by the Envoy's instructions, which did not authorise the use of naval force, he made no progress with the Sultan, though the latter was manifestly uneasy. Barghash was afraid of his Arabs, who had made up their minds from the first that they would not have the contemplated treaty, and hoped that it might be averted by the intervention of a Foreign Power. Moreover, they had a lingering doubt whether they would be left in peace if the Treaty were signed. "Twice did you raise your demands in Seyyid Said's time," Barghash had told the Envoy; "again in Seyyid Majid's time; now this fourth time you have come to me, Barghash, with still more crushing exactions, and if I grant this, God only knows what the fifth demand may be. How do I know this is final? Is there nothing beyond?"

With Dr. Kirk, Barghash returned to metaphor, the form of controversy which best suits the hesitating, reflective nature of the Arab. Slowly and deliberately addressing the Agent, he said: "When you find you have heaped a load upon your camel that it cannot pass the city gate, do you not lessen the burden and gain your object? Now lessen this heavy burden the Government have laid upon us, be it ever so little, and we are your servants, and you will gain all you desire; give us some respite and we will accept the Treaty."

On March 15 Dr. Kirk requested from the Sultan a final answer to the many letters he had received at the hand of the Envoy, whereupon Barghash wrote a circular note "to the Queen, the Wazeers, the Governor-General, and the Governor of Bombay," saying that he had replied to his Excellency as he was able, and concluding as for the prohibiting of the transport of slaves to Arabia, we will endeavour as much as we can, but let it not be hidden from your knowledge that there are thieves everywhere."

Sir Bartle Frere failed in his main purpose, but his mission was by no means barren of results. Visiting the ports of the continental coast, Madagascar and the Comoro Islands, he ascertained the methods of the slave traders, the customs dues collected on slaves, the limits of the traffic, the extent of the Sultan's authority over the more remote parts of his dominions, and the influence of the Indian traders. "England, through India," he wrote, "has an immense practical hold on East Africa. The Sultan and his Arabs can do nothing for good or evil without the Indian capitalist. Throughout our whole circuit, from Zanzibar round by Mozambique and Madagascar, and up to Cape Guardafui, we did not, except at Johanna, meet half-a-dozen exceptions to the rule that every shopkeeper was an Indian."

The hurricane of 1872 had destroyed Barghash's navy, so that his hold on his African Coast possessions, always limited, had become little more than nominal. In the southern portion of those dominions the chief port was Kilwa, which, hidden behind unsurveyed reefs, out of sight of cruisers, flourished on the slave trade, exporting annually, in spite of the Treaty of 1845, about 35,000 raw slaves. Since those days the coasts and islands have been surveyed (Under Captain Wharton in 1873-78, and under Commander Balfour in 1888-90), but at the time of Sir Bartle Frere's visit the navigation was dangerous for all except Arab dhows, and the Arab chiefs felt secure in their position. When Sir Bartle landed at this port and invited the Governor to meet him, that functionary replied: "Let him come here and sit here. I will not move to see him." English," he afterwards said, in the interpreter's hearing, "show force to Seyyid Barghash and come here to show force to me, but I will meet force with force." Whereupon he sent six Arab soldiers to the Custom House, where the Envoy was sitting, with the apparent object of putting this threat into execution, but no violence was offered. The coarse behaviour of this man towards the British Envoy clearly showed the attitude of the Arabs with respect to the proposed Treaty, and made it plain that Barghash had ground for his apprehension of danger when he said: "A spear is held at each of my eyes; with which shall I choose to be pierced?"

The hope to succeed by persuasion, beyond which the Mission had no authority to go, was foredoomed to failure, and the British Government found it necessary to adopt the argument of force. On May 15 Earl Granville instructed Dr. Kirk, who had now been invested with plenipotentiary powers, to inform the Sultan that if the Treaty were not accepted and signed by him before the arrival of Admiral Cumming, who was ordered to proceed at once to Zanzibar, the British naval forces would blockade the islands. Even then Barghash would not comply, for he and the Arabs hoped to see a French war vessel come to support them. Had the opportunity occurred, he would have tried to go to Paris and open negotiations there, and he had to be convinced of the vanity of such expectations. In putting pressure on the Sultan, Dr. Kirk always had the Arab chiefs present and addressed arguments to them all, but, even when the crisis was most acute, no one showed animosity against him. The Sultan, in fact, was not a free agent, the consent of the chiefs being indispensable; so that Dr. Kirk, without forfeiting their goodwill, found it necessary to suggest vague alarms, far beyond the inconveniences of a blockade. So effectually did he work on the fears of the Arabs that they joined their influence to his and urged the Sultan to sign. The good feeling of Barghash was plainly shewn at these interviews. When Dr. Kirk one day was explaining what a blockade meant, no letters in or out, no fresh meat from the mainland, and if a French man-of-war should arrive, no permission for Barghash to leave, the Seyyid leant over and whispered in his ear, "Then I will come and live with you at the Agency."

Thus, before the arrival of Admiral Cumming, Dr. Kirk, by his firmness and prudence, had the Treaty duly signed. When the formality was complete the Sultan said, with great relief: "Now my head is safe on my shoulders; it is your head that is in danger." But Dr. Kirk, knowing better than he did the views of the Arabs, replied, "There is no fear of my head."

On June 6 Dr. Kirk was able to send to Earl Granville the Treaty signed and ratified. It bears date June 5, 1873, and it was signed by John Kirk, Political Agent, Zanzibar; "The Mean in God's sight, Nasir bin Said bin Abdallah;" "The humble, the poor, Barghash-bin-Said."

It provided for (i) the total cessation from that date of the export of slaves from the coast of the Mainland of Africa, whether destined for transport from one part of the Sultan's Dominions to another, or for conveyance to foreign parts; (2) the closing of all public slave markets in the Sultan's Dominions; (3) the protection by His Highness of all liberated slaves; (4) the prohibition by Her Britannic Majesty of all British India subjects from possessing slaves and from acquiring any fresh slaves. A Treaty in similar terms, but relating to the Dominions of the Sultan of Muscat, was signed by Sir Bartle Frere and Seyyid Turki bin Said, Sultan of Muscat, on April 14, 1873.

Mr. Clement Hill, in a short sketch dated January 17, 1873, has provided us with a glimpse of the slave market in Zanzibar as it last appeared before being for ever closed. "The Slave Market," he wrote, "is no longer in the Square which it so long occupied, as within the last few weeks Her Majesty's Acting-Consul, Dr. Kirk, took advantage of the old site having been bought by a British Indian subject, to prohibit his allowing the continuance of the scandal. The site now occupied is a small square, surrounded on three sides by buildings, and the approach to which is, on the one side, through the Bazaars, where the trade is carried on chiefly by Indians, and on the other, through more open streets leading to the outskirts of the Town. . . .

"On entering the market we passed by wooden sheds, under which sat, on the left, some half-caste Arabs, on the right, some half-clothed Negroes. The market was comparatively empty when we arrived at half-past four in the afternoon, so we had a good opportunity of seeing the slaves who were already there. They were seated in rows round the square, each batch sitting packed close together, and herded by an Arab or Negro (for the Negro seems to forget the miseries he once underwent as a newly-captured slave, or, like a schoolboy bullied as a youngster bullies again when able), who forced into position the luckless wretch who stretched his stiffening limbs beyond the limits allowed him. We counted at that time ninety, of all ages and of both sexes. Many wore a set and wearied look, many were fat and gay, while two young men and a boy alone confirmed, by their skeleton frames and looks of misery, the sensational tales often written of these markets. The impression left upon the mind at this time was that the process of sale was not more debasing to the Negro than were the statute hiring fairs of recent English times to the servant class of England. Most of the slaves were naked, save a clout round the waist of the men, and a cloth thrown loosely over the women. I say 'naked,' for one can hardly consider as clothing what some evidently held to be full dress, viz.: the scars and slashes on their faces, and the rings in their ears and noses. Some, however, of the women, chosen probably for some attraction which, great doubtless to Zanzibarite eyes, were hardly appreciable, by Europeans, were gaudily dressed in coloured robes, with short-clipped hair, eyes and eyebrows painted black, and henna-dyed foreheads, while the rings and armlets they wore were heavy and large.

"About five o'clock, the frequenters of the market, the lounge of the true Zanzibaris rolled quietly in, Arabs and half-castes, Persians of the Guard in their long caps, and all armed with matchlock, sword or dagger. At once the salesmen woke up, and all was bustle. And now came a cruel time. With a true knowledge of business, the sickliest and most wretched slaves were trotted out first, led round by the hand among the crowd, and their price called out. The price of one boy was seven dollars; he was stripped and examined by a connoisseur, his arms felt his teeth examined, his eyes looked at, and finally he was rejected.

"The examination of the women was still more disgusting. Bloated and henna-dyed old debauchees gloated over them, handled them from head to foot before a crowd of lookers-on, like a cow-seller or horse-dealer; and finally, when one was apparently satisfactory, buyer, seller, and woman all retired behind the curtain of the shed to play out the final scene of examination.

"I cannot say that the subjects of this searching examination seemed to object to it; on the whole, they appeared perfectly callous, neither caring whether their merits were dilated on nor apparently sensible of the notice they were attracting from the bystanders.

"The prices we heard mentioned varied from sixtyseven dollars for a woman to seven dollars for the boy whose case I have mentioned. We saw no deals actually effected, and were told that the presence of the Mission in Zanzibar had sensibly affected the commerce in slaves as well as in the ordinary articles of trade.

"This being the close time, the market was not at its full height, though there must have been at least two hundred slaves there before we left.

"No rudeness was shown to us by anyone, though I have been told that some officers of the squadron now here have been insulted and hissed by Arabs."

To supplement this account we take the following from Captain Colomb's "Slave Catching in the Indian Ocean." It refers apparently to the year 1872:

"The market was well on when we arrived. There were perhaps twenty auctioneers, each attending a separate group and selling away as hard as possible. One of the officers counted over 300 slaves present, and it was clear several groups had only just been landed. My former friend with the bullet-head was dozily naming his eighteen or twenty dollars, as the case might be, altogether untouched by the excitement which seemed to govern some of his brethren or rivals.

"One of these strongly attracted my notice. He was a young man, not altogether Arab in appearance, and with a not unpleasant cast of countenance. His counter was laid out with a choice selection of goods from the continent, and he was selling them like a steam-engine.

"His 'lot' appeared to be lately imported; they were all young boys and girls, some of them mere babies; and it was amongst them that the terribly painful part of the slave system was to be seen. I mean the miserable state, apparently of starvation, in which so many of these poor wretches are sometimes landed. The sight is simply horrible, and no amount of sophistry or sentiment will reconcile us to such a condition of things. Skeletons, with a diseased skin drawn tight over them, eyeballs left hideously prominent by the falling away of the surrounding flesh, chests sunk and bent, joints unnaturally swelled and horribly knotty by contrast with the wretched limbs between them, voices dry and hard and 'distinctly near' like those of a nightmare-these are the characteristics which mark too many of the negroes when imported. All, however, are by no means so. I have seen in the same batch some skeletons, and others as plump as possible. In this very group it was so.

My Arab auctioneer was working away at a boy when I first noticed him. He had reached sixteen dollars, but there seemed to be no advance. I knew my friend to be selling, when I could only see his back, by the steady periodical working thereof, caused by his vigorous declamation.

" 'St-asher; St-asher; St-asher; St-asher; St-asher; St-asher * etc., thus the auctioneer, not looking at anyone in particular, or seeming to attach any definite meaning to what he was doing. Only the 'St-asher' came out of him like a jet of steam, and shook his whole body and the body of the slave boy on whom his hand rested.

"I addressed him through the interpreter:

"'When did they land?'

"Auctioneer: 'St-asher-two days ago-St-asher-St-asher, etc.'

"I: 'What will you let him go for?'

"Auctioneer (he never leaves off): St-asher-St-asher-twenty dollars-St-asher, etc.'

"No advance appearing on 'St-asher,' the boy was made to sit down and a little girl, about six years old, put up.

* **Sitashara-sixteen (dollars).** † **Sabatashara-seventeen.**

"A wizened Arab, with a quiet face and one eye, was amongst the buyers. He looked at the child's little hands, and then stooped down and spoke to her with a smiling face. The child smiled in return, and I could not think that my wizened Arab would treat her *very* badly if he bought her. She was soon worked up to the regulation 'St-asher,' and two or three more bidders chimed in. The steamengine worked faster and faster; he had got to 'Sebba-t'asher; Sebba-t'asher'; † and in his hurry and work could only pluck at the dresses of probable purchasers.

"Wizen-face and the rest of the buyers are all very calm, and do not trouble their heads much about the matter, but the steam-engine will certainly burst his boiler if it goes on much longer. Wizen-face, impelled by a strong pull at his dress, advances a quarter of a dollar ; steam-engine plucks him again, with an advance of another quarter, and goes on working madly. Wizen-face, however, is not inclined to go further, and moves away. Steam-engine plucks him harder by the dress, and never leaving off his 'Sebba-t'asher-noos,' which is now the price, stoops down and gathers the child up in his arms, seeming to say, 'Come, take the little thing-she is only an armful.' Wizen-face will not buy, however, after all, and steam-engine blows off his steam, and sets the little girl on the ground preparatory to getting the steam up over a fresh article.

" At this moment my attention was attracted in another direction, by hearing a sound as of a drowsy humble-bee chanting in monotone. Passing through the crowd in the direction of the sound, I became aware of a string of some eight negro girls, standing in a row and facing me. These girls were decorated in the highest style of the fashion before described, but they each had, besides, a sort of mantle of blue muslin thrown lightly round their shoulders, which, it struck me, they were rather proud of. The humble-bee from whom the buzzing proceeded was the auctioneer in charge of the sale of these girls. In appearance he looked like a benevolent edition of Mr. Fagin, as we first make his acquaintance in the pages of 'Oliver Twist.' His beard was white and flowing, his nose hooked and prominent, and his eyes half closed and dreamy. He carried the regulation cane under his arm, was sauntering round and round his stock of goods, and making undecided changes in the 'sit' of the girls' attire with his disengaged hand. The drowsy buzzing which proceeded from his lips resolved itself into distinct sounds when I got near enough to analyse them.

"The sounds were: 'Thelatha washerin wa noos'; 'thelatha washerin wa noos'; which when separated into proper words became Swahili for 'twenty-three and a half,' twenty-three and a half dollars being the upset price of each or any of the lot before me.

"This humble-bee differed from the other auctioneers, "inasmuch as he did not seem to connect his buzzing chant with his stock-in-trade.

"'Thelatha washerin wa noos, thelatha washerin wa noos, thelatha washerin wa noos'; it was more a song to pass away the time than an announcement of the upset price of his lots, as he sauntered backwards and forwards, now re-settling a fold of muslin which he had unsettled on his last passage, now patting the shoulder of this one, and now altering the position of the arm of that one, and never ceasing to chant the while.

"I studied the faces of these girls very closely to try and detect what their feelings were on the subject, but it is almost as hopeless to penetrate the thoughts of a negro through his expression as it is to get at those of a sheep by the same process. I could see neither pleasure nor pain, any other active sentiment in their demeanour or expression. Absence of thought, rather than presence of indifference, pervaded each countenance, and I could not help speculating whether it were more true that the thoughts which we, in our state of mental energy, would consider proper to such an occasion were really present in these creatures' minds, but hidden from me by the negro conformation of features, or whether the thoughts were really absent. If I am to judge by what I have seen of the negro in his natural state, I must give it that the thought is absent.

"I got my interpreter to ask one girl whether she liked it or not, but the only answer obtainable was that careless jerk out of the chin, which we associate with sulky indifference."

Approached by narrow, tortuous alleys of Indian shops, the depths of the bazaar, the English Cathedral now is on the site of the market where these slaves were herded and sold.

Seyyid Barghash bin Said.

CHAPTER IX

SEYYID BARGHASH-VISIT TO ENGLAND-REVIVAL OF THE SLAVE TRADE-LIEUTENANT MATHEWS

BARGHASH, after the signature of the treaty for the abolition of the slave trade, and the closing of public slave markets within his dominions, adhered loyally to his engagements. On June 5, 1873, the very day of the signature, the slave market at Zanzibar was cleared and closed by messengers sent from the Palace, and on June 8, a proclamation was posted up prohibiting under penalties the transport of slaves by sea. This proclamation Barghash did not suffer to remain a dead letter, but, of his own initiative, imprisoned not only those slave-dealers who actually transgressed but also those who were preparing to do so.

At the same time the blockade by the British ships was strictly maintained, slave-runners being handed over to justice, their dhows confiscated and their slaves set free. For a while the shipments of slaves from the mainland coast fell off, and at Zanzibar and Pemba the price of slaves doubled. There were, however, 4,000 slaves for sale at Kilwa, and in July half-a-dozen large slave caravans were expected in accordance with the usual course of things. The dealers were doing their best to work off their stock sending gangs of slaves northwards along or not far from the coast that they might be shipped at some port opposite Zanzibar or Pemba. This was, in fact, the system which Dr. Kirk, acting through the Sultan, had to combat. The slave trade as a legitimate trade had ceased to exist, but, as foretold by Dr. Kirk long before the signing of the treaty, the result was that smuggling on a large scale sprang up and continued for many years, 10,000 or 12,000 slaves being annually taken across the channels, from 30 to 45 miles in breadth, separating Zanzibar and Pemba from the mainland coast.

After these events, Dr. Kirk, who was suffering in health, obtained leave of absence, and during the year 1874, had opportunities of discussing with the representatives of the Foreign Office the working of the Treaty and the general condition of affairs in Zanzibar. The result was that when, in April 1875, he returned to his post he was the bearer of an invitation from the British Government to the Sultan to come to England. The advantages of such a visit were obvious; for the ruler of Zanzibar was the centre of Legislative and Administrative Authority in his dominions, and if he and his chief advisers had ocular demonstration of the power and wealth of his ally, Great Britain, where no slaves existed, they would have less hesitation than they had hitherto shewn in yielding to British influence.

Arrangements were soon completed. An Arab Chief, Ali bin Soud, was appointed as Regent during the absence of Barghash, while the Prime Minister, Nasur bin Said bin Abdullah, and four other Arab Chiefs, besides Sir Tharia Topan, the most important member of the Indian trading community in Zanzibar, with friends and a retinue of servants, were to attend him on his visit. At Zanzibar the place of Dr. Kirk, who was requested by the British Goverment to accompany His Highness, was to be taken by Major Euan-Smith, appointed by the Viceroy of India.

Before setting out, Barghash executed a deed (subsequently superseded by a more liberal instrument) emancipating all his domestic slaves at his death. This he did, as the deed itself testified, that he might obtain acceptance of God, and in His name, and that he might escape from punishment.

On May 9, 1875, the Sultan and his party embarked and proceeded on their way. They were requested to put in at Lisbon to greet the King of Portugual, and Admiral Seymour was ordered to Lisbon with the Channel Squadron to salute Barghash and afford him an opportunity of estimating the naval power of Great Britain. Barghash was displeased with the smallness of his suite and, in going ashore, Dr. Kirk, who was in the leading boat, was horrified to see in the procession a number of the Sultan's menials dressed up as grandees of the suite, evidently destined to accompany their master into the presence. The Agent was, however, able to prevent this scandal by posting himself at the door, and at the moment of their entry cutting off the kitchen contingent, and directing them into an adjoining room. The King invited Barghash, but no one else, to sit down. The Arabs, observing the Queen seated, remarked to one another in Arabic, that their dignity would not allow them to remain standing while a woman was sitting, so they all sat down too. The Agent remained standing at Barghash's side; the King had his Foreign Minister standing on his left, and they conversed in French. But the King and his Minister exchanged occasional remarks in Portuguese, and Dr.

Kirk, who was not supposed to know Portuguese, heard them discussing their plans.

They would entertain the Zanzibar monarch at a reception, have a display of fireworks, and afterwards try and get him to settle the boundary question. The Agent remained motionless at his post, his eyes fixed on the wall in front of him, but when the visit was over he went on board the flagship and arranged with the Admiral that they should leave Lisbon that night. When the King had returned the visit, the Minister, hearing of the Projected departure, went on board the *Canara*, and endeavoured to get the conversation round to the question of the boundary. But the Monarch was not to be caught in this way. " These things," he said, no doubt calling to mind their conflicts in the past, "these things are drawn with the sword, not with the pen."

The party reached Gravesend on June 15, whence they went up the river in one of the Thames Steamboat Company's boats. On landing at the Westminster Palace steps the Sultan was welcomed by representatives of the Foreign Office and many other distinguished men. Among these were Sir Bartle Frere, whom he knew well, the Rev. Dr. Badger, a friend whose acquaintance he had first made during his compulsory visit to Bombay, and Mr. (now Sir) Clement Hill of the Foreign Office, to whom had been entrusted the delicate duty of making arrangements for the hospitable entertainment of Barghash during his stay in England.

Next day the Sultan began the round of business and of amusement (even more exhausting), which continued without intermission for more than four weeks, in the course of which he visited the Queen at Windsor, and the Prince and Princess of Wales at Marlborough House. He afterwards declared that the pleasantest sight he had seen in London was that of the children of their Royal Highnesses. Day after day he became acquainted with the varied forms of British hospitality. He received and was received by Royal Dukes and Ministers of State. He was fêted at balls and concerts and garden parties; he listened to deputations headed by bishops and noblemen who enlarged on the excellence of the Bible, bewailed the evils of slavery, and extolled the beneficial work which was carried on by British Missionaries within His Highness' dominions. He was thus brought face to face with some aspects of religious life in England, but he did not relax his observance of his own religious customs. He performed his devotions regularly twice a day, and behind his hotel in Piccadilly he had a private slaughterhouse and a private kitchen where his native butcher and four native cooks prepared his repasts.

His love of horses was gratified in Hyde Park and at Ascot, whither he was taken in the race week. He saw "Blue Beard" at the Globe Theatre, heard "Lohengrin" at Her Majesty's Opera, and "Acis and Galatea" at the Crystal Palace. He had an agreeable presence, and showed his approval of performances and also of plaudits intended for himself by a graceful movement of the arm, so that he became not merely fashionable but popular. At the Crystal Palace, when the choir rose to sing, he, with Arab politeness, rose also, and then the vast audience, following his example, got on their feet. There was general bewilderment as to what the movement might mean, and goodnatured amusement when it was discovered to be a mistake due to the Sultan's ignorance of English customs.

At the British Museum Barghash shewed intelligent appreciation of old Arab manuscripts, and of the results of archaeological exploration of Oriental cities, but at the Postal Telegraph Office, where attempts were made to explain the working of the apparatus, he shook his head in despair. His attitude towards London novelties was that of an intelligent, good-humoured man, willing to be entertained but without false pretence. He paid visits to Brighton, to Aldershot, to Woolwich Arsenal, and to Birmingham, Liverpool, and Manchester. Returning to London he figured at the Guildhall, where an elaborate address in a costly casket was presented to him, and at the Mansion House, where he was feasted. He had learned that in his numerous speeches (which had been translated by Dr. Badger) the critics had remarked on a good deal of sameness. To this his reply at the Mansion House was: "How can I help it? It is the fault of the English people. You all welcome me; you all tell me I have done something for the abolition of the slave trade, and you hope I shall do more; what can I say but thank you, thank you, thank you."

After a month so crowded with incidents, it was no doubt a welcome change to cross the Channel. On July 15, he went from Folkestone to Calais, where he was received by representatives of the French Government, who took him to Paris. There he spent a few days; then travelled to Marseilles, where he took ship for Zanzibar, reaching his home on September 19. In letters to the Queen, to the Prince of Wales, and Lord Derby, the Foreign Secretary, he expressed his thanks for the many tokens of friendship he had received during his visit.

One result of these doings was a supplementary treaty signed on July 14, by Lord Derby and Nasur bin Said bin Abdullah, on behalf of their respective

Governments. This treaty was at once ratified by Barghash, and on September 20, the ratification by Queen Victoria was delivered to the Sultan at Zanzibar.

The treaty provided that domestic slaves in personal attendance on their masters, or in the discharge of the legitimate business of their masters, might be conveyed by ship without rendering the vessel liable to confiscation; but if they were being taken against their will such slaves would be set free. The first of these provisions was not found to work satisfactorily. Many hundreds of domestic slaves annually accompanied their masters in their pilgrimage to Mecca, the great centre of the slave trade for Turkey and Persia, and only a small proportion of them were brought back. Barghash, though he was persuaded to make some concession to the Arabs, ostensibly to encourage them in the observance of religious duties, was still acting in good faith, and in the following year he freed his household slaves, giving them carefully drawn up deeds of manumission, duly executed, and this step helped to guide Zanzibar opinion on the question of slavery in the right direction.

But the problem was, how to stop the traffic in raw, newly-caught slaves between Kilwa and Pemba. This traffic had assumed a dreadful character. The miserable victims of the slave dealers' rapacity were now marched, often at night, through jungle paths to Bagamoyo, and, when it was unsafe to ship them there, they were driven further north to Lamu and even to Somaliland, 700 miles from Kilwa. When it became dangerous to march them along the coast northwards, the wary dealers conveyed them partly by sea and thus escaped observation where they were looked for on land. Severe punishments were tried. In one case the master of the dhow, the crew, and the slave owners were taken and handed over to Dr. Kirk, who caused the six slave owners (three of them being pure Arabs) and the captain to be secured in their own slave chains, and marched through the streets. Then they were flogged in front of the Palace, Arabs and Negroes being treated alike. This method of punishment had the advantage of driving the traffic in Zanzibar into the hands of the lowest classes; it made it less reputable and thus more easily dealt with. The slave runners were treated as common degraded criminals, and the population of Zanzibar could hardly respect men who suffered such treatment.

Still the smuggling from the mainland was not extinguished, but there was evidence that the Sultan had impressed on his Walis the necessity of exerting themselves to the utmost to put it down. In a slave dhow, captured with 129 slaves on board by the boats of the *London*, there was found a private letter, which, when translated, ran as follows: "This letter comes from the harbour of Tanga, and, my dear friend, if you ask about Seyyid Barghash I tell you His Highness has stopped the buying and selling of slaves at Kilwa and Bagamoyo, and imprisoned the dealers in irons; this is the news, and at Bagamoyo the agents are sending back their money."

Some of the Walis were evidently acting up to their instructions, but, notwithstanding the statements in this letter, the authorities at Kilwa were (as we shall see presently) deeply implicated in the slave trade, so that further steps were necessary.

The next move made by Dr. Kirk was to induce the Sultan to issue the two proclamations of April 18, 1876. One of these prohibited the conveyance of slaves by land, under penalty of severe personal punishment and forfeiture of property and slaves; the other prohibited the approach of slave caravans from the interior, from Nyasa and elsewhere, under similar penalties. It was mainly against the inhabitants of Kilwa that these proclamations were directed, for that town was the centre of the traffic in raw slaves. At this time Dr. Kirk, after careful investigation, estimated that 12,000 slaves were annually smuggled into Pemba, as many were marched over-land further north, and some also shipped to Zanzibar. Allowing for the loss of life among the slaves caused by their long marches and terrible privations, the number actually brought to the coast was not less than 35,000, representing an annual loss to the interior of Africa of perhaps 350,000 of the population, as the direct result of slave-raiding with its attendant murder and disease. The number annually sold at Kilwa was over 35,000, the prices received for them amounting to over 120,000 lacs. It was on this traffic that the whole population of the town directly or indirectly depended. The proclamations were duly posted up, but the inhabitants defied proclamations, and the local chiefs continued as usual to levy dues on the caravans.

Energetic measures were therefore taken to enforce the Sultan's orders, and the British war-vessel *Thetis*, commanded by Captain Ward, was sent to Kilwa with instructions to remain there as long as was necessary. Where force on any considerable scale was likely to be required, it was unsafe to trust entirely to the Sultan's troops. The slave-hunting and slave-running Arabs were reckless ruffians of the lowest class, often foreigners from Arabia with no purpose except to secure the profit of slavecatching. To cope with them, men of stronger character were required than the levies raised by Barghash. Hence the presence of the *Thetis* at Kilwa. Dr. Kirk also went, and the Sultan sent special orders to the Governor, Said bin Abdullah, who was himself directly implicated in the traffic, to arrest and send to Zanzibar as prisoners all the chiefs of Kilwa, providing him for this purpose with a force of 212 soldiers. On May 15, 1876, the *Thetis* arrived in time to prevent confusion. The raw slaves had accumulated to the number of about 6,000, but had been removed inland out of the reach of confiscation. They were gradually taken north and during the next three months were shipped in small numbers from Bagamoyo. There was always a stream of boats, most numerous at night, crossing to Pemba, carrying three or four slaves at a time. But on the whole it was clear that, for the present, the people of Kilwa considered themselves beaten in the contest. They moved northwards to Bagamoyo in large numbers, for the trade, was not extinct. Those who remained behind betook themselves, at the instigation of Dr. Kirk, to the collection of rubber which was very profitable. The fitting out of slave caravans was (for some' months at least) stopped.

In the end of that year, however, and the beginning of 1877, the traffic revived The rubber trade continued prosperous, yet there were Arabs at Kilwa who could not refrain from slave-hunting, and others who could not hold aloof from its gains. On this occasion the Governor, Said bin Abdullah, was the person chiefly implicated, both as slave owner and receiver of bribes. He was promptly removed from his office, and he went, apparently of his own free will, to Zanzibar. Soon afterwards a dhow with a gang of his slaves was captured at Pangani and brought to Zanzibar. The investigation before Dr. Kirk, as judge of the Vice-Admiralty Court, clearly shewed that the ex-Governor was the culprit. The slaves in charge of the gang gave evidence against him, and an old slave who had been put into the gang to be sold, made the state of matters still clearer. The slaves were all sent before the Sultan who, at the time, was sitting in Baraza with the ex-Governor beside him. When confronted with all these men, the ex-Governor had no defence to make, and at Dr. Kirk's request he was at once arrested, put in slave-irons, and sent to the common prison. Thus a wholesome lesson was given with the utmost publicity, and the Sultan sent out letters to Governors, threatening them with severe punishment if they neglected their duty with respect to the slave traffic; a warning which had good results.

The British vessel which, in those years, was commanded by the chief naval officer at Zanzibar was the *London*. She had reached Zanzibar in November, 1874, commanded by Captain G. L. Sulivan, who was succeeded in September by Captain T. B. Sullivan. The *London* was used as a stationary ship at Zanzibar while her boats cruised for the suppression of the slave trade. To this ship Lloyd W. Mathews was appointed as lieutenant, on August 27, 1875, and he at once proved himself an able and energetic officer. The work of dhow catching was often dangerous, and from the Admiralty reports it seems clear that sometimes the young officers in the boats of the *London* displayed more of the spirit of enterprise than of prudence, and owed occasionally to good fortune escape from "accidents" which might have brought the punishment of murder on whole villages. The names of three lieutenants, O'Neill, Mathews and Lang, were specially mentioned for commendation in the reports of Captain T. B. Sullivan who, on August 2, 1876, wrote: "Although constantly brought into contact with the Arab slave owners at Pemba who have suffered these losses, such has been the tact shewn by these officers that in no case has friendly intercourse between them been affected."

In a letter to his mother, dated July 29, 1877, Lieutenant Mathews wrote: "I returned a few days ago from a cruise of 26 days having captured three slave vessels, and expect to leave here (H.M.S. *London*) to-morrow for a few days to try and track one out that I have information about. Tracking them is rather like what children play-Hide and Seek-as we sometimes have to go 40 or 50 miles out of our way from the place at which we expect to find them, and then we find them stowed away up rivers or creeks, and have to get at them dead or alive as best we can. They are in the most awful state when we get at them (the slaves); just stewing together, packed like herrings, and one mass of small-pox; many often dead; and they and the living cooped up as tight as they can fit in. We deal with the owners first, and sort out the poor devils afterwards!" And again he wrote: "The slave dealers are an ugly lot. You have to be ready to put a bullet through them at all times, and it is sometimes impossible to bring them back without disabling them if you mean to return with a whole skin and the cargo of poor devils you've rescued."

In August, 1877, Barghash, acting on the advice of Dr. Kirk, resolved to have a new military force of about 500 men, armed with Snider rifles and drilled in European style. Hitherto his force had consisted of an undisciplined and lawless Persian Guard and Arab irregulars from Hadramaut, on whom little dependence could be placed, whereas the new force would consist of negroes who could be made amenable to discipline and would certainly not combine with the Arabs. Captain Sullivan of the *London* was applied to for assistance in this matter, and, being told that Lieutenant Lloyd Mathews had volunteered to drill the men, he gave permission for this officer to do so at such times as his services could be spared. This offer was accepted by the Sultan, and the enrolment and instruction of the Zanzibar recruits went on satisfactorily.

Mr. Richard Vause, of the *Natal Mercury*, who paid a visit to Zanzibar in 1877, recorded his impressions of these recruits in the following terms: "Attracted by the martial sound of fife and drum, we follow its direction, and soon come upon a string of black recruits, at the run to their rendezvous. Filing with them into the police barracks, we find Lieutenant Mathews, R.N., of H.M.S. *London*, in the drill shed, from whom we gather that he is engaged on behalf of the Sultan in converting the raw material present into food for powder, *alias*, soldiers, by drilling them every afternoon.

"Lieutenant Mathews has a quiet happy knack with him, drills them in English, and they take to soldiering as naturally as ducks do to water. To-day he has four sections of 80 men each, and though 'irregulars' in everysense of the word, they really do not look half amiss in their short black jackets, white trousers and jaunty red caps. They go through their exercise with excellent precision, and Lieutenant Mathews is quite sanguine they will prove very efficient. In fact, by last mail, one of our letters says they are making great strides, and becoming a well drilled body of men. It was impossible, though, to restrain a smile at the wooden weapons, shaped like muskets, with which they 'present arms,' possession whereof the fellows all seem not a little proud, carrying them about even when off parade. The Arab officers, who give the word of command in good English, in their gold and silver lace and blue frock-coat and trousers, look great swells. In conversation with some of the 'raw material,' we find them utterly unable to understand what the motive impelling the Sultan to make soldiers of them is, or what purpose they are to serve. They evidently look upon it as connected with some strategic operation on the opposite mainland, as there is, according to their view, no conceivable use to which they can be put on the island itself."

The British Government entirely approved of the formation of this force and, on April 12, 1878, intimated that, to signify their approval of the Sultan's action with respect to the slave trade, they had ordered 500 stand of Snider rifles, with bayonets and ammunition, and also seven Whitworth guns, to be shipped for Zanzibar for His Highness' use. On June 22, the arms arrived and were formally placed in the hands of the soldiers, who were then inspected by the Sultan. The men, all of whom had been trained by Lieutenant Mathews, and were under his sole command, had made highly creditable progress and the companies first formed were ready to commence practice with the new rifles.

The Sultan was the owner of a great number of slaves who worked on his plantations and with whose services, in the condition of things then existing, he could not easily dispense. In the persistent smuggling of slaves across the channel, it was almost certain that not a few were landed on his private grounds; but these surreptitious proceedings were due to the connivance of his overseers to whom it was difficult to bring home actual complicity. So far from encouraging these irregularities, Barghash shewed by his private as well as his public acts that he was in sympathy with the movement against slavery. In January, 1879, an Arab of Lingah on the Persian Gulf trading by dhow with Zanzibar, sent a complimentary letter and presents to the Sultan. The presents were Oriental in their character, a Bahraini donkey (the donkeys of Bahrain are still valuable), two dresses and an Abyssinian male slave. The Sultan dismissed the bearer of the letter, declining the presents, but freeing the slave.

His Governors of the Somali coast acted in accordance with the spirit as well as the letter of his instructions to them. There slavery had been nominally abolished by the proclamation of January 15, 1876, and now active Walis endeavoured to make the proclamation effective. At Barawa, the Wali, ceasing to recognise the status of slavery, at every opportunity which the exercise of his judicial duties afforded set the slaves free. If a slave came before him with a complaint of cruelty on the part of his master; if two men disputed in his court the ownership of a slave; or if any other circumstance brought the question of slavery before him in concrete form, it was the slave who got the benefit, for he was declared to be free. Consequently, slave-owners became cautious and careful neither to give slaves occasion for complaint, nor to make too much of their title to property in them.

The proceedings of the missionaries were frequently a cause of embarrassment. Their sympathies were, of course, in favour of liberty, and they took little account either of law or custom. At Rabai, near Mombasa, at the end of 1879, they had about 150 slaves who had run away from their masters. These slaves had not been freed, but they had built houses for themselves and they worked for their own support. Their masters claiming them, it was only by the interposition of the Sultan that the dispute was settled without violence.

The Sultan was a man of ability and saw that neither his own interests nor the prosperity of his dominions depended on the slave trade. Before the treaty of 1873, his revenue had been largely derived from duties on imported slaves; in 1875, the duties being farmed, the rent paid to the Sultan amounted to 350,000 dollars annually: in 1880 the rent was increased to 500,000 dollars.

In June, 1880, the command of the military force, and the management of police force were entirely in the hands of Lieutenant Mathews. In consequence of troubles at Pimbivi, including the murder of Captain Carter and his companion Mr. Cadenhead of the Belgian expedition, he was sent on August 13, with his troops to occupy stations inland. The expedition was away three months and, though military in form, had an entirely pacific purpose, being intended to protect the inhabitants against passing plunderers and to prepare routes for traffic. Occupying an entrenched position at Mamboia, 120 miles from the coast, it put matters in a satisfactory condition, settling difficulties respecting run-away slaves.

Towards the end of April, 1881, the Wali of Pangani was reported to be remiss in suppressing the exportation of slaves to Pemba, and Dr. Kirk applied to the Sultan for his removal from office. The Wali, being at the time in Zanzibar, was not allowed to return to his post, but two men were sent secretly to watch at Pangani and find out what was going on. Two days later, Mathews, with an armed force on board a native vessel, entered Pangani harbour. He duly met his two "inquiry agents," who briefly made their report and enabled him to decide on the spot what course he should adopt. Guided by the two men, be marched his soldiers under the Sultan's colours to the houses of the slave-dealers and had them and their slaves promptly secured. In his operations he was assisted by the Sultan's officials, and was able to arrest the principal offender, on whom the whole of, the slave traffic at Pangani depended, and to seize the vessels engaged in the trade. Then he went to Tanga, but the rumour of his doings went before him, and the slave-dealers were prepared. He was delayed and obstructed by the officials and no slaves could be found. However, he had the chief dealer arrested and sent to Zanzibar, and his dhow seized. In these proceedings Mathews was supported by the Sultan. Offenders were punished, slaves were set free, and for further operations on the coast an Intelligence Department under Mathews was organised.

These incidents, however, had other and more important results. When Mathews had paid to Tanga the surprise visit which proved to be no surprise, there were no slaves there, not because there was no slave traffic, but because the slave runners had removed their stock inland to escape detection. When Mathews left they did not bring back their gangs to Tanga, but took them to Mtangata, a small port between Tanga and Pangani. There they found a northern Arab fishing dhow and putting 80 slaves on board, set sail on May 5 for Pemba. The night was dark and one of the boats of the *London* approaching hailed her at 30 yards' distance. As no answer was given, a blank cartridge was fired to which the dhow replied by a volley of bullets into the boat. The boat was a whaler with only four English seamen and an interpreter on board; there was no officer in command and, in the confusion which followed the unexpected attack, there was some delay and two oars were lost. The dhow continued to fire on them, but the boat, following at a distance, returned the fire till the dhow, apparently intimidated, lowered her sail. By that time the whaler's crew had almost exhausted their ammunition and, dreading foul play in seizing the prize, turned away to look for help. The dhow re-hoisting her sail, soon reached Pemba where the slave-owners and their cargo were safely landed. When the *London's* steamboat came on the scene the dhow was again standing out to sea, but at once put about and ran on to the beach where she was captured, though the crew escaped. Owing to some mismanagement on the part of the captors the vessel was suffered to be broken up before condemnation, and thus the difficulty of her identification was much increased. At Dr. Kirk's request the Sultan at once wrote to Mohammed bin Jama, one of his agents in Pemba, requiring him to do his utmost for the arrest of the persons concerned in this shipment of slaves. The man on whom suspicion fell was an Arab of good family, a proprietor who had recently returned from Oman. When Mohammed called him to meet the charge he at first complied but afterwards refused to appear, and, lest force should be used against him, he collected his friends and armed his followers. The Arab chiefs of Pemba in those days did not regard the Sultan as their ruler, but only as a leader whose authority was derived from themselves. Living at a distance from the seat of Government at Zanzibar, they had no practical acquaintance with the centralised administration there, but adhered to their antiquated usages and sought to uphold their ancient rights. An order from the Sultan addressed collectively to these chiefs, each of whom considered himself as his equal, was hardly to be endured, but when delivered through an agent, whom they considered of an inferior tribe, it seemed little short of an insult, and therefore they set the Sultan's command at defiance. Mohammed, being in a difficulty, applied for further instructions, and the Sultan, advised by Dr. Kirk, resolved to seize this opportunity of correcting abuses, and to crush the power of revolt which the Arab chiefs possessed. He sent Lieutenant Mathews at the head of a body of regular soldiers with authority to arrest the man who was accused of slave trading, and, without referring to Zanzibar for further instructions, to shoot down every Arab who offered resistance. Acting on this authority, Mathews speedily brought the island to submission, and the power of the Arab chiefs collapsed. The chief who had been accused of slave running quietly gave himself up, but the evidence of his guilt being insufficient he was, after a fair trial, discharged.

In july 1881, Mathews, having been permitted to retire from the British Navy with the rank of lieutenant, was confirmed in his command of the Sultan's troops. He was often brought into association with civil and naval officials, both British and foreign, and that he might be able to support his position, the Sultan appointed him to the rank of Brigadier-General in Zanzibar.

Sir Lioyd Mathews, K.C.M.G.

CHAPTER X

SEYYID BARGHASH-THE DEATH OF CAPTAIN BROWNRIGG AND ITS RESULTS

CAPTAIN BROWNRIGG in August, 1880, took over the command of H.M.S. *London*, as Senior Naval Officer at Zanzibar, and he at once displayed the ability and zeal which earned for him the high approval of Admiral Gore Jones under whom he served. The captures of slaverunners effected under his orders were numerous, as shewn by the many formal documents, decrees, certificates, receipts, and reports concerning them. Documents relating to similar matters are probably now issued nowhere, and before long they will doubtless be regarded as curiosities. The seizure of each slave dhow was brought to the cognizance of the Court of H.B.M. Consul-General at Zanzibar and was followed by a close investigation into the circumstances. In all cases there was strict impartiality, and where injury had been inflicted on the innocent, full compensation was made. Usually, however, guilt was clear and condemnation followed. In case NO. 33 of 1881, the Decree was as follows:

"Our Sovereign Lady the Queen against the native vessel named "Mambo Sasa" sailing under Zanzibar colours and having no papers, whereof Mahomed-bin-Jaribu is the owner, and Salim-bin-Bougene Master, her tackle, apparel, and furniture; and also against ninety-one male and forty-six female slaves, seized as liable to forfeiture by C. J. Brownrigg Esq., a Captain in the Royal Navy, and commanding Her Majesty's ship "London," before Lieutenant Colonel S. B. Miles, Her Majesty's Acting Agent and Consul General at Zanzibar, on the 18th day of October, 1881.

"Appeared personally Sub-Lieutenant Robert H. Travers, R.N. of H.M. ship - "London" and produced his sworn declaration setting out the circumstances under which the native vessel "Mambo Sasa," under Zanzibar colours of the description and dimensions set forth in the annexed certificate of admeasurement taken by the captors, was seized by him, together with ninety-one male and forty-six female slaves off Pemba on the 15th day of October, 1881. I, the said acting Agent and Consul-General, having heard the evidence and examined the witnesses, and having found sufficient proof that the vessel at the time of her capture was engaged in the slave trade in contravention of Treaties existing between Great Britain and Zanzibar, do adjudge the said vessel, her tackle, furniture and apparel, and also the ninety-one male and forty-six female slaves found on board thereof to have been lawfully seized, and to be forfeited to our Sovereign Lady the Queen, and do condemn the same accordingly."

Then follows the certificate of destruction, signed October 23, 1881, by the Sub-Lieutenant, R. C. Travers, and approved on October 24, by Captain C. J. Brownrigg. After this comes the certificate of admeasurement (prize money being awarded according to the size of the vessel captured) bearing, besides the signatures of the Captain and Sub-Lieutenant, that of the Coxswain of the "London's" launch; and that is followed by the Consul-General's receipt for slaves, in this form:

"RECEIVED from Captain C. J. Brownrigg, R.N., commanding H.M.S. "London," ninety-one male and forty-six female slaves, taken by the boats of that vessel and condemned in this Court in case NO. 33 of 1881, Zanzibar Admiralty Court file."

Captain Brownrigg's own account of the matter states that "at 5 a.m. on October 15, Sub-Lieutenant Travers sighted a dhow and gave chase, coming up with her about 7 a.m. On closing her it was noticed that there were a number of Arabs on board, and that they had arms and were making preparations to use them to prevent them boarding the dhow; but, on a shot being fired close to the dhow, they laid down their arms, and the Chief Arab waved his sword to say that no resistance would be offered. On boarding her she was found to contain 137 slaves, 10 Arabs in charge, and 12 passengers, besides her crew of 8 hands who were armed as well as the Arabs and passengers; the dhow was towed into Fundu (depôt at Pemba) and in transhipping them from the dhow to the sailing boat "Alexandra," one dinghy full capsized, and Enoch Lightbourne, A.B., and Thomas Melhuish, Ordinary, specially distinguished themselves by the promptness they displayed in jumping overboard and saving the slaves, who were in an emaciated condition and unable to swim, and some would undoubtedly have been drowned had it not been for these two men, especially Melhuish, who, on one of the female slaves sinking, dived and brought her to the surface."

Bounties for the capture of slaves and dhows, it should be mentioned, were distributed among officers and men, through the Naval Prize Fund. For each slave taken the bounty would be as much as £5 and for dhows it ranged from 30 shillings to £5 10s. per ton. The total amount awarded varied, of course, with the condition of the slave traffic. When few slave dhows were running, it might not exceed £2,000 but when the trade was brisk it would reach £12,000 in the course of the year.

On November 26, 1881, Captain Brownrigg proceeded from Zanzibar to Pemba in the *London's* steam pinnace *Wave* on a visit of inspection and for the examination of the bays and creeks on the eastern side of the island, where it was suspected slaves were landed. He was expected back at Zanzibar on December 6, but on the 4th his body and that of a seaman, together with five of the crew of the pinnace, were brought from Pemba to Zanzibar.

The circumstances of Captain Brownrigg's death were as follows:- On the morning of December 3, he, with the coxswain, 4 seamen, 3 stokers and 2 natives, was cruising on the west side of Pemba near Kokota Gap. He was not supposed to exert his efforts personally in the work of capturing slave dhows, but if one came in his way he willingly availed himself of the opportunity. Two dhows were sighted, examined, and allowed to pass, and then a third came in sight. This dhow was small, and it was noticed that she was flying French colours, a circumstance which seems to have inclined Captain Brownrigg to be specially careful not to give offence. He was sitting near the tiller beside the coxswain, Yates and the interpreter, and, when the dhow was about 1,000 yards distant, he said "I intend going alongside that dhow." He then put on his uniform but not his sword, holding the latter by the scabbard in his left hand. He next said to Yates, "I do not want to go on board her, but you go forward and take the hookrope, and when we get alongside you jump on board the dhow and make the hookrope fast, at the same time take a quick look round and see if you can see anything" (meaning slaves). Then he took the tiller, and Yates asked if he should get the arms ready, to which he replied, "All right, I'll see to that; you go forward." Then Yates went forward and stood ready with his hookrope. As the pinnace was nearly alongside the dhow, her captain was seen standing on the poop with some papers in his hand, but no opportunity was given of examining them. The two vessels got abreast of one another, and Yates was in the act of stepping on board when he noticed about eight Arabs crouching with rifles ready, and at once shouted to Captain Brownrigg. The Arabs fired but missed him, and he with his hook and rope knocked one of them to the bottom of the dhow. Two Arabs then rushed at him with their rifles clubbed, but one of them slipped and fell, and Yates, ducking, caught hold of the rifle of the other. Standing with one foot on the *Wave* and the other on the dhow, he grappled with the Arab till both fell over the gunnel of the dhow and then rolled into the sea. Yates was eventually saved, but in the meantime the Arabs, firing a volley into the pinnace, killed or wounded four of the crew, and almost at the same moment Captain Brownrigg, having seized a loaded rifle, killed two of the Arabs at one shot. Then the crew of the dhow streamed over into the *Wave*, where no one but the captain opposed them. Brownrigg then gave the order, "Full speed ahead," but neither the stoker, who had in fact been knocked overboard, nor anyone else responded, and the fight had to be fought to the end. He had his empty rifle and, using this as a club, he knocked down several of the Arabs. He was a powerful, resolute man, and, had he been in any degree supported by his crew, he would have been too strong for the Arabs. Of the survivors of his crew, most were wounded, only two being left in the pinnace; the others had fallen or been driven overboard, and, being shot at by the Arabs, two were hit and sank. Still Brownrigg fought on, his limbs and hands gashed and bleeding, and no other weapon being within his grasp, he felled an Arab with his telescope. Some of his assailants were in front and some above on the awning, while he stood exposed in the stern sheets. The Arabs above slashed at him with their long Omani swords, and one cut him across the face, blinding him. He asked his wounded Goanese servant for water but received none, and then, utterly exhausted, he was shot through the heart and fell. The Arabs then proceeded to kill or mutilate such of the wounded as they found on board, or in the dinghy which was towed by the pinnace, but the captain's servant escaped by feigning death. Then they tried to wreck the machinery and sink the pinnace, but without success, and, as soon as they were gone, the stoker, who had been swimming about, scrambled on board, got up steam, and, after rescuing others, took the boat to the naval depôt, whence, next day, the remains of the captain and one seaman were taken by Lieutenant Travers to Zanzibar, together with five of the survivors, two being left behind. Next morning, December 5, the remains of Captain Brownrigg and the seaman Aers were buried in the old English cemetery at Grave Island in the harbour of Zanzibar with the honours which were due.

The dhow in the meantime had reached Wete, and having landed her cargo of about 100 slaves, she was taken to a place of concealment. The Arab, Hindi bin Khatim, who was suspected as the leader in this outrage, was wellknown. He belonged to a band of Muscat slave dealers and had been shortly before released from prison, having been acquitted on a charge of slave dealing for want of sufficient evidence. No time was now lost in arranging for the apprehension of the whole crew. On the morning of December 5, General Mathews, with a force of 100 men and accompanied by H.B.M. Consul, Mr. Holmwood, and a representative of the French Consulate which was interested in the matter, set out from Zanzibar on board the Sultan's steamer *Star* for Pemba.

Next morning the *Star* was off the Port of Wete, but though twice stranding was unable to land the force till evening. However, a sailing boat of the *London* came and reported the capture of the dhow by Lieutenant Target, who, accompanied by one of the seamen, and by Cockroach, the interpreter, who had witnessed the conflict, had gone up the Wete Creek and found the missing vessel in charge of two men, who at once ran away. The dhow was towed round to Funzi, whither Mr. Holmwood and M. Greffulhe, of the French Consulate, proceeded to examine her. There were not only clear indications that she had carried a large cargo of slaves, but also evidence of recent bloodshed. A blood-stained garment, pierced by a bullet, seemed to have been worn by a man who had fallen, shot through the heart, by the one shot fired from the pinnace. No French colours or papers were found on board.

When Mr. Holmwood returned to Wete he found that General Mathews, having failed to obtain from the Arabs any information about the whereabouts of the fugitives, was on the point of sending out parties of troops to search the road, grounds, and houses for Hindi or any one who seemed to be associated with him. This method of procedure was not in accordance with the views of the Consul, who, not only then, but subsequently, liberally supplied the General with advice and with offers of help. But Lloyd Mathews knew the Arabs he had to deal with, and the soldiers he commanded. He refused to arrest Arab Governors and chiefs merely on unsupported suspicion, and rejected the reinforcements which were pressed upon him. During that night his men were scouring the country and, in the morning, when near Chake Chake, he received a letter from M. Greffulhe stating that one of his officers had arrested Suliman bin Abdullah, a near relation of

Hindi, with whom, a few days before, he had been seen. Mathews offered Suliman a reward of 500 dollars for such information as would lead to the capture of the fugitive, and this offer was professedly accepted by Suliman who, however, said that he required time. Mathews gave him till next day (December 8) and then, convinced that be was playing false, seized his property, burnt his houses and sent him, along with some other Arabs, to Zanzibar. No further progress was made till the following day, when, after mature deliberation, Mathews arrested Naser bin Ali, the Arab chief of Wete, and sent him on board the *Star* for conveyance to Zanzibar. It was through this man's plantations that the 100 slaves from the dhow had been led, and it was near his house and in charge of his people that the dhow had been left; and all this time he had refused information. But he was not strong enough for the part he played, for now, when the anchor was being weighed, he said that he knew the hiding place of Hindi, and would deliver him up within forty-eight hours. On giving security for the performance of this promise, including landed property worth £20,000, he was released. Next afternoon he sent word that Hindi was hiding in a wood close by, indicating the spot, and Mathews at once set out with his men to prevent escape; but on reaching the place he found that Hindi had fled towards the eastern coast of the island. Mathews procured a guide who knew whither Hindi had gone, and tracked him to Chimba, to the house of an Arab, Saleh bin Rhabish, a slave dealer, but not one of Hindi's crew. By that time it was dark, and there was difficulty in effectively surrounding the house. Mathews, however, posted his men and went forward to summon those within to surrender. The slave dealers were armed with swords, and at once rushed to the attack, Saleh charging at Mathews, who was compelled to shoot him down. Two (not belonging to the dhow crew) were captured unwounded, and one managed to escape. Inside, there was still one man, and to get at him it was necessary to break down the wall. He proved to be no other than Hindi, and, when called on to surrender, he cut down the officer who summoned him. His resistance only ended when his sword-hand was shot away and one leg was torn with two bullets. Two surgeons from the Philomel found it necessary to amputate the hand and then the leg, but he made no recovery. The shock was too great for him, and he died on the evening of December 12, glorying that he had slain so redoubtable a fighter as Captain Brownrigg who, he declared, had killed two of his men with one shot.

On December 19 Hindi's brother, Khalfan, was caught along with another

Arab, Massoud, and these two were brought to trial for actual participation in the murder. It was found that the dhow had had only seven or eight of a crew, one of them being a slave. Of the crew two were killed at the time of the attack, Hindi died of wounds nine days later, two were prisoners, and one either escaped or died of wounds. The slave of course was not dealt with.

The report sent from Pemba by Mr. Holmwood, on December 12, concerning the more important of these proceedings, concludes with the following generous tribute to General Mathews and his native force:" I cannot close this report without remarking upon the steadiness, good behaviour, and patient endurance of the Sultan's native force. They have had to keep guard day and night over a considerable village and its approaches, also to furnish patrols and outposts; yet they have always been ready at a moment's notice to march on the expeditions, generally occupying the whole night, which their leader has ordered. General Mathews himself has worked indefatigably; indeed, I fear he has over-exerted himself. If the remainder of his troops are equal to the small body here present, he has reason to be proud of the force under his command, and no officer could better deserve the confidence which he has inspired among his men."

We extract the following from the official report addressed to the Sultan by General Mathews :

"We started immediately after sunset, and the following morning while searching the roads to Chake Chake, and within half an hour's march of that place, I received a letter from the French Vice-Consul, telling me of the return of one of my officers with a relation of Hindi bin Hattam, named Suliman bin Abdullah, whom he had arrested. I immediately returned and found that he had been seen with Hindi the night after the fight. On searching his house a second time, we found several guns, slave-chains, and neck-rings, and amongst his papers, a French pass for a dhow named *Zura*, 41 tons, owned by Hindi bin Hattam, from Mayotte to Mozambique, one passenger, Mohamet bin Ali. This vessel, by Hindi bin Hattam's statement, was lost at Kondulhi, and the dhow now captured was bought for him by an agent whilst at Zanzibar . . . . .

"On Sunday, December 11, at midnight, we captured Hindi bin Hattam at Chimba, in the house of an Arab named Sali bin Rabish, but not without bloodshed, as the Arabs discovering us before the house could be properly surrounded, attempted to cut their way through us. Eventually Sali bin Rabish was killed, Hindi bin Hattam mortally wounded, two were taken unhurt, and one, who was wounded, fell into the river and could not again be found.

"We carried Hindi bin Hattam and the body of his companion to Waite, where he confessed that at one time he sailed under French colours. Having lost his dhow he bought the present one through an agent at Zanzibar, taking over his colours and papers, but without entering it at the French Consulate. He stated that his reason for fighting the English steamboat was that he had shewn them his colours and papers as they came close to him, and that a shot was fired from the boat which killed two of his men. As soon as he saw his men fall he gave the order to fight the boat, and killed the Captain and three of the crew; the remainder jumped overboard. He states two were killed in the dhow by the first shot from the boat, and the second shot wounded another badly and injured his own left arm which I saw was scored as if by a bullet. Another of the crew had his skull fractured. As soon as the fight was over he made for Waite, running into the creek to the southward of the harbour. On grounding the dhow he told the remainder of the crew who were unhurt, viz., his brother Halfan bin Hattam, and one of the sailors, to escape from the island, and that he would see to the wounded. He also stated that afterwards, seeing they were so badly wounded, he left them to their fate. When I asked him if he thought they were dead or alive, he said they must have died. We could find no trace of them, so it is possible they may have been found dead in the dhow before her capture, and thrown into the creek or buried in the jungle. The dhow had 100 slaves on board. Hindi bin Hattam died about 9 p.m. on the night of the 12th December.

"The Arabs of Pemba after the capture and death of Hindi gave us every assistance. On the 19th December Halfan bin Hattam and the one remaining Arab of the crew were captured. Halfan bin Hattam stated that he was in the dhow as steersman, and that when the English steamboat came up with them, his brother showed the colours and papers and told them to keep off and not to board him, as he was a French dhow, but they came alongside and fired a shot, killing two of the crew. He states that they then fired into the boat, and afterwards attacked with their swords; but that he himself had nothing to do with it. After the fight he threw the dead bodies of the Arabs overboard. The other two wounded he left with his brother in Waite Creek, telling him they were unable to move, one being wounded in the head, and the other in the leg. Being told by his brother to escape if possible he then left with the last of the crew. From that time until captured, he had not seen his brother, nor heard of his death, as they had lived hiding in the jungle or sea, on the east side of Pemba, coming out only at night to steal sufficient food from the nearest plantation. He states that the crew of the dhow were seven Arabs, including his brother and a slave to assist. The Arab sailor captured with him confessed that he was in the dhow.

"The second day after the taking of Hindi bin Hattam a dhow was stolen at night from Sittini Creek. I believe some of Hindi bin Hattam's friends, fearing consequences, escaped, as many Arab slave-dealers were found by the searching parties hidden with their recently-imported slaves in different jungles and out-of-the-way huts. . . .

"H.B.M. ship *Philomel*, her boats, and the boats of H.B.M. ship *London*, blockaded the west side of Pemba. Lieutenant Target, of H.B.M. ship *London*, was always ready with his boats in giving us every assistance."

The prisoners, Khalfan bin Khatim and Massoud, the sailor, along with Suliman bin Abdullah, were, by arrangement with the Sultan, sent, on December 29, to the British Consulate to have the question of their guilt or innocence inquired into. The first two were identified by several of the crew of the pinnace, and they acknowledged that they were on board the dhow, but alleged that they acted only in self-defence after the attack had been made by the men in the pinnace, an allegation which was disproved not only by the evidence of the British crew, but also by the condition of the arms on board the pinnace. These two men were clearly guilty, and the British Consul General demanded their public execution. To this, however, the Sultan demurred. He would express no opinion as to the guilt or innocence of the men, but at all events they were Moslems, and, according to Mohammedan law, Moslems ought not to be put to death for the murder of a Christian. He was willing that they should be imprisoned for life; if this was not sufficient, let the British authorities take them and deal with them as they thought fit. This was not satisfactory, and there was lengthy correspondence between Zanzibar and London, until in April, 1882, the British authorities abandoned the demand for capital punishment and insisted only on the Sultan's carrying out the sentence of imprisonment for life. Barghash's response was as follows:-

"Your letter has reached me in which you state you are instructed by the great Minister, Lord Granville, to require that Khalfan and Massoud should be kept in prison till death. From that day we have kept them with the other murderers, and it is not possible for us to allow them to leave the prison except for their burial.

We request you to inform the Minister that we are full of thanks to him for his kindness to us and-Salaam."

The circumstances leading to and rising out of the murder of Captain Brownrigg have received fuller statement than is required for ordinary incidents in the suppression of the slave trade. One of the features of this case was the abuse of the French flag by a slave dhow, an incident not uncommon but difficult to deal with. A careful investigation made by M. Greffulhe, the French Vice-Consul, showed that the French flag and French papers used by the captain of the dhow had been granted in respect of a different vessel and that the culprits were not to be considered as under French protection. There was lengthened correspondence between London and Paris as to the right of search in order to verify the flag in such circumstances, but the result was unsatisfactory, the French Government adhering to their refusal to admit the right.

The decisive action of General Mathews in bringing swift retribution on the murderers and in arresting the slavedealing Arabs who were more or less implicated, had far-reaching results in the political development of Zanzibar. It completed the downfall of the power of these semi-independent chiefs, so that the Sultan was freed from their dominion and became an autocratic ruler. But while the power of the Sultan was increased by these events, so was the personal influence of General Mathews who, at the head of his small but devoted military and police force, had absolute mastery over the Arab population. He was so strong and swift, and adhered so rigidly to practical justice, that the Arabs, where he had to be reckoned with, accepted his will without dispute. Yet his action excited no permanent hostility; he was not regarded with malevolence, and it was only to breakers of the law and to evildoers that he was a terror. On the civil and legislative side the absolute authority of the Sultan was controlled by the British Consul-General, Dr. (now Sir John) Kirk, under whose prudent direction vast strides were made in the economic, commercial, and social development of the islands. Though he showed constant hostility to the slave trade, and probably did more for the suppression of slavery than any other man; though he was daily employed in thwarting slave traders, handing them over to the Sultan for punishment, confiscating their dhows, and liberating their slaves, yet he never incurred the hostility or dislike of those against whose selfish interests he laboured. The overthrow of the Arab chiefs and slave dealers gave freer play to these two men and their successors, and the events which led up to it form a landmark in the history of Zanzibar.

I had the privilege of accompanying Sir Lloyd on what proved to be his last journey to Pemba in July, 1901, three months before he died. We went in the SS. *Barawa*, sister ship to the *Kilwa*, the two famous little boats that created some sensation in 1895, when they were chartered by the French Government to convey troops to Madagascar.

We anchored the first night under Ras Nungwe, and at daybreak crossed to Makongwe, south of Pemba. Our destination was Wete, but Sir Lloyd, wishing to avoid or to postpone the fuss that would be made as soon as the people of Wete knew of his presence on board, proceeded leisurely up the coast till it was dark, and then dropped anchor two miles from the town, among the reefs and islands that had sheltered him in those slave-cruising days, twenty years before. But half an hour had scarcely elapsed before the swish of oars was heard, and the next moment the Wali of Wete and half-a-dozen of the leading Arabs came on board. Sir Lloyd was annoyed, but he was careful not to let the Arabs detect this when he received them on the upper deck. Arabs are very discreet in anything like a formal interview, especially if it be with a European in authority-speaking only when they are spoken to, and then making but the briefest conventional replies. But on this occasion they seemed to me to be especially on the alert and apprehensive-keeping their keen black eyes fixed upon Sir Lloyd's face, their whole attitude one of uneasiness, as if still smarting from the chastisement which, years before, he had administered. Sir Lloyd, long used to their ways, had trained himself to meet the Arabs as they met him. No line of his countenance betrayed the business upon which he had come; he kept his eyes on the deck, lifting them for a brief remark to one or another, and then immediately dropping them again. As all such interviews with Arabs are, it was one of silence, with only an occasional interruption.

To celebrate the death of Captain Brownrigg, the people of Wete decorated their town, and all Pemba rejoiced at the triumph over the European, but the island wears a different aspect now. Having accomplished their task and set free the slave the British laid aside their weapons and hastened to succour those whom they had delivered and those whom they had punished. Pemba has passed from tyranny and enmity to freedom and tranquillity, for the Arab no longer looks upon the Englishman as his foe but as his friend. And where the oppressor prevailed, the missionary now labours.

In 1880 the British Consul-General had recommended that vice-consuls should be appointed to various ports on the continental coast, where they might aid in checking the movement of slaves both on land and by sea. This advice was not acted on at the time for, from various causes, there was now and then a partial cessation of the traffic. It might be that the slave owners were discouraged by the persistent watchfulness of the British boats, or the slave hunters were deterred by the firmness of the Sultan in punishing law breakers, or it might be that, for quite other reasons, there was no demand for slave-labour, as in 1882, when Zanzibar was well stocked, while in Pemba, owing to a fall in the price of clove, the price of slaves was insufficient for the risk involved. However, in October, 1883, three vice-consuls were -appointed, Commander Gissing, R.N., to Mombasa; Mr. J. G. Haggard, formerly Lieutenant R.N., to Lamu; Lieutenant C. S. Smith, R.N., to Kilwa. Twelve years later, namely, on March 23, 1895, Dr. O'Sullivan-Beare, the first British official to reside on the island, arrived at Chake Chake, having been appointed vice-consul for Pemba.

In August, 1883, Sir John Kirk returned to his post after a two years' absence on leave, and the hearty welcome with which he was received by the Sultan was an indication of the influence which he wielded at the Palace. The British Agent had been commissioned to invest His Highness with the insignia of the Order of St. Michael and St. George, a distinction which he highly appreciated, and it was resolved that the investiture should be made with all due formality on September 10. Admiral Sir W. Hewett with a fleet of eight war-vessels entered Zanzibar harbour, and this naval display, the finest ever seen there, added to the favourable impression which had been produced. The naval officers were presented at the Palace, and, on September 14, with the support of the Admiral, the investiture was made in an impressive manner, and was followed by festivities. Next day the Sultan and his suite were received with honours on board the flag-ship *Euryalus,* and the friendly feeling already existing was strengthened. To Lord Granville Barghash telegraphed, "I am rejoiced at this mark of cordiality, and thank Her Majesty heartily. I pray Almighty grant your Lordship long life, and may the British Empire continue to prosper."

Another event to be recorded was the transference of the control and payment of the Political Agency and Consulate-General at Zanzibar from the Indian to the Imperial Government. This step, which was completed on September 1, 1883, was taken in order that means adapted to the suppression of the slave-trade might be more readily put in operation.

When Mr. Haggard went to Lamu he found there was trouble a short distance inland with the Arab chief Ahmet (surnamed Simba, or the Lion), who, with his sons Fumo Bakari and Fumo Amari, was the curse of the region. He had been in receipt of a pension from the Sultan, but this did not satisfy him and his marauding followers, who were armed with swords, knives, bows and arrows, guns being very scarce. When, in 1881, he had been asked to disperse his men he had replied with a demand for a supply of gun-powder. The coast Arabs had marched against him, and the Sultan had sent a force to subdue him, but Simba was not to be overcome, and a temporary peace was made. In 1884 Mr. Haggard found that he and his men were kidnapping slaves from Lamu and bartering them to the Somalis for gun-powder; but, worse than this, there was famine in the land, and the natives, rather than die of hunger, were going into slavery. So from Mombasa it was reported that the coast people were selling their children for food in the hope of redeeming them when better times should come.

Young naval officers appointed to consular positions might well be perplexed with the intricacies of judicial procedure, as was Mr. Smith at Kilwa. He, however, found a competent adviser in Mr. Cracknall, a barrister who, two years before, had entered on his duties as assistant political agent at Zanzibar. Under his direction Mr. Smith made such progress in judicial attainments that within a few weeks, much to his surprise, the Khathi of Kilwa practically left to him not only the capture but also the disposal of slaves and even of slave-dealers. In May, 1884, his report seemed to show that rubber-collecting was of more importance than the slave trade, but in July he seized a slave gang which was on the point of marching north. In October, parents were selling their children for food, and slave-running broke out with great vigour. Slaves were abundant and cheap owing to famine, for natives were kidnapping from neighbouring villages and selling the victims to agents on the coast. In those months many slave dhows were taken, some with over a hundred slaves on board. One taken in December in the Pemba Channel had 163 slaves and many passengers. They were all starving Wazaramo, emaciated skeletons, from a district where the population was dying of hunger and disease. No food had been taken for the voyage and the slaves had had nothing to eat. The boat of the Ospprey in making the capture, had to keep at a safe distance, for there was a rush from the dhow which would have swamped it. Even after the suffering had been relieved, several died.

In many districts famine and slavery were caused or increased by the ravages of marauding bands who reduced the country to a wilderness. So it was in 1884 in the region between Kilwa and the Rovuma River, and also inland from Tanga, where the Masai killed 10,000 people and drove away 15,000 head of cattle.

In March, 1885, General Mathews was sent by Barghash on a mission of inquiry to the country between Pangani and Kilwa, and he found abundant evidence that the slave dealers had profited by the famine. Wazaramo people had been kidnapped and sold, even by their own tribesmen, and handed over to Arab agents from South Arabia and Oman. The slaves thus acquired were set to work in large numbers on the sugar and rice fields at Pangani, while others were smuggled across to Zanzibar and Pemba. In these doings many of the Sultan's officials were implicated, but the chief culprits were the Arab agents, and Mathews had them promptly and suddenly arrested and sent to Zanzibar. It was intended that this inquiry should be extended to the coast further south, but before this purpose could be executed the Sultan heard of the proceedings of the Germans in the Kilimanjaro country, and sent Mathews there to forestall, and, if possible, to thwart them.

Thus, with many fluctuations, the slave traffic went on, slaves being rescued and set free sometimes by hundreds at other times by twos or threes. Usually the slaverunners quietly submitted to the loss of captured dhows and slaves, but when fortune seemed to favour them, they were ready to make a bold fight. Two instances of unusual aggressiveness on the part of Arabs occurred. On the morning of May 30, 1887, Lieutenant Fegen of the *Turquoise*, being in command of the cutter, sighted an Arab slave dhow. He summoned her to haul to, but she steered straight for the cutter and tried to run her down, the Arabs firing a volley and wounding one sailor. The rigging of the two vessels became entangled together and a hand-to-hand fight took place. Seven Arabs were ready to board the cutter, but Lieutenant Fegen, running forward, promptly shot two of them with his revolver, and ran a third through the body with his cutlass. While thus engaged he was wounded in his right arm by an Arab, whom an able seaman, J. W. Pearson, at once ran through the body. Three of the cutter's crew were lying wounded, but Fegen and the other three of the crew continued fighting. When the vessels got clear of each other, nine of the thirteen Arabs on the dhow had been killed, and the four who were alive, with seven other armed men, tried to make their escape in their dhow. Fegen, however, kept up the chase till the Arab helms-

THE DEATH OF CAPTAIN BROWNRIGG AND ITS RESULTS

man was shot, and the dhow broaching to, capsized in shallow water. Two Arabs reached the shore, but one escaped, and the other died of wounds. Fifty-three slaves were rescued.

Another Arab attack was made on October 17, 1888, off the Island of Pemba, where Lieutenant Cooper of the *Griffon* was cruising in the steam cutter with a crew of six men. About ten o'clock in the evening he observed a dhow which, on being required in the usual manner to heave to, at once opened a heavy fire, wounding Lieutenant Cooper and two of the crew. Cooper was shot through the chest, but told Bray, the ship's corporal, to do his best and not mind him. The three unwounded men kept up a steady fire for half-an-hour, till the dhow and the cutter both grounded, about ten yards apart. Then the Arabs jumped overboard unseen and escaped, 74 slaves being rescued. The cutter, however, had hastened back to the ship with Lieutenant Cooper who, two hours after receiving the wound, died just as he came alongside of the Griffon.

It was to the memory of this gallant young officer that the Naval canteen and recreation ground, known as the Cooper Institute, outside the town of Zanzibar, was founded.

The creek, Weti.

Sir John and Lady Key and Miss Taylor at Weti.

CHAPTER XI

SEYYID BARGHASH-THE GERMAN SURPRISE OF 1885

THE time has passed when patriotic motives need influence our judgment as to the aggression which Germany initiated in East Africa in 1884, or prevent a fair consideration of the question whether that aggression has or has not been beneficial to those regions. There can be but one answer to that question. Since it was inevitable that sooner or later European domination should assert itself in those regions it was a good thing that Germany succeeded in establishing herself there. The Portuguese had held and oppressed the country for 190 years (1508-1698); the Arabs who succeeded them had brought prosperity to some of the coast towns, but had conferred no benefit on the inland regions. There they had not governed, but only traded and enriched themselves, their traffic being mainly in slaves. After the Arabs, the British, had they so desired, might have come into power in East Africa, but, while recognising the importance of retaining political influence over the Sultans of Muscat and Zanzibar, they had no wish to acquire burdensome possessions for the advantage or at the expense of either. Great Britain had, as we have seen, engaged in 1862 with France, then the only other important colonising Power, to respect the independence of these two rulers, and showed no wish to change its policy. Both Seyyid Said and Seyyid Barghash offered to place Zanzibar and her East African possessions under the protection of Great Britain, and Barghash gave Dr. Kirk a declaration in which he bound himself not to cede territory to any other Power than Great Britain; but these offers, like the Mombasa Treaty of 1824, were quietly ignored, and British statesmen, while expending blood and treasure for the suppression of the slave trade, made no effort to secure a permanent hold over the region. It was only when the Germans came on the scene, asserting rights over wide inland tracts, to the exclusion of Zanzibar and Great Britain alike, that the British Government perceived the importance of securing a foothold where British merchants and travellers had already been active.

Whatever sympathy with the motives, and whatever satisfaction with the achievements of the Germans in East Africa, we may now have, it is impossible to approve of the manner in which they began their work. A "Society for German Colonization" employed as its agent for the purpose of making treaties with East African chiefs Dr. Karl Peters, who visited the inland regions and easily obtained the signatures of local chiefs to documents of which the following, dated November 29, 1884, is a specimen:

"Mangungo, Sultan of Msovero, in Usagara, and Doctor Karl Peters, Sultan Mangungo simultaneously for all his people and Dr. Peters for all his present and future associates, hereby conclude a Treaty of eternal friendship.

"Mangungo offers all his territory, with all its civil and public appurtenances to Dr. Karl Peters, as the representative of the Society for German Colonization, for exclusive and universal utilisation for German Colonization.

"Dr. Karl Peters, in the name of the Society for German Colonization, declares his willingness to take over the territory of the Sultan Mangungo with all rights for German Colonization, subject to any existing suzerainty rights of Myweyi Sagara.

"In pursuance thereof, Sultan Mangungo hereby cedes all the territory of Msovero, belonging to him by inheritance or otherwise, for all time, to Dr. Karl Peters, making over to him at the same time all his rights. Dr. Karl Peters, in the name of the Society for German Colonization, undertakes to give special attention to Msovero when colonizing Usagara.

"This Treaty has been communicated to the Sultan Mangungo by the Interpreter Ramazan in a clear manner, and has been signed by both sides with the observation of the formalities valid in Usagara, the Sultan on direct inquiry having declared that he was not in any way dependent upon the Sultan of Zanzibar, and that he even did not know of the existence of the latter."

The proceedings of Dr. Karl Peters were approved by the German Emperor, who, on February 17, 1885, granted a Charter of Protection to the "Society for German Colonization," and "accepted" the suzerainty of Usagara, Nguru, Uzeguha, and Ukami.

The Emperor's proclamation fell like a bolt from the blue upon Barghash, who immediately telegraphed to him his protest, and was only dissuaded by Sir John Kirk from proceeding in person to Berlin. The only stations held by

Barghash in these districts were Mamboia, which had been occupied by General Mathews in 1880, and two small stations behind Bagamoyo. These he began to strengthen with additional troops, and he despatched Mathews on a mission which had for its object "the definite incorporation with the Zanzibar dominions of the hill regions about Kilimanjaro," including Chaga, Taveta, Taita, and Arusha. This was really a move to cut out the Germans who, under Juhlke, the successor of Peters, were moving through the Bondei country, towards that rich prize Kilimanjaro, making. "treaties" as they went. "Sultan" Fungu, a Bondei village headman, made a statement to Juhlke which presents the case from the native point of view:

"The land which I with my own power, together with my race, have taken possession of belongs to the great district of Bondei. I myself, however, came from Useguha and have settled here. In Bondei itself there is no great Chief, but there live there well-known rulers over territories like mine, and no one has hitherto disputed either my lordship or theirs. I am neither a subject of the Sultan Seyyid Barghash nor of any person, nor has the Sultan either possessions or fortresses in my country, neither does he send any soldiers as far as here. As, however, we all know that the Sultan is a powerful man, who knows what is the law, we have voluntarily repaired to his Government in Pangani when disputes have arisen amongst us, so that he should tell us what is right. But I know very well that the white man knows that just as well and better, and I and my race should be very glad if white people would settle among us, for we believe that they have the power to protect us, and that we ourselves should derive great benefit from them. Then fighting between the black people would cease, and the Masai would no longer make predatory excursions into our country. If you will bring white people into our country we will let our disputes be settled by you, and go no more to Pangani. Moreover, we will give to the white people all the land they wish to have, and, so far as lies in our power, help them in building their houses, in occupying the land, as well as in all other works."

Having failed to cajole any of the real chiefs of the Bondei, Juhlke was compelled to exploit this "Sultan" Fungu, the headman of a small village; who had no power or land to bestow outside his own compound, but who was held to have surrendered to the German East Africa Company for ever "all the rights which according to European ideas are comprised in the sovereign rights of a Prince." In return for this the Company consented to "bring their wise people, German colonists," into the country.

General Mathews had, meanwhile, lost no time in carrying out the mission entrusted to him by Barghash.. The Sultan had received the German Emperor's proclamation on April 27, 1885, at the hands of Herr Rohlfs, German Consul-General at Zanzibar, who had been sent out specially to conduct the negotiations, and who was at the same time the bearer of a letter from His Majesty, in which the latter proposed to enter into a treaty with the Sultan for the benefit of their respective subjects. One month later, on May 30, Mathews had obtained from the Chiefs of Chaga and Kilimanjaro a declaration, in which they professed that they and their people, and those of Taveta and Taita were subjects of the Sultan of Zanzibar and were loyal to him and his flag. A few days after the departure of Mathews, Juhlke turned up, and in long and elaborate statements and "treaties" succeeded in upsetting on paper all that Mathews had accomplished on paper. "I beg thee," said Mandara, Chief of Mochi who had also signed the Declaration, "to bring with thee a better flagstaff than General Mathews brought with him."

The dispute, however, was now being adjusted in London and Berlin between Lord Granville and Prince Bismarck. It has been held that in virtually supporting Bismarck, Granville acted timorously; but to form a just estimate of the course he took one must consider the interests which Great Britain had at stake in other parts of the world. In Egypt she had just entered upon her career of occupation and control and had made of France, if not an enemy, an angry and jealous opponent; in the Transvaal the restless Boers had only two years before signed the famous Convention. It would obviously have been inconvenient, if not dangerous, to have Bismarck intriguing with France in Egypt, or with the Boers in the Transvaal, and Great Britain no doubt decided wisely in accepting facts and bowing the Germans into their new possessions. Germany was, moreover, justified in her desire to annex these territories. Great Britain had allowed her opportunity to go by, and it was too late now to grumble about it. Barghash was therefore compelled to acquiesce, his grievance being the more bitter because, as he explained in a letter to Prince Bismarck on June 12, 1885, the treaty-makers: "these same Germans have only got there by means of sovereign letters of recommendation which I gave them to my officials there." On August 7 Commodore Paschen and a German fleet entered the harbour, and on the 11th the Commodore demanded from the Sultan a recognition by him of the Emperor's Protectorate over Usagara, Uzeguha, Nguru and Ukami, as well as over Witu, and to withdraw his men from those places. The formal submission of the Sultan to these demands was sent to the Commodore on August 14.

On May 25, that is, four months after the despatch of the German Consul-General with the Emperor's letter to Barghash, Earl Granville had written to Sir E. Malet, our Ambassador in Berlin, incidentally requesting him to inform Prince Bismarck that a scheme had been started in England by some prominent capitalists for a British Settlement in the country between the coast and the Lakes which are the sources of the White Nile, and for its connection with the coast by a railway. This referred to the British East Africa Association, the parent of the Imperial British East Africa Company, which, founded by Sir William Mackinnon, obtained its Royal Charter on September 3, 1888.

The British East Africa scheme was based on concessions granted to Mr. (now Sir Harry) Johnston by agreement with the local chiefs of the Taveta country in the neighbourhood of Kilimanjaro on September 27, 1884, treaties which also possessed priority over those of the Germans. The German Government, not satisfied that this British enterprise would not conflict with the interests of the new German Protectorate, requested Lord Granville that any decision respecting it might be deferred. In November, 1885, the German Government were informed that no further step had been taken towards the assertion of the British claims, but that the original cession had been made over to the President of the Manchester Chamber of Commerce. In the following December, and January the German Government repeatedly expressed the hope that the English enterprise, since it had not yet been entered on, would still be deferred so that it might not interfere with a definite arrangement, but that the German Company, being already active, should be allowed a free hand. The reply given by Lord Rosebery, Foreign Minister, was that the English had held back at the request of the Germans in order that the two Governments might come to an agreement on Zanzibar questions; but, seeing the activity of the Germans in the Kilimanjaro region, the British Government could not restrain the English Company from asserting its rights there. These symptoms of jealousy subsided, however, as the negotiations advanced.

Zanzibar coast with Beit al Ajaib before 1896.

CHAPTER XII

SEYYID BARGHASH - DELIMITATION - PORTUGUESE AGGRESSION

THE question which now demanded settlement was this: What territory on continental East Africa was under the jurisdiction of the Sultan of Zanzibar? It could scarcely be maintained that his authority was either acknowledged or asserted far inland, except along the great trade routes and at some trade centres of the interior, and his claim on the allegiance of the Kilimanjaro tribes, even though allowed by them, had no success. That he had possessions on the coast was not disputed, but the Germans held that these were limited to a few towns, and they laid claim to long stretches of coastline as included in their concessions. Over Witu also, far to the north, the Germans asserted rights on the ground of the protection of the Empire vaguely accorded to the Chief of that town. This so-called Sultan was an old man of the Wagunia race of Nabahan-Arab descent; his name was Ahmet bin Sultan Komlut, but he was commonly called Simba (or the Lion). He had spent most of his life in fighting for possession of the island of Patta, but being at length driven out by the Sultan of Zanzibar, he had for fifteen years been living on the mainland, first at Kau on the coast, then at Witu, a short distance inland, where, according to the report of Mr. Haggard, the British Vice-Consul at Lamu, he had a following of "malcontents, bankrupts, and felons," who lived by plundering the Swahili villages and by selling the inhabitants as slaves, so that the country became more and more desolate. The Germans, however, had a different estimate of Simba's character and history. They regarded him as a hero, struggling against Arab domination, and eager for the prosperity of his subjects. They discovered that Simba had abolished slavery, and that his civilising influence was such that the natives had been induced to abandon their nomadic life and settle down to agricultural pursuits. The Germans produced no treaty with Simba, but they stated that his predecessor had, in 1867, through a German traveller,

119

requested the Prussian Government to take him under their protection, that negotiations had recently begun for treaty relations, that Simba, was now their *Protege*, and that Germans bad settled in his territory. It was on such grounds that, when Barghash, who regarded Simba and his crew as outlaws, sent in May, 1885, a military force to the neighbouring island of Lamu, which would serve as a convenient base for the suppression of the commotion at Witu, the German Government promptly interfered, threatening to use force against Barghash if he did not desist. Lord Granville interposed to prevent further imbroglio, and Barghash did not attack Simba. The British in this, as in other matters, allowed the Germans to take their own way, with what result will appear at a later stage.

The British Government, while exerting, through Sir John Kirk, its restraining influence on the Sultan, arranged for a joint commission, British, German, and French, to delimit the continental possessions of Zanzibar; but Barghash, though not opposing this commission, refused to appoint an agent to look after his interests. For the proposed delimitation the British Commissioner was Lieutenant-Colonel Kitchener, the German was Dr. Schmidt, and the French M. Lemaire.

The first appointment was made in October, 1885, but delay occurred from various causes, and when the reports of their proceedings were rendered, the result was too indeterminate to form a basis for actual delimitation. There was serious difference of opinion among the commissioners, the English and French recognising the Sultan's title to the whole coast-line which he claimed, while the German Commissioner recognised his right to certain ports, but did not admit it over the intervening coast. The Commissioners proceeded to the coast independently of one another, to examine each to his own satisfaction the extent to which the Sultan's authority prevailed. But when they reassembled the German Commissioner insisted that only in those points on which they were unanimous could a decision be come to, thus virtually leaving the final word to the Germans. The results of the Commission were practically nil. But on June 9, 1886, they sent in a report, recording the points on which they were unanimous. This was accepted *pro tanto* by the British and German Governments, and the disputed questions were subsequently discussed and settled at a conference of British and German officials in London.

At length an Agreement was drawn up and signed, October 29 and November 1, 1886, by the representatives of Germany and Great Britain respectively. Under this Agreement the two Governments recognised the Sultanate of Zanzibar over the Islands of Zanzibar and Pemba, Lamu, Mafia, all the islands of the coast, and a continuous line of coast from the River Miningani, at the head of Tunghi Bay, on the south, up to Kipini on the north, this coast-line having a breadth of ten nautical miles from high water-mark. To the north of Kipini the Governments recognised as belonging to Zanzibar the places Kismayu, Barawa, Merka, and Mogadishu, each with a radius of ten miles, and Warsheik with a radius of five miles. The Agreement provided, also, that the German sphere on the coast should extend from the Rovuma to the Umba, and the British from the Umba to the Tana. Germany further engaged to adhere to the Anglo-French Declaration of the Independence of Zanzibar. On December 4 the arrangement under the Agreement was formally accepted by Barghash, and on December 8, the French Government intimated that they raised no objection to the proposed delimitation of the Zanzibar Sultanate.

With respect to the accepted delimitation, two points require notice, viz. : the southern boundary on the coastline and the exclusion of Witu from the Zanzibar dominions. We shall here deal only with the question of the southern boundary, leaving Witu for another chapter.

In the Anglo-German Agreement the southern boundary was carefully described as commencing from the mouth of the Miningani River, at the head of Tunghi Bay; following that river for five miles, and then following the line of latitude to the right bank of the Rovuma. The Germans, having on November 1, 1886, acknowledged the Miningani as the southern boundary of the Zanzibar coast territory, made, on December 30 of the same year, without the knowledge of the British or of the Zanzibar Government, an agreement with Portugal, acknowledging the mouth of the Rovuma as the most northerly point of the Portuguese coast-line, the Rovuma being about twenty-five miles to the north of the Miningani. It was these two agreements which brought the dispute to a crisis, but the German Government disclaimed all responsibility in the matter and left the disputants to settle their quarrel as best they could. The dispute was further complicated by the fact that hitherto Portugal had claimed the coast up to Cape Delgado, between the two rivers. The disputed territory was of no great value, though it contained the village of Miningani, which was an outlet for the ivory trade, and the town of Tunghi, where there was a fort, occupied by a Zanzibar Wali and about thirty soldiers. Whatever may have been the merits of the quarrel, the action of the Portuguese was precipitate and unjustifiable. The commotion they made seems now little more than a storm in a tea-cup, but it shows the excitability of those who were interested in East African questions, and serves to justify the caution uniformly observed by the British Government.

An attempt at a settlement had been begun in April, 1886, when Barghash had written to the King of Portugal, suggesting that commissioners should be appointed to arrange matters in Zanzibar. The negotiations then commenced were carried on by the Portuguese Consul-General, Major Serpa Pinto, who unfortunately had, through failing health, to return to Europe before a conclusion was reached. In January, 1887, Captain Castilho, the Governor-General of Mozambique, was appointed Portuguese Commissioner, and he at once announced by telegram to the Sultan his intention of visiting Zanzibar to dispose of the boundary question. His telegram was, on January 17, supported by one from the King of Portugal, who expressed the hope that the question would be satisfactorily settled. On January 20 Captain Castilho arrived on board a Portuguese corvette, and next day he paid a visit of courtesy to the Sultan. On the day following he paid another visit and proceeded to open the question in dispute. Being requested by the Sultan to transmit in writing anything to which he expected a reply, he had recourse to the German and British Consuls-General. The latter of these officials, Mr. Frederic Holmwood, explained to him that, in the circumstances, the Sultan could scarcely take the responsibility of discussing any change in his boundaries without the sanction of Great Britain and Germany. On January 29 Captain Castilho wrote to the Sultan, who in reply stated that he accepted as final the delimitation made by the Commissioners of the Powers. The Portuguese did not (as they might have done) refer to the three Powers for an explanation of their procedure, but at once took measures to enforce their claim.

On February 11 Captain Castilho, acting on instructions, sent the Sultan an Arabic letter, demanding that, before noon next day, the territory in dispute should be handed over to him, otherwise he should haul down the flag from the Portuguese Consulate and take his departure. Next day the Sultan replied, referring the Portuguese Government to the Governments of Great Britain and Germany. The Portuguese Commissioner at once broke off relations with Zanzibar, and set out in the corvette for Tunghi, where, on February 14, he found a Portuguese gunboat waiting at anchor. Next day the Sultan's steamer *Kilwa*, with a German captain, German officers, and a German cargo which had been loaded at the request of the German Consul-General, to be forwarded to Usagara (in the

German Protectorate), entered Tungbi Bay and, by order of the Portuguese, anchored between the two Portuguese. warvessels. The captain was told to consider his ship, himself, and his crew (twenty-seven in all) as taken in war: the ship's papers were seized; all the men were transferred to the corvette, and ultimately, to Zanzibar; an inventory was made of everything on board, seals put on the hatchways and magazines, and the Portuguese flag hoisted. Next day, under Portuguese officers, the vessel left for Mozambique, where her cargo was landed under charge of the German Consul, so that she was free to be used in the Portuguese service. Then Captain Castilho began operations against the coast. On February 18 the corvette commenced the bombardment of Tunghi, and the gunboat attacked Miningani. This village was inhabited mostly by peaceful British-Indian traders, who, accustomed to British protection, looked for compensation for injury. On the 23rd an armed boat's crew landed and fired into a mango grove without result. On the evening of that day, however, the bombardment having been resumed, the Miningani village was seen to be in flames, and the complete rout of the inhabitants was inferred. For three days more the bombardment of Tunghi was continued, off and on, and on the evening of February 27, a detachment of riflemen and marines landed unopposed and destroyed the place. Then the *Kilwa*, now serving as a Portuguese transport, entered the bay with a cargo of provisions, and a reinforcement of sixty native soldiers. Thus, with much noise but with no bloodshed, for there was no opposition, the occupation was completed, and on March 2 Captain Castilho, on board the corvette convoying the *Kilwa*, returned to Mozambique.

When tidings of these things reached the Sultan he was naturally indignant, and many of his Arab subjects urged that he should at once resist the Portuguese aggression. Barghash, however, had learned the advantage of submitting to wiser counsels, and he referred the whole matter to Great Britain and Germany. He was prepared to repel attack on Zanzibar, keeping steam up and a force of 1,000 well-trained men, under General Mathews, ready for action. But he would not take the offensive, and the battle, so far as it went, was thenceforth carried on by diplomatists in Europe. The Portuguese threatened further depredations on Zanzibar trade, even on trade with India, but were easily convinced that such proceedings would not be tolerated. Lord Salisbury demanded the restoration of the *Kilwa* to the Sultan and this was tardily conceded. On May 21, 1887, the vessel was handed over to the British and German Consuls at Mozambique; on the

31st the Sultan's steamer *Barawa*, with the former captain and crew of the *Kilwa* on board, reached Mozambique, and took over the vessel in the name of its rightful owner.

The main question being still unsettled, a commission was agreed on and amicable relations were ostensibly restored, but when the commissioners met they could agree to nothing. Arbitration was suggested by the diplomatists, but the Portuguese would have none of it. Then in December, 1887, negotiation by ministers at Lisbon was tried, but this also came to nothing. So convinced were the Portuguese of the correctness of their proceedings, that they contemptuously refused to compensate the threescore and ten Hindis whose houses and property they had wantonly destroyed.

The dispute was at length settled by the Treaty of September, 1894, between Germany and Portugal, which decided that the boundary begins on parallel 10° 40' south latitude, and runs from the coast westwards till it meets the river Rovuma, which thence becomes the common boundary. Thus Germany now holds the mouth of the Rovuma and Kionga Bay, while Portugal retains Tunghi Bay and the villages which she had bombarded.

We are now approaching the end of the career of Barghash, and, before he vanishes from the scene, we may briefly consider his character and his attitude towards the changes which took place during his reign. On the death of his father Said, who ruled both Oman and Zanzibar, in 1856, Barghash, as we have seen, had tried to anticipate his brother Majid in seizing the Throne of Zanzibar. In those days there were rival British and French interests in the island, and of the rivals for the Throne, Majid favoured the side of the British while Barghash was anti-European, though he was inclined to look to the French for support. The British (or, rather, British-Indian) Agent promptly had Barghash arrested and shipped off to Bombay, where, as has been recorded, he was kept under supervision until Majid's seat on the Throne was quite secure. Then he was permitted to come back to Zanzibar, where he lived in peace, enjoying more liberty than in after years he allowed to his brother Khalifa. At his house overlooking the sea he was, from 1866 onwards, frequently visited by Dr. Kirk to make sure that he was not intriguing against Majid, and also that Majid was not plotting against him; for had these two brothers not been watched, each in the interest of the other, one of them would have been put out of the way. At that time Barghash, as we have seen, professed to have abandoned his hopes of French support, alleging that he was a sincere friend of the British policy, and unlike Majid desired the suppression of the slave trade. As soon, however, as he felt his seat secure, Seyyid Barghash suddenly repudiated his promises, became what was known as a *Mtaawa*, a pious, devout person, told the Consul that any promises he had made as a private individual were void now that he had become a Ruler of the Faithful, for as such he had a mission from Allah. He no longer favoured the suppression of the slave trade, but, in defiance of the British Agent, supported certain British Indians, who, that they might own slaves, wished to be regarded as Arab subjects. This policy was met by measures which resulted in imprisonment of the Indians for slave holding; and a heavy reduction of the Sultan's revenue, through a more stringent reading of certain clauses of the Commercial Treaty which were being set aside, brought him to compliance; but it was not till after the signature of the Treaty of 1873 that he became thoroughly convinced of the effectiveness of British power, and became a loyal supporter of the British policy.

Over the native inhabitants of Zanzibar, the Sultan had, from the first, sufficient power, the foreign or Indian traders being under their own consular jurisdiction. The wealthy Arabs, however, living like feudal barons with their slaves about them, on their estates in Zanzibar and Pemba, formed an exception. Holding traditions brought from Arabia, they did not regard the Sultan as their Sovereign, but only as the first among equals, and their spokesman in all matters affecting other Powers. Over them the Sultan had in fact very little power. There is significance in the fact that the Sultans of Zanzibar do not dress differently from the Arabs, except in the use of the peaked turban, though this is assumed by all members of the ruling house. For the establishment of order and tranquillity, and especially for the effective observance of the slave trade Treaty of 1873, it was necessary that the independence of these chiefs should be limited. The military force organised by Mathews and the march of these troops through Pemba in pursuit of the murderers of Captain Brownrigg crushed the Arab power, and rendered the Sultan supreme, subject, however, to British influence. The Arab chiefs who up to 1873 had dominated the courts of the Palace, were completely discarded, and under the guidance of the British Political Agent the Sultan's administration became prosperous. Not that Barghash suffered himself to be led in ignorance; he was a strong-minded man, who could take a wide view of things and, without assistance, initiate and carry out measures for the advantage of his people. He had a passion for building. At Chukwani, six miles south of the town, he built a Palace on a commanding headland, upon which he lavished money; at Chuini, six miles to the north, he built himself another palace, in the river bed, constructing a costly artificial foundation to enable him to keep the building low, thereby securing a flow of water. Here he established a sugar factory, principally for amusement. He built two other sugar factories in the interior of the island, but they are all three now in ruins. The valuable crown plantations, which at the death of Seyyid Said were divided among his children, Barghash recovered for the state, adding thereto many others. By a system of conduits he tapped a spring three miles away and brought fresh water to the town; he built roads and made a light railway to Chukwani. His roads have been improved and extended, but his railway disappeared long ago. He wasted money on many foolish enterprises, but here and there among the ruins monuments remain to testify of his energy and masterfulness. One of his most important acts was the creation of a cheap steam transport service between Zanzibar and Bombay, a measure which, at first, on account of its cost, seemed to be a doubtful venture. When, Dr. Kirk pointed out to him that he was running the steamers at a loss of £20,000 per annum, he replied: "True, that is the result if you regard the ships alone, but you forget the increase of revenue from customs duties on imports, in consequence of the higher standard of living which cheap freight has introduced among the Indians," an answer which Dr. Kirk acknowledged to be sufficient.

At the time of his accession the Sultan's revenue amounted to about £70,000 per annum; at the time of his death it had increased to over £200,000. His revenue increased, notwithstanding the suppression of the slave trade, which had been regarded as fatal to the prosperity of the place, and this provided a fulcrum on which the British Agent could always work, especially because, as in comparatively recent times in our own country, there was then no distinction between the public revenue and the private income of the Sovereign. When Seyyid Said, Barghash's father, died, all the property which he had acquired for public purposes (ships of war, arms of troops, etc.) was valued and treated as private property, each of the brothers and sisters being allotted a share. Barghash preferred to have the spending of a large revenue rather than of a small one, and this natural desire, when prudently guided, was to the advantage of his people.

Early in 1888 the health of Barghash caused anxiety; he went to Mogadishu in the hope of benefiting by the change, but returned to Zanzibar worn and ill. There were springs at Bushire, near Muscat, which it was thought might be beneficial, and, intending to visit them, he cabled to Lord Salisbury, pathetically requesting him to telegraph to the British Consul at Muscat to regard him favourably, though, as he alleged, he and his brother Turki, the Seyyid of Muscat, were friends. The favour was of course at once granted, and on February 23 he set out, leaving General Mathews in charge. At Muscat he met his brother, who telegraphed to Zanzibar: "Have seen Barghash, he is much better." He spent a week at the springs, but finding no improvement in health, he returned to Zanzibar and died on the morning of March 27, 1888.

A Jahazi sailing.

CHAPTER XIII

SEYYID KHALIFA-RISINGS IN THE GERMAN SPHERE-THE BLOCKADE

IT had been resolved by the British Government that Seyyid Khalifa should be accepted as the proper successor to the Sultanate. He was a brother of Barghash, who he had made a feeble attempt to oust from power, the only result being that he himself was put in irons, and when released from custody, kept under surveillance.

The interval between the decease of a Sultan and the appointment of a successor by the Arabs had always been a time of disorder in Zanzibar. But, though on the death of such a ruler as Barghash trouble might have been expected, everything now went smoothly. General Mathe, who was in control of the administration, at once informed the various foreign representatives of the Sultan's death and then, with the troops, took possession of the square in front of the palace. The British Agent, Colonel Euan Smith, communicated to the French and German Consuls the views of the British Government, and found that their instructions were in harmony with his own. The crowds gathered thick within the palace square, but they were perfectly orderly, the stillness of the air being broken only by the wailing of the mourners within the palace. Khalifa, since the departure of Barghash for Muscat, had been living in confinement in the country, and had to be sent for, his brother Ali being, in the meantime, informed of the choice that had been made. Ali and the Arabs plainly signified their agreement. When Khalifa heard the announcement that he had been chosen as Sultan, he was at first quite dazed, like a prisoner released suddenly from a dungeon, but requested General Mathews to serve him as he had served his brother Barghash. His peaceful accession was welcomed by all.

Notwithstanding the Treaty signed by Barghash for the suppression of the slave trade and of slave markets, and in spite of the efforts of the British Government to make the treaty effective, the detestable traffic still flourished, if not in the island, at all events in the continental possessions of Zanzibar. When Khalifa became Sultan, British men-of-war were patrolling the coast and many slave dhows were captured every year. For the trade was lucrative and those engaged in it could afford occasional losses. The area over which the traffic was spread was not limited to the Zanzibar dominions, but extended northwards to the Red Sea coast and Muscat, and southwards to the Comoro Isles and Madagascar. It might have been supposed that the extension and consolidation of French influence on the Somali coast and in the African islands of the Indian Ocean would tend towards the extirpation of the slave trade, but it proved otherwise. Slaves captured among the southern Danakil races were marched overland to Tajourah whence, under the eyes of the French officials, they were shipped in hundreds to Jeddah or Mocha on the Arabian coast of the Red Sea, or to ports on the South Arabian coast. There was great demand for slave labour in Mayotte and Madagascar, and this was supplied by slave dhows which carried large consignments of slaves from Lindi and other Zanzibar continental ports as well as from the Portuguese territory. The French Government had no wish to encourage this traffic, but their naval force in these waters was small and, while their officials in Mayotte and Madagascar with too much facility permitted the use of the French flag to Arab dhows, the French Government strenuously refused to the British vessels the right to search any dhow flying the tricolour. Thus it came about that British cruisers could only look on while dhows, nominally French but evidently carrying slaves, passed outwards from Zanzibar ports with impunity. The political situation was delicate and British captains had to take great care not to ruffle French susceptibilities even in endeavouring to prevent the misuse of the French flag. Added to all these difficulties was the fact that the men who, all along the coast, carried on this detestable traffic were fanatical Arabs, many of them from Muscat, who thought that Africans were made to be their slaves. These men, no less than the British sailors, enjoyed a spice of danger, and desperate encounters might at any time take place.

The nature of the work of dhow catching has been sufficiently shown in earlier portions of this book. The slaverunners were prepared for any emergency, to resist, to flee, or to surrender unconditionally; but the victims of their rapacity had no choice. They sat below, huddled together, men, women and children, in nakedness and filth, often stuffed compactly between decks which were so close as hardly to allow a sitting posture. In view of possible capture by the British, the slave-runners contrived to make their raw victims believe that not they but the white men were the dangerous enemies. "White men eat black men," they would say, and, if any slaves happened to be employed on deck, would point to the smoke from the funnel of the pursuing cutter as evidence that a fire was being prepared to roast them. Thus it was not strange that, when the dhows were beached in the dark in wellknown creeks, and the Arabs betook themselves to the beach for refuge, they had no difficulty in taking with them their living cargoes. Only when the victims were in the last stage of hunger would they willingly trust themselves in the hands of their deliverers.

There was another difficulty in the way of the British crews. Both officers and men were ignorant of the languages, Arabic and African, spoken on board the dhows, and had to trust to interpreters who were not always worthy of confidence. These men were usually of Arab blood, and they served the British merely for the sake of the small pay offered. In their work they incurred the odium of their fellow countrymen, odium which they could and did mitigate by occasional misrepresentation of words spoken. No doubt deliberate and gross perversion of the truth was rare, but in more than one case it was proved that absolutely false statements had been made for the sake of gain, so that severe punishment, with flogging and imprisonment, was inflicted. In course of time the evil abated, but its possibility had always to be taken into account.

While dhow-catching operations were in progress Seyyid Khalifa showed himself not unfavourable to the suppression of the slave trade. Not only were dhows destroyed and slaves set free, but gangs of Arab slave dealers were sent to prison. In one case, five of these men were condemned to six months' rigorous imprisonment, but were soon able to escape by the connivance of their gaoler, who did not report the matter. The men went to Pemba, where they were recognised by a British naval officer, who duly reported them to his superior. The affair was thus brought to the knowledge of the Sultan, who had the culprits re-arrested and sentenced to 12 (instead of six) months' hard labour; nor was this all, for these five slave traders, lest, having the sympathy of their fellow countrymen, they should again escape, were by arrangement transferred from Zanzibar to Aden, where they served their term of imprisonment.

Notwithstanding the activity of the British and the loyal support of the Sultan, the slave traffic did not diminish but rather increased, and the misery of which it was the cause seemed more widely spread than ever. More systematic operations were necessary operations which were required also for other reasons.

The Germans had had no difficulty in imposing their treaties on the simple-minded natives inland, but they soon found that it was a harder task to secure their permanent good-will. They proceeded vigorously to develop the resources of the country, and to Germanise the institutions of the tribes so far as that seemed requisite, until, before the middle of the year 1888, the Chiefs of the Usambara were in full revolt. Moreover, the German East Africa Association had, on April 28, 1888, obtained from the Sultan a fifty years' concession of the coast from the Umba to the Rovuma, including the administration of justice, the customs, lands and buildings, the transference to take place on August 15 of that year. When, however, they began to take over their concession, they found that not only the Sultan but also the bellicose Arab chiefs of that region had to be reckoned with. These Arabs, while loyal to the Sultan, did not consider that they were bound at his bidding to transfer their loyalty to strangers whose habits and methods of administration were utterly distasteful to them. At Bagamoyo, when the Germans began to assert themselves, the populace would endure no tampering with the Sultan's flag, and the German flag could only be hoisted on the intervention of a German gunboat. At Tanga also there was violent opposition, the Arabs firing on the boat in which the Germans approached, till a German gunboat promptly, but imprudently, bombarded the town and a party of marines landing, drove the Arabs into the bush. At Pangani when Herr Vohsen, the Director of the German Company, attempted to land, he was fired upon and returned to Zanzibar for the purpose of bringing a man-of-war to take vengeance on the inhabitants. Fortunately he found none, and, before further mischief was done in that quarter, the Sultan, whose loyalty was unjustly suspected by the German Government, sent General Mathews to Pangani to attempt a pacification. There Mathews found an organised rebel force of 1,000 men whom he succeeded in temporarily appeasing, urging the chiefs to lay their grievances before the Sultan and the German Consul-General. This course they adopted, sending five deputies who accompanied General Mathews to Zanzibar; but at the interview the deputies showed themselves resolute, speaking plainly of German insult, and declaring that they would not accept German administration except in the matter of the customs. The Sultan offered to appoint Arab officials, but, before any clear course could be entered on, things went from bad to worse, and when Mathews went again to Pangani, though personally highly popular among the Arabs, he was told that since he was acting in the interests of the Germans, he must at once depart on pain of death. And there is no doubt the Arabs would have killed him had he stayed; as it was, his great personality alone saved him; any other man than Mathews would probably have been killed. At Kilwa two German officials were slain after having killed 21 of their assailants, while eleven natives employed there by the German Company were put to death. From other southern ports the Germans escaped. At Bagamoyo and Dar es Salaam there were German officials, but they were only able to remain because they were protected by German gunboats. All along the coast, the hatred against the Germans was bitter and deep, a hatred which naturally was sometimes extended to other Europeans, but neither against British nor French was there anything like the same intensity of feeling.

It was in those days (October 9, 1888) that the Concession given by Barghash in 1887 to the Imperial British East Africa Company was renewed and extended by Seyyid Khalifa, and the work of the Company in East Africa inaugurated. Considering the state of feeling in the region, the time was critical. At Mombasa there happened to be a riot between Zanzibar porters and the townspeople which might have easily grown to serious dimensions, but by the skilful use of the Sultan's authority and by prudent management, tranquillity was preserved. The violent opposition offered to the Germans they, perhaps excusably, attributed to the efforts which had been made to suppress the slave trade, but there can be no doubt that it was due chiefly to their own imprudence. The Arabs felt aggrieved at British interference with this lucrative traffic, but they never, at least in this region, displayed such animosity against British subjects, whether European or Indian, as they now exhibited against the Germans.

Nevertheless, ostensibly, it was mainly with a view to the absolute suppression of the traffic in slaves that agreements were now made for operations of a more comprehensive and systematic character. It was agreed by Great Britain and Germany, and ultimately by Italy and Portugal, that the importation of arms and ammunition and the exportation of slaves should be prohibited, and that for these purposes the mainland coast from Witu in the north to Pemba Bay on the coast of Mozambique in the south should be blockaded.

The French Government still refused unlimited right of search, but, now that operations of a warlike character were being instituted, they were willing to regard this as one of the incidents of a blockade, so that at length it was possible that the French slavers should be boarded and brought to book.

The formalities preliminary to the blockade were somewhat lengthy, and were strictly observed. Arrangements had to be made between the British and German Admirals; proclamations had to be issued by the Sultan to his own subjects and to the Walis, Sheikhs, Akidas, Elders and others in authority; similar proclamations and warnings had to be made for the information of all the British Indians within the Sultan's dominions, and circulars had to be sent to foreign consuls and others within the region concerned. At length, on November 29, 1888, the declaration was issued by the British Rear-Admiral Fremantle, and the German Rear-Admiral Deinhard, in the name of the Sultan, in accordance with instructions from their respective Governments, announcing the purpose and the limits of the blockade, and intimating that it would be in force from noon of December 2, 1888. For dealing with vessels captured for breach of the blockade, authority was given by Order in Council to the British Consul-General to proceed judicially in matters of prize.

The arrangement between the Admirals was that the British should blockade the coast north of Wanga, and also that from Lindi to the Rovuma, the intervening strip being left to the Germans. The British and German Admirals had each twelve boats for blockade work, but the British had, in addition, about half-a-dozen boats to watch the Island of Pemba. To the southern part of their coast-line the Italians sent a cruiser, and subsequently other Italian vessels took part in the blockade. The French Government stood aloof, but kept a ship at Zanzibar to watch events. French officials seemed anxious not to make difficulties, but to discourage the abuse of their national flag.

The blockade had not been long in force when the German corvette *Carola* captured a slave dhow off Pangani with 80 slaves on board. The Arabs were not yet familiar with the German war-vessels which were painted black, the English being white, and the dhow, expecting no harm, sailed close up to the *Carola* so that it at once became a prize. But it was with events on the mainland that the Germans were chiefly concerned.

The leader of the hostile movement, which need not be described as an insurrection, was Bushiri, an Arab, who was capable of showing disinterested kindness to friends and also of perpetrating, or at least of tolerating, the infliction of barbarities on his enemies. His headquarters were first at Pangani, but, after that town had been bombarded and occupied by the Germans, he removed to the neighbourhood of Bagamoyo. He had no purpose which might not be accounted straightforward, for at Bagamoyo be sent to inform the Germans that if they would quit the country they would suffer no harm that they might even farm the customs duties without objection, provided they made no attempt to exercise any authority over the coast tribes. These terms, however, received no consideration from the Germans. Bushiri had about 2,000 armed men, most of them having breech-loaders, and he was provided with three small cannon. The Germans had a stronghold in the town, they had their war vessels in the offing, and at night they landed a guard of sailors. From the 4th to the 7th of December there was much fighting, the natives having over a hundred killed, and the Germans only one; but Bushiri was able to take and fortify a stone house close to the German quarters. There he mounted his guns and, having placed his men between the Germans and the sea, appeared resolved on the destruction of his enemies. But during the night a panic seems to have risen among his men who had been told that the ground beneath them was honey-combed and laid with mines. They suddenly left the positions they had taken up and set about pillaging and destroying the houses which were still intact, smashing doors and windows, wrecking all they could lay hands on, and plundering men and women alike. Worse than this, they attacked a company of Unyamwezi porters who, having fought their way to the town with a valuable load of ivory, had placed themselves under the protection of the Germans. They surrounded the house which the Germans had allotted to these men, took their ivory, and seizing their leaders, gave them the choice between death and supporting their cause. Many of the porters who refused to join in the movement were killed on the spot, and others had their hands cut off. Then Bushiri, abandoning his three cannon, withdrew five miles to the west, leaving Bagamoyo without a single inhabitant. The population of the town had to take refuge at the Mission of the Black Fathers, a mile or two away, where assistance was given without distinction to all the homeless and the starving. About 2000 natives were fed there daily, and no one ever sought to molest the members of the mission.

While Bushiri remained watchful, ready to attack the Germans either at Bagamoyo or Dar es Salaam, there was confusion at Kilwa, Lindi, and other ports, the local chiefs, for a time, robbing and oppressing the traders. In the British sphere, not far distant, all was quiet, though there was cause for anxiety. At the mission stations near Mombasa in December there were harboured about 1,420 runaway slaves, of whom about 870 were claimed by their owners, and 550, so far as appeared, were ownerless. To harbour slaves was illegal and created intense dissatisfaction among the Arabs, and yet it seemed inhuman to turn these refugees adrift.

The British Company's Administrator, Mr. (now Sir George) Mackenzie, made and carried out an arrangement which quelled all discontent. The 870 slaves who were claimed were set free, and their owners were compensated at the average rate of 25 dollars per slave, while the 550 who were unclaimed received a certificate of permission to remain in the mission till claimed, when each case might be inquired into. At the same time the missionaries were enjoined to harbour no more slaves except on humanitarian grounds apart from the general question of slavery, an injunction which they did not rigidly observe. The total amount of compensation granted was £3,500, an expenditure which conciliated the whole population, especially the Arabs.

On German territory, however, things got worse. In January, 1889, Mr. Brooks, a lay missionary, on his way to Saadani, was murdered, with many natives belonging to his caravan, when about 12 miles from the coast. At Dar es Salaam and at Pugu there were Catholic and Protestant Mission stations where runaway slaves were harboured. In January these missions were attacked. From Dar es Salaam the missionaries themselves escaped on board the German gun-boat, but the natives were captured and carried off by the Arabs. From Pugu, of the nine Europeans, only two escaped, while three men and one woman were shot and two men and one woman were taken prisoners. The prisoners, however, were liberated on March 11 in exchange for Arab slave-runners who had been captured, and a payment of 6,000 rupees.

The rescued slaves at Pugu, sent thither by Germans, were once more at the disposal of their captors. There was now, in fact, a glut of slaves, and a slave market, too abundantly supplied, was opened at Bagamoyo where sales were offered in great numbers, but at very low prices. The French Mission at Bagamoyo was not interfered with; it was still feeding thousands of the destitute, but nevertheless it began to be in danger, its security depending on the protection of Bushiri. There were British missions inland at Mamboia and Mpwapwa, and their safety seemed doubtful; but the chief use which Bushiri made of his opportunities in such matters was to secure exchange of prisoners, or to extort ransom. The mission owed its safety, to a large extent, to the assistance rendered personally by Nasur bin Suliman, a man of wealth and influence, who had for 15 years been Governor of Bagamoyo. In these trying times he exerted his influence and even risked his life in the interest of the missionaries.

While the Germans are preparing to crush this revolt, we may, for a little, look back and see how Seyyid Khalifa regarded the progress of events. In the main he followed readily enough the injunctions which he received from Colonel Euan Smith, but, being an Arab, he could scarcely be in complete accord with him. He knew perfectly well that the Arabs of the Mrima, or continental coast, had just cause of complaint, and on November 8, 1888, he wrote, as he had done before, that the causes of the disturbances were the removal of the Zanzibar flags, contempt shewn towards the mosques, and the new administration introduced by the German Company which differed completely from that which the people had been used to under their Sultan. "We," he said, "use courtesy in governing our people and not force. If people become refractory through oppression of our officials, we can keep them in order. By the help of God they listen to us. We wrote to you before that, by the help of God we can pacify these disturbances without men-of-war, but you did not agree with us. As to the materials of war, they do not come from any other places than yours. You may give orders to your subjects not to sell these things at all, and about the Proclamation, inshallah, we will write and send it to our subjects, but as to the subjects of others, you do the same."

The Sultan's complaints, followed by his compliance, must command respect and sympathy, but now and then he displayed less forbearance. On one occasion, in December 1888, during an illness, when he seemed to have fallen under fanatical influence, he ordered 29 slaves, accused of murder, to be put to death. These men and women had never been tried, but they were to be executed in batches on successive days. Of the first batch, one escaped, but four were clumsily decapitated in the public market. There still remained 24 prisoners under sentence of death, and, in spite of Colonel Euan-Smith's remonstrances four more were executed three days later amid a pitiless crowd of all nationalities. Then it was discovered and acknowledged that one of the first batch had been executed by mistake, and that various irregularities had taken place with respect to those who still awaited death. Nevertheless after an interval of another day, orders were given for the execution of three men and two women. This was too much, and

Colonel Euan-Smith knowing that irreparable wrong was being perpetrated, went to the Sultan in the morning and extorted his consent that this and the remaining executions should be countermanded.

In another matter he was intractable. Five slaverunners, accused of murdering Lieutenant Cooper, had, with the connivance of the Wali and other officials of Pemba, been allowed to escape. The facts were notorious, and, through the Sultan, a fine of 10,000 dollars was exacted of the Pemba officials; but the five delinquents were so serviceable in procuring slave labour for Pemba, that the Arabs would rather have paid double the amount of the fine than have had them arrested. The Sultan, however, professed to regard the fine as unjust and only paid the amount on compulsion and under protest.

In January 1889, Captain Wissmann, who had already spent eight years in Africa and had twice crossed the Continent, was appointed Imperial Governor of German East Africa, and was directed to take command of the military operations which were to be undertaken for the restoration of order. The troops to be employed for this purpose would be, to a large extent, natives of Africa, and the Governor was required to proceed by way of Egypt where he would enlist Sudanese soldiers. These preparations, however, caused delay, and in the meantime the Arabs were not idle. They descended on Dar es Salaam, looted the bazaar, drove out the British Indians and attacked the German officials. The Germans proclaimed martial law at Dar es Salaam and Bagamoyo, and prohibited the import of provisions along the coast between Saadani and Kilwa. On March 23, they bombarded Saadani to punish the inhabitants for the murder of Mr. Brooks; but the bombardment did little damage, as the natives having removed the thatched roofs of their houses had betaken themselves to the bush.

At length, in the beginning of May, Captain Wissmann with ample force to quell the disturbance, appeared on the scene. He was somewhat hampered in commencing operations by fear of jeopardizing the lives of the European missionaries who were still at the mercy of the Arabs; but when it appeared that they were tolerably safe he set to work with vigour. Under his command were about 1,000 men, comprising 120 of the European staff and noncommissioned officers, 200 German blue-jackets, 80 Zulus and 600 Sudanese and other black troops. Bushiri had for months been hanging about the neighbourhood of Bagamoyo, and it was there that, on May 8, 1889, Wissmann fell upon his stockaded camp. Bushiri is said to have himself withdrawn before the assault was made, but, before his men gave up the contest, the Germans had 40 black soldiers killed, besides a German officer and 2 men, while on the side of the Arabs, 80 were killed and 20 taken prisoners. This defeat was a fatal blow to Bushiri's cause. His Arab companions deserted him, crossing in friendly dhows and in small parties to the Island of Zanzibar as they found opportunity. At the same time the native tribes of the coast melted away Bushiri wandered from village to village, trying to arouse the tribes, but his efforts had no success.

Saadani had been already bombarded, but still the inhabitants refused to submit to the Germans. On June 5, they had an opportunity of shewing that they were unsubdued. The boats of a German ship were seen approaching and the natives, rushing down to the shore, received them with a heavy fire. It was resolved that this village should be attacked both by sea and land. Two days later a heavy bombardment was opened from the ships commanded by Admiral Deinhard, while Captain Wissmann with 1,000 men landed on the north side. The natives had entrenched themselves on the beach, but when they were attacked by the land force they retreated inland. Wissmann at once began the pursuit, leaving the town in flames behind him; but, failing to overtake the foe, he returned to the coast at Bagamoyo. In this fight it seems that the Germans lost five men killed and wounded, and the Arabs four. There was little more serious fighting in this region. The Germans occupied Pangani on July 8, and Tanga on July 10, and by that time, things were beginning to revert to their normal condition. Caravans with ivory were arriving at the coast towns, and the Indian traders who had taken refuge in Zanzibar were hastening back to resume their share in the traffic. Still Bushiri was at large, and it was not till the month of December that he was captured and executed, to the satisfaction of the German administrators. In the South, at Lindi and Kilwa, where disaffection against the Germans was strong, and also amongst the tribes to the west, the disturbance was not suppressed till six months later.

In November, 1890, the rights of the Sultan of Zanzibar over the Continental coast within the German sphere were purchased in the name of the German East Africa Company for a payment of 4,000,000 marks or about £200,000, this sum being handed to the British Government on behalf of Zanzibar which receives annually the interest accruing from this sum.

Boats in Zanzibar Harbour.

Boats infront of Zanzibar Stone Town.

CHAPTER XIV

WITU AND THE BRITISH COAST-MBARUK REBELLIONS

SEYYID KHALIFA died on February 14, 1890 and was succeeded by his brother Ali bin Said, the fourth of the sons of Said to rule in Zanzibar. Ali, during his brief reign, quietly accepted the reforms which he found in progress, and offered no opposition to the extension and consolidation of European power on the mainland. It was during his reign that Zanzibar became formally a British Protectorate, and its administration was brought under the direct guidance of British officials. He died on March 5, 1893, and was succeeded by Seyyid Hamid bin Thuwaini, whose accession was not altogether unopposed. Khalid, the son of Barghash, made an attempt to secure the succession for himself, but the disturbance on this occasion was not serious, and Hamid reigned securely till his death, August 27, 1896. This ruler, though he did not willingly conform to the ways of his British advisers, had too little power to be able to cause mischief. The political influence of both Ali and Hamid was unimportant.

In the report of the Delimitation Commission of 1886 there was, as we have seen, no agreement as to whether the town and territory of Witu belonged to Zanzibar or not. In 1887 the Sultan of Zanzibar abandoned his claim to the territory, and its boundaries were determined by a Commission representing the German and Zanzibar Governments. Upon this a German Company was formed to develop the resources of the territory, but the venture had no success, and in 1889, the German Government made a demand on the Sultan of Zanzibar for a concession of the neighbouring island of Lamu, alleging a promise of this concession which was denied. This and other disputes were settled by the arbitration award of Baron Lambermont in August, 1889, an award which was (in this matter) unfavourable to the German claims. There were other causes of disagreement, especially with respect to a customhouse which the Germans claimed the right to administer, and it seemed as if the British and Germans were about to come to blows in that region. The representative of German interests there went so far as to present to the chief six hundred muskets and large quantities of ammunition, a present which there was soon reason to regret. Altogether German prosperity in Witu seemed precarious, when on July 1, 1890, the Anglo-German Agreement was made, under which the control of the region was to pass to British hands, though the sovereignty of the Witu Sultan was to be recognised by Great Britain. The Sultan Fumo Bakari, was weak and fanatical, and his territory was, as in Simba's time, a refuge for the violent and the needy. Among these people there was not unnaturally, a growing dislike of Europeans in general, and of Germans in particular. In August, 1890, a German, named Küntzel, who had formerly lived in Witu for many years, reached Lamu on his way back to Witu, where he meant to erect a steam saw-mill. He had neither right nor authority to exploit the Witu forests, and at Lamu he was warned that he had better not go forward. But, being provided with half a score of German workmen, he persisted in his purpose. When he put his men to work in the forest, the Witu Sultan ordered them to desist, there being signs of danger to which Küntzel gave too little heed. When the danger could not be ignored he and his men came together into the town, and, on the morning of September 15, found that the ground near their house was occupied with soldiers. Küntzel demanded an interview with the Sultan, but was told to wait. Being a man of violent temper, he went out to the soldiers and remonstrated with them in Swahili, using strong language, and after breakfast the company, eight in number, made for the town gate, which they found barred, though five of them managed to get through. The soldiers then began to fire upon them. They ran and were pursued, the soldiers firing at them from behind the bushes, the Germans returning the fire as well as they could. All the five Germans fell, but one of them who was wounded in the leg subsequently made his escape. Next morning the natives took the German youth who had been left to watch the saw-mill, eight miles from Witu, and one held his arms while another cut his throat. The Somali interpreter, who was in the pay of the Germans and saw this, had difficulty in escaping, but was rescued by other Somalis in Mkonumbi. On September 18, at a place twenty miles from Witu, the natives killed another German, one who was entirely unconnected with Kuntzel's party, and there was destruction and looting of the property of Germans at other places. But when the Sultan was asked by Herr Toeppen, the official German representative, to permit the burial of the dead, he refused the request. Clearly the massacre had been arranged with the connivance at least of the Witu Sultan, and the news reaching Europe, there was much indignation. The German Government seemed to think that the British authorities had somehow been remiss, and they demanded that the British Government should interfere, punish the guilty, "protect Germans at once," and exact compensation for losses of property. In dealing with these rather peremptory demands, Lord Salisbury shewed that not the British but the German Government was responsible; that the British had not yet taken over the Protectorate, but were waiting for the Germans to release the Witu Sultan from his engagements with them. Nevertheless, the British undertook the task of bringing the Sultan into subjection. Letters were despatched to Fumo Bakari summoning him to Lamu; requiring him to make restitution of the property of the murdered Germans and to deliver up the murderers to justice. The replies to these letters being unsatisfactory, the British Agent, Colonel Euan-Smith, in accordance with his instructions, asked Admiral Fremantle to take steps for the infliction of punishment.

The admiral was quite prepared to act. There were four villages whose inhabitants were implicated in the murders, and the first step was to punish them. From the *Boadicea*, the *Cossack*, and the *Brisk*, which were lying near Lamu, two armed parties, accompanied by the comrades of the murdered Germans, proceeded, on October 24, 1890, up the two creeks on which the villages stood. They met with no serious opposition, for when the sailors landed, the inhabitants took to flight. The sailors burned the villages and returned to the ships with no casualty to report.

Next morning the Admiral sailed to Kipini, where he had nine war vessels lying in the roadstead; a steamer belonging to the British East Africa Company had also arrived, bringing porters and 150 Indian troops. That day was spent in landing bluejackets and marines, and in the evening an advance party of 200 men with field guns was pushed forward about three miles on the road to Witu. On the morning of October 26 the remainder of the expedition, which contained altogether 950 fighting men, set out from Kipini under the personal command of Admiral Fremantle, and that night they encamped at a place about three miles from Witu. Next day they advanced against Witu, which, after encountering some opposition, they occupied about nine o'clock in the morning. The Sultan had about 3,000 fighting men, but they were half-hearted and easily dispersed. The town had, in fact, been evacuated, and the work of the expedition during the day was simply demolition. They blew up the gunpowder and ammunition which they found, and burned the houses to the ground. In conspicuous places among the ruins the Admiral set up a notice offering a reward of 10,000 rupees for the apprehension of the Witu Sultan. On October 28 the expedition, with twelve men wounded, returned to the coast. Of the natives of Witu, seventy or eighty were either killed or wounded.

These events, however, were only the beginning of troubles. The territory was in confusion; the Sultan had still a large following, and it was absolutely necessary to restore order. On November 15, the British Protectorate was proclaimed, but still no provision was made for regular administration. The British East Africa Company hesitated to undertake this *damnosa hereditas*. Then Fumo Bakari died and his younger brother, Bwana Shelle, was elected to succeed him. But Bwana at once announced his intention of surrendering the murderers and making peace with the British, whereupon he was deposed and imprisoned, another brother, Fumo Amari, being put in his place. It seemed pretty clear that a settlement would be difficult, but yet Sir C. Euan-Smith managed to patch up a peace, offering pardon to all except the actual murderers, and promising honourable treatment and subsistence to Fumo Amari, whom, however, he did not recognise as Sultan.

In March, 1891, agreements were signed on the part of the British Government, the Imperial British East Africa Company, and the notables and people of Witu, whereby a new order of things was to be introduced. The British Company undertook the administration, a competence being assured to Fumo Amari; and among other excellent measures adopted was the abolition of the Status of Slavery, though the actual process of liberating the slaves was not to be completed till 1896. But it soon became clear that the peace would not last. Fumo Amari and his supporters took up a position at a place called Jongeni, in the northern forest, whence, they continued to harry the surrounding country. In July, 1891, Captain Rogers, who was in command of the police, and Mr. Jackson, the Company's superintendent, desirous of conciliating these outlaws, went unarmed to Jongeni and remonstrated with them but without success. In spite of all the efforts of the Company, there was no peace; trade and agriculture were at a standstill and anarchy prevailed. In March, 1892, the Company's officials attempted to compel submission, making an attack on Jongeni, but with an insufficient force and without field guns. They had to retire from the stockade with the loss of three killed and ten wounded. Mr. Gerald Portal supplying them with guns and ammunition, they made another attempt, but though they drove back the natives into the forest, they could not destroy their stockades nor make any permanent impression on them. But in April, with the British ship *Philomel* at Lamu, and the British Commissioner in Witu, the recalcitrant chiefs were intimidated and dispersed their forces, while Fumo Amari went to the village allotted him. A month later, however, Fumo had again betaken himself to the forests and had at his command hundreds of men whose vocation was fighting. In February, 1893, he became openly defiant and demanded the release of his men who had been arrested for raiding. The Company, face to face with troubles for which it was not responsible and without adequate means for the restoration of order, found it necessary to withdraw, and on July 31 Witu was placed under the Sultan of Zanzibar.

In the meantime on July 20 the British Consul-General, Mr. Rennell Rodd, with three men-of-war, had arrived at Lamu, accompanied by General Mathews and an Arab envoy from the Sultan of Zanzibar. Next day the Sultan's steamer *Barawa* arrived with General Hatch and about 170 soldiers on board, and preparations were made for an advance inland. The expedition reached Witu on July 26, and to that place Fumo Amari was summoned. But neither he nor his associates came, and it was decided to advance against their forest stronghold at Pumwani. Reinforcements were sent for, and the party when complete consisted of Mr. Rennell Rodd, General Hatch with forty Nubian and forty Zanzibari soldiers, Captain Lindley commanding the naval brigade of four companies of bluejackets and one of marines, with the field gun and the rocket and guncotton party in the centre. General Mathews, Captain A. S. Rogers, and Dr. Rae accompanied the expedition, the two latter being familiar with the country. They set out from their camp at Mkumbi on August 6, and the following day, when they approached Pumwani, they encountered a determined fire, their assailants being hidden in the bush. They advanced along a forest road at the end of which they saw a strong gate of piles and cross-beams, and a stockade extending right and left into the forest. The field gun and guncotton did their work at the gate, and when this obstacle was removed, the bluejackets rushed through and found the stronghold deserted. About two hours after the first of the enemy's shots had been heard, all was quiet. The next day, August 8, was spent in destroying the fortifications, riflepits, and crops of the forest outlaws, and on the following morning, just before the expedition began its return march to Mkumbi, the ruins were fired and the forest entrance was converted into a lane of fire. Of the members of the expedition two were killed and fifteen wounded.

At Jongeni, not far from Pumwani, there was another forest stronghold under a native chief, and on August 10 Mr. Rodd sent a despatch demanding its surrender. The journey to Jongeni and back to Mkumbi only required seven hours, and, the messenger not having returned, the march against the stockade began on August 12. The day following the fortifications and the villages were taken and destroyed, only three members of the expedition being wounded. The party reached the coast on August 16, and there they found the messenger who had not returned to Mkumbi. He was in a state of great excitement, for the Jongeni natives had imprisoned him and sentenced him to death, and he had only been able to escape with the assistance of his friends.

To provide a measure of protection for the peaceable villages against the raids of bandits whom it was impracticable to follow into the forest, Sudanese and Zanzibari soldiers were disposed in suitable localities, and at the same time the general administrative arrangements for the coast region were published. One of the regulations prohibited the sale of slaves, and the separation of slave children from their mothers, and decreed that slaves could be inherited only by the lawful children of their owners. These provisions probably indicate the utmost that could be done towards the suppression of slavery at that time, though apparently falling short of the total abolition pronounced two years before.

There were signs that affairs were becoming more settled, but the outlaws, unwilling to abandon their predatory life, made one or two raids in the month of September, and had to be repressed. For this a force of 140 men from the British ships and 85 men under General Hatch from Zanzibar sufficed. This party, like the earlier one, did its work quickly, surprising the outlaws and burning their stockades. At length, in 1894, the reign of the Sons of Simba was for ever abolished, and the long lingering resistance to law and order disappeared.

The Sultanate was retained, but it was made only subordinate to that of Zanzibar. The chief who was raised to authority was Omar bin Hamid, an offshoot of the Nabahan dynasty to which Simba, Fumo Bakari, and Fumo Amari had belonged. He had, with ability and good faith, acted as Wali of Witu under the Zanzibar administration, and on July 7, 1895, he was formally installed as Sultan of Witu. Accredited to him as Resident is a British Officer, who is under the control of the British Commissioner for East Africa, the first Resident having been Mr. A. S. Rogers, now Regent and First Minister of the Zanzibar Government. In the once turbulent little state affairs are now quietly conducted, and the region is one of the most peaceable and prosperous portions of the British Protectorate in East Africa.

On an area of 1,200 square miles it contains a population (mostly Swahili and other natives) of over 16,000, of whom about 6,000 are in the town of Witu and 1,000 in Mkonumbi. The northern part is covered with thick forest, yielding rubber; in the east there are many villages and plantations. Administratively Witu forms part of Tanaland.

To the Imperial British East Africa Company there still remained a long stretch of coast-line to the south, and in the neighbourhood of Mombasa fresh troubles with the Arab chiefs arose. Mombasa, as we have seen, had been the capital of the Mazrui family, who claimed independent sway over the region till, in 1837, they were overthrown by Seyyid Said. Though the power of this family was broken it was not extinguished, for one branch had founded a small state at Gazi, about thirty miles to the south of Mombasa, and another branch had set up a similar state at Takaungu, about as far to the north.

To the leadership of the Gazi Arabs Mbaruk bin Rashid succeeded, and he proved a thorn in the side of Zanzibar. Again and again he rebelled, until in March, 1882, General Mathews was sent against him. The Arab chief driven from Gazi, betook himself to his stockaded stronghold of El Hazam on Mweli Hill, about eighteen miles west of Gazi and there Mathews with a force of 1,200 regulars and irregulars closely besieged him for eighteen days. An attack was then made and the fortress taken, together with about 390 prisoners, but Mbaruk was able to cut his way through with 300 of his men. It was thought that Mbaruk would never recover from this overthrow, but he seemed little the worse, and eventually he even regained the pension or subsidy which the Sultan of Zanzibar had granted. This subsidy was continued (ostensibly for services to be rendered) by the British East Africa Company, for whose leniency Mbaruk had little respect.

In 1895 a dispute arose regarding the succession to the leadership of the Takaungu branch, which was possessed of authority similar to that held by Mbaruk of Gazi. The British Company, apparently with general consent, nominated Rashid bin Salim, a son of the late chief, but this nomination was speedily resented by the late chief's brother, Mbaruk bin Rashid (not the Gazi chief of the

147

same name). There were long and fruitless negotiations between Mbaruk of Takaungu on the one hand and the representatives of the Sultan, the British Government, and the Imperial British East Africa Company on the other, and eventually an expedition was sent to suppress the violence to which Mbaruk had recourse. The chief was defeated and pursued from place to place, till at last he took refuge with his kinsman of Gazi, leaving behind him his brother Aziz, who vigorously continued the war, burning and looting towns, villages, and plantations.

At this stage, on July 1, 1895, the East Africa Company handed over their troubles to the British Government, in whose name Mr. Hardinge, the Consul-General at Zanzibar, took over the administration. Mr. Hardinge wrote to Mbaruk of Gazi requesting the surrender of his namesake of Takaungu, and, the Gazi chief consenting to an interview with the Consul-General, they met on July 8, but though Mbaruk spoke fair and made promises there was no result. A week later Aziz attacked and half burned the town of Takaungu, but was repulsed by the native garrison, with Captain Raikes at their head. He then betook himself to Sokoki, whence, being repulsed by an expedition from the British ships, he fled southwards to Mbaruk of Gazi for refuge. The Gazi chief promised to hand over the fugitives at Gazi, and Mr. Hardinge, with Sir Lloyd Mathews and a force under Admiral Rawson, set out overland from Mombasa to receive them. But on the way they learned that Mbaruk and his guests had gone to Mweli, where, as we have seen, there was a strong hill fortress.

Mr. Hardinge, leaving Gazi to be defended by a Sudanese guard under Captain Rogers and a landing party from the *Phoebe*, which was lying off the coast, returned to Mombasa, and wrote to Mbaruk requiring his submission. Though the Gazi chief had, in the meantime, been burning and slaying, his reply, without offering satisfaction, professed loyalty. It was clear that he was only trifling with the British, and therefore on August 12 the expedition, fully equipped, set out against him. It was under the command of Admiral Rawson and consisted of 220 blue-jackets, 84 marines, 60 Sudanese, and 50 Zanzibaris, arranged in two divisions, under the command of Captain Egerton of the *St. George* and Captain MacGill of the *Phoebe*. The Sudanese were commanded by Captain Rogers, whose temporary position as Governor of Gazi had been assigned first to Captain Raikes and then to Captain Festing of the Blonde. The force was provided with a 7-pounder, four maxims, and a supply of war-rockets, and there were 700 porters for transport work. A diversion, which succeeded in misleading Mbaruk as to the direction from which the attack would be made, was arranged under Captain Raikes, and Captain Marx of the *Barrosa* was sent forward to form a camp about half-way. The expedition was accompanied by Mr. Hardinge and by Sir Lloyd Mathews, who was not only a skilful guide, familiar with the country, but also managed the commissariat and recruited the porters. The distance to be travelled was about thirty miles. When, on August 16, they had gone more than half-way and were passing under a hill called Ndolo, they were suddenly fired upon, a Sudanese soldier and a porter being killed and Sir Lloyd Mathews and a sailor of the *Phoebe* slightly wounded. The Arab assailants were, as was afterwards learned, led by Eyoub, a son of the Gazi chief, but were quickly driven off. Two days later the expedition reached Mweli, and at once set to work with the 7-pounder and the rockets to destroy the northern stockade. A general attack was made and the stockade taken, the enemy offering but a short resistance, though their leader remained at his post to the last and was shot through the head by a Sudanese soldier. The southern gate also was quickly captured, and two hours after the fighting began, the place was in the hands of the British. The stores and ammunition found within were either buried or blown up, the houses were razed to the ground, and then, after spending three days in wasting the resources of the enemy, the expedition returned to Mombasa.

Mbaruk of Gazi went north to the Takaungu region and the troubles continued both in the north and in the south. On October 16, Captain Lawrence, in command of native soldiers at Gazi, was killed in attempting to arrest one of Mbaruk's chief men; on November 2, a camel caravan was attacked and plundered, and a mission station at Rabai, near Mombasa, was attacked. There were raids and murders all along the coast, and the military force at the disposal of the authorities being too small to cope with the state of things which had arisen, on December 30, an Indian contingent of 300 men, under Captain Barratt, was landed at Mombasa, but in the operations which ensued these men were at a disadvantage through their ignorance of the country.

In January, 1896, Freretown, in Mombasa harbour, was attacked by 300 rebels, and the Indian troops sent against them, being misled by treacherous guides, narrowly escaped perishing of thirst. In February, Malindi was similarly attacked, and the assailants were routed, but when pursued they always vanished. North and south the country was raided by this elusive enemy, and the officials, both civil and military, were baffled beyond endurance. At Sokoki, near Takaungu, Captain Harrison held a strong stockade with 100 men to restrain the rebels in that region; among the tribes, Mr. MacDougall, whose proper duties were civil, not only gathered the Elders for "shauris" or discussions, and induced them to remain at peace, but also marched at the head of soldiers in pursuit of the rebels, or directed the garrisoning of stockades against their attacks. In the south General Hatch, with 205 men, was active, chasing the rebels and burning their villages. Sometimes he seemed on the point of capturing Mbaruk, who was known to be now in the Mweli region, but he never succeeded.

To put a speedy end to this troublesome condition of things, an Indian regiment (the 24th Baluchistan) of 720 men, all ranks, under Colonel Pearson, was landed at Mombasa on March 15, 1896. A few days later Colonel Pearson began to dispose his men so that one line of posts stretched westwards from Mombasa along the Uganda road, and another westwards from Wanga along the Umba, while supplies were stocked in the Shimba district for the flying columns which should scour the intervening country. It was known that Mbaruk was within this region; he could scarcely escape to the west where there extended the wide waterless Taru desert, beyond which the tribes were hostile to him. It had been arranged with Major von Wissmann, the Governor of German East Africa, that if Mbaruk crossed into German territory he and his men should be disarmed forthwith and moved southwards away from the frontier. On March 21, the operations of the flying columns began on April 10, Mbaruk was trying to get across the German frontier, and on April 16 he surrendered to the Germans. He did not at once understand his position, but on April 20 and succeeding days he and about 1,600 of his followers laid down their arms. He was shipped to Dar-es-Salaam, but all the rest, except ten who had been active leaders and were excluded from the general amnesty, were at liberty either to return to their own villages or to settle in German territory on ground which would be allotted to them. Many went back to their old homes, while those who remained in the German sphere were distributed over thinly peopled regions and formed a welcome addition to the population.

So ended the last of the mainland rebellions, with which this narrative is concerned. Since then there have been serious risings in the interior, especially among the Ogaden Somalis in the Jubaland region, to the west of Kismayu; but these territories were not within the Zanzibar dominions.

Within the British East African Protectorate the dominions of the Sultan of Zanzibar are: A strip of coast-line ten miles broad from the German frontier to Kipini, the Islands of the Lamu Archipelago, and an area of ten miles round the port of Kismayu. A purely British administration has been established, but the territory being within the Sultanate of Zanzibar, foreigners have certain territorial rights, and profit by the stipulations of Zanzibar treaties with the countries to which they belong.

North of the Juba, the ports of Barawa, Merka, Mogadishu, and Warsheikh were ceded to Italy in August, 1892, and the administration was taken over by Italy in September, 1893.

Seyyid Hamed bin Thuweini.

CHAPTER XV

THE END OF SLAVERY

THE work of the blockading squadrons for the suppression of the slave traffic had been unremitting. In the middle of the year 1889 there were ten British war-vessels engaged in those waters; their boats being always on the look-out for dhows, of which over 1,200 were boarded and searched monthly. The slaves actually found on board were few, not because the traffic was at an end, but because the Arabs were wary and, when there was risk of capture, would land their living cargoes on the mainland coast and make off with them to the bush. There were also the usual attempts to smuggle slaves into the islands in small numbers, attempts which no doubt were mostly successful and would be continued as long as slavery existed.

In the Island of Zanzibar the slave population was largely in excess of the free, and prudence required that the extinction of slavery should not be enforced precipitately. The step now taken for this purpose was the agreement of September 13, 1889, between Seyyid Khalifa and the British Government, whereby all persons entering the Sultan's Dominions after November 1 of that year should be free, and likewise that all children born after January 1, 1890, should be free; but the latter part of this agreement was not embodied in any proclamation. In return for these concessions on the part of the Sultan, it was agreed that the blockade, as then maintained by the British squadron, should be raised without delay. The raising of the blockade, however, was not to assist the slave-runners, for by Proclamation of September 20, 1889, the Sultan announced that he had granted to Great Britain and Germany a perpetual right of search, of all Zanzibar dhows, boats, and canoes, in Zanzibar waters. By a Proclamation, issued by the British Consul-General, this right of search was extended so as to include dhows, and boats belonging to British subjects; various proclamations of local application

153

were also made.

The next important step was the issue of the Decree by Seyyid Ali, August 1, 1890, which, while retaining the legal status of slavery, prohibited under severe penalties all buying and selling of slaves, and pronounced the immediate liberation of all slaves of owners dying without lawful children. At the same time slaves were allowed, like freemen, to bring their complaints before the Kathis, and those who were proved to have been grossly ill-treated were to be liberated. Since the year 1860 no British subject in Zanzibar had been permitted to own slaves; since November, 1888, no British subject had been permitted to make any contract with owners for the hire of slaves, and by this decree of August 1, 1890, the prohibition against slave-owning was extended to husbands and wives and children of British subjects, and also to all persons who, once slaves, had been freed by British authority. Thus great numbers of slaves were at once declared free, and the clause forbidding any change in the ownership of slaves, except through the succession of children, was not only beneficial in itself but provided an easy way out of difficulties which threatened to rise subsequently.

The Decree originally contained a clause enabling slaves to purchase their own freedom on fair terms, with or without the consent of their masters; but, three weeks later, this provision was rescinded. To the Sultan and the Arab slave-owners this power of redemption seemed dangerous, for the slaves "might get big heads," that is, become insubordinate and insolent, and might even commit robberies to provide themselves with redemption money.

Still the slave dealers made persistent efforts to continue the illicit traffic and were only frustrated by the watchfulness of the British boats. In one case of capture in June, 1891, 53 slaves were liberated and the slave-runners sentenced to "thirty cuts and the chain gang." The number of slaves liberated through the action of the British boats in the year 1892-93 was 175.

Before this, another evil of long standing became serious. Liberated slaves were in many cases not unnaturally disinclined to work, and the supply of labour available for agricultural and other purposes was far short of the demand. Not only so, but there was a constant drain of men from the island for continental purposes. Zanzibar porters were employed by the authorities of the German sphere, the English sphere, the Congo Independent State, and Natal, and by innumerable Arab and European traders and travellers in the interior of Africa. Within a few months nearly 2,000 men had, either by persuasion or compulsion, been withdrawn from Zanzibar, which was regarded as an unfailing reservoir of willing or unwilling labour. This out-flow of the population was a very serious matter, both for the porters themselves and for the prosperity of the island, for of the men thus drafted off many never returned. The course proposed by Mr. Gerald Portal to the Sultan and accepted by him was the issue on September 11 1891, of a decree whereby all recruiting or enlistment of soldiers, coolies, and porters for service beyond the Dominions of His Highness was strictly forbidden.

In May, 1892, the Brussels Act was put in force, and the registration of dhows sailing under Zanzibar or English colours was begun. These dhows were all marked and numbered on the sail and stern with figures two feet long. They were not allowed to put to sea unless provided with the necessary papers, and their crews and passengers were mustered and examined before the port officer, who was a British naval commander.

In the same year the traffic in arms and ammunition was put under control, and the sale of guns and gunpowder to natives was stopped. By these measures it became easier to check slave-smuggling, but still many dhows which visited Zanzibar escaped registration, and it was chiefly by such vessels that such illicit traffic as still lingered was maintained. Thus, on April 22, 1893, the boats of the British war-vessel *Philomel* found a dhow flying French colours about 12 miles off Zanzibar. Authority to search was obtained from the French consulate, and, on board the dhow, which was bound for the Persian Gulf, there were found about 50 slave-children who had been kidnapped. This incident was used at the time by partisan writers as a basis for insinuations of remissness on the part of the British officials, to whose activity both on shore and at sea the detection of the slaverunning Arabs was due. Other attempts of similar nature were made and frustrated, for the slave trade died hard. The Admiralty report for 1893 showed that the traffic by sea had scarcely any existence; even the dhows overhauled on the South Arabian coast contained neither slaves nor preparation for their reception. The police on shore and the boats at sea had been too vigilant for the Arabs, and, in the opinion of Admiral Kennedy, the suppression of the traffic was partly attributable to "the general march of civilization in what formerly used to be unfrequented parts of the globe."

But even yet smuggling had not ceased. The slave system entered not only into the agricultural and other out-door operations of the Arabs, but also into their domestic and family life, and, as most of the slaves were childless, the importation of fresh supplies was difficult to stop. In the beginning of 1895, the number of slaves annually brought into Zanzibar and Pemba was estimated by Sir Lloyd Mathews at from 1,000 to 1,500. They were landed at night in twos or threes far from towns, and distributed among the inland villages and plantations where they were sold without difficulty. To meet this state of matters, police were stationed at the small ports and inland villages, and small captures were effected from time to time.

Of the number imported some hundreds were annually exported, though seldom in a manner which could be shewn to be illegal. Many of the Arabs went annually on pilgrimage to Mecca attended by slaves who expressed no unwillingness to go, but when the masters returned they were attended by few of the domestics who had departed with them. Both for importation and exportation of slaves, the law, as it now stood, provided remedies; but the slaves were kept in ignorance of their rights, and the Mohammedan law courts, while dealing fairly with cases brought within their cognizance, did not, or could not, initiate measures to prevent particular abuses.

The question how slavery itself should be brought to an end was still unsettled. Among Europeans there was no dispute as to the desirability of its abolition, but there was much discussion as to the methods by which that end should be reached. There were abolitionists in Great Britain with agents in Zanzibar who, in this delicate and difficult condition of affairs, clamoured with perfect selfconfidence for complete, absolute, and unconditional emancipation, and protested against any system of compensation to slave-owners, as tending to retard and complicate the carrying out of abolition. Ordinary considerations of prudence and of fair dealing required that abolition should be brought about without dislocation of the economic and social conditions of the islands and without injustice. There were no statistics either of the number of freemen or of slaves (for Mohammedans may not number the people), but competent judges estimated the free at 70,000, and the slaves at 140,000. The slave population was the main source whence labour was obtained for the working of the agricultural estates, and they were mostly engaged in the cultivation of cloves. On the successful development of this industry depended not only the welfare of the slaveowners and other freemen, but of the slaves themselves and even the solvency of the State. Inconsiderate intererence with the existing order of things might at once plunge the islands into confusion. It was necessary to consider also what harm might result from the sudden liberation of multitudes of ignorant native labourers who had been victims of oppressive cruelty, and of thousands of young women who were either domestic slaves or concubines. Could such a measure be of advantage to the women? or would it tend to the general welfare? Further, concubinage was a recognised institution, and the lot of concubines was in general an easy one. Should one bear a child to her master, her future freedom and independence were secured; her child would inherit from the father and she herself would enjoy the benefits of the inheritance. As regards the slave-holders it could not reasonably be maintained that owners of property in its nature lawful from time immemorial, legally acquired and legally used, should be deprived of it without compensation.

The method recommended and insisted on by Sir Arthur Hardinge, to whose foresight is mainly due the peacefulness of the transition to freedom, was similar to that which had been followed in India in 1843. By the Decree of Seyyid Hamoud, April 7, 1897, the legal status of slavery was abolished. The courts of law would no longer enforce any alleged rights over any person or the services or property of any person on the ground that he was a slave. If, however, anyone could prove that he was till then in lawful possession of such rights, he should receive just and reasonable compensation for the loss of them. In view of the action which had long been taken for the liberation of slaves, and especially of the Decrees of 1889 and 1890, which had declared the freedom of great numbers, it was improbable that compensation could be claimed for the loss of any very large proportion of those who were still held in the position of slaves, and all claims would have to be strictly proved. As, already, slaves could not be sold or alienated in any way, so now it was provided that compensation money, being the equivalent for lost rights over slaves, could not be seized for debt. To check idleness and vagrancy on the part of freed slaves, it was provided and published that they would all be liable to taxation like other subjects of the Sultan; that they were bound, on pain of being declared vagrants, to show that they had a regular domicile and means of subsistence; and that when such domicile was on another man's land they would have to pay a just rent to the owner. With respect to the position of concubines, it was decreed that such persons should be regarded as inmates of the harem in the same sense as wives, but could demand and obtain the dissolution of this relation on proof of cruelty. But any concubine who had not borne children might, with the sanction of the Court, be redeemed.

The effective articles of the Decree were as follows:-

(1). From and after this 1st day of Zilkada, 1314 (April 7th, 1897), all claims of whatever description made before any court or public authority in respect of the alleged relations of master and slave shall be referred to the District Court within whose jurisdiction they may arise, and shall be cognizable by that Court alone.

(2). From and after this 1st day of Zilkada the District Court shall decline to enforce any alleged rights over the body, service, or property of any person on the ground that such person is a slave, but wherever any person shall claim that he was lawfully possessed of such rights, in accordance with the Decrees of our predecessors, before the publication of the present Decree, and has now by the application of the said Decree been deprived of them, and has suffered loss by such deprivation, then the Court, unless satisfied that the claim is unfounded, shall report to Our First Minister that it deems the claimant entitled, in consideration of the loss of such rights and damage resulting therefrom, to such pecuniary compensation as may be a just and reasonable equivalent for their value, and Our First Minister shall then award to him such sum.

(3). The compensation money thus awarded shall not be liable to be claimed in respect of any debt for which the person of the slave for whom it was granted could not previously by law be seized.

(4). Any person whose right to freedom shall have been formally recognised under the 2nd Article shall be liable to any tax, abatement, corvee or payment in lieu of corvee, which our Government may at any time hereafter see fit to impose on the general body of its subjects, and shall be bound, on pain of being declared a vagrant, to shew that he possesses a regular domicile and means of subsistence, and where such domicile is situated on land owned by any other person, to pay to the owner of such land such rent (which may take the form of an equivalent in labour or produce) as may be agreed upon between them before the District Court.

(5). Concubines shall be regarded as inmates of the Harem in the same sense as wives, and shall remain in their present relations unless they should demand their dissolution on the ground of cruelty, in which case the District Court shall grant it if the alleged cruelty has been proved to its satisfaction. A concubine not having borne children may be redeemed with the sanction of the Court.

(6). Any person making any claim under any of the provisions of this Decree shall have the right to appeal from the decision of the District Court to Ourselves, or to such Judge or other public authority as we may from time to time see fit to delegate for the purpose.

In order that the change from slavery to freedom might be accomplished smoothly, the old administrative divisions of Zanzibar and Pemba were, by a second Decree, abolished, and new districts were created with District Courts and Arab judges from whom there was an appeal to the Sultan or, in fact, to Sir Lloyd Mathews, the First Minister of the Sultan.

The Decree was made known first to the Arab chiefs in Zanzibar; then it was published and explained to officials throughout both islands, who set forth its provisions both to slave-owners and slaves. English Slavery Commissioners (Mr. J. T. Last for Zanzibar and Mr. J. P. Farler in Pemba) were appointed to watch over its execution, to give advice when asked, and to report to the central Government, and a Zanzibar Government Agent Mr. Herbert Lister-was appointed to Pemba, to control vagrant freedmen.

A movement was made among some of the slave-owners to have their slaves shipped to places beyond the jurisdiction of the Sultan, but this, being anticipated and provided for by Sir Lloyd Mathews, never assumed serious proportions. The form it usually took was a futile attempt to pass off natives as domestic servants and personal attendants on a journey to Oman. A few slaves were sent in French dhows to Muscat, and a few were taken to the German coast. Some Pemba Arabs even tried to make an arrangement with the German Governor of Tanga whereby they might obtain land on which to settle with their slaves. They were told they might obtain land if they surrendered or sold their estates in Pemba, but that no immigrants would be received on the condition of having one foot in the German and the other in the British Protectorate. These terms did not please the slave-owners so they went back to their shambas in Pemba to face the new order of things.

The liberation of the slaves proceeded slowly. There was no rush for freedom, no serious unsettlement of the prevailing economic conditions. For a time the slaves did not grasp the significance of the legal change, but understood clearly enough that their masters would not now be allowed to treat them harshly. They came before the Walis with complaints of cruelty (often trivial), and, when the specific wrongs were redressed, went back to their work well satisfied.

The owners found it was to their advantage to keep the slaves out of the courts, and therefore abandoned the infliction of personal chastisement, the slaves being permitted to work or not to work, very much at their own pleasure.

In the Island of Zanzibar by the end of June no more than 120 persons (about 40 per month) had claimed their freedom, but the number had been gradually increasing. It was chiefly among town slaves, men who worked as servants to Indians or as artisans, bakers, fishers, or small dealers, that the desire for freedom first spread. Slaves of this description were hired out by their owners or allowed to labour in their own vocation, but of their earnings one half went to their masters. When the unhired artisans or trading class obtained their liberty their position was vastly improved, for they at once received double for their labour. With the slaves who were hired out however, the case was different. Their employers were generally Indian, keen at a bargain. They pointed out to freed slaves that now, since they could keep all their earnings to themselves, it was proper that the wages should be reduced by half, and on this principle the Indians reaped the profit intended for the slave.

Apart from this provocation, there were not a few town freed slaves who did not understand their position as freemen. They readily undertook work, but were idle and neglectful in its performance, and when urged to shew a moderate degree of diligence they threatened an action before the British Consul-General. European merchants found difficulty in controlling the men they employed, and there was some consultation with the authorities on the subject. The idea of a Government labour bureau was seriously suggested, but Sir Lloyd Mathews with the approval of Sir A. Hardinge, stationed a few askaris about the town, to arrest the indolent and refractory; a measure which ensured order among the freed men.

In the Island of Pemba things moved more slowly, for, in the first eleven weeks following the issue of the Decree, in only one case had slaves claimed their liberty, and this they obtained on the ground of cruelty, so that the owner, an Arab lady, received no compensation.

After the Decree had been in operation for a year the number of slaves who in both islands, had taken advantage of its provisions, was 4,278. Of this number, 2,000 had obtained their freedom, and 2,278, had, without claiming papers of freedom, made contracts with their masters as free labourers.

In and about the town of Zanzibar the slave-owners were of three classes: the wealthy Arabs in whose service there was distinction, luxury and security-few slaves of these men applied for or desired their liberty; the middle class natives who could confer no privileges and could provide no luxuries-between them and their slaves the bond was in many cases soon dissolved; the artisans and small traders who associated familiarly with their slaves and treated them almost as equals-few of the slaves of these men claimed their freedom.

In country places and especially in Pemba the plantation slaves gave some trouble. They wished to enjoy the ease and comfort which they associated with freedom, but, at the same time, they were disinclined to leave their old homes, and the shambas with which their masters had provided them, and the coconuts which were produced on the shambas. They would go to the Wali and claim their freedom. The Wali would ask, "How are you to earn your living?" and they would say, "Cultivating our shambas." "But if you live on your master's shamba, you must pay rent." This they had never thought of, so they took time to consider. Sometimes the passionate young Arabs would become impatient and indignant at the idleness and insolence of their labourers, and would there and then administer condign punishment, after which the slaves would hale them into court, accuse them of cruelty and forthwith be declared free men. Or the trouble might take a different turn. The master, disgusted with the laziness and dishonesty of his men under the new conditions, would bring a batch of them into court, requesting that they should be freed forthwith and himself compensated. Then the slaves would decline to be set free and assert that they belonged to their master who was bound to provide for them. What claim had the owner to compensation for losses on which he, and he alone, insisted?

But, on the whole, the transition stage passed in both islands without serious difficulty. In Pemba, under the influence of Mr. Farler, the best of the masters and the best of the slaves had no difficulty in coming to terms which, without the use of formal papers of freedom and without compensation to the slave-owners, were settled as between free men. To the labourer an allotment was made, the produce of which was his own. Instead of paying rent he worked for four days a week, six hours a day, on his master's land; all work done outside that period being paid for in coin or in kind by the master. These arrangements were usually in writing, for a period of two years; latterly they were required to be in writing and registered by the courts. The Sultan set the example of this system and, of thousands of slaves living and working on his lands in Zanzibar and Pemba, not one asked for freedom.

Among the smaller and poorer proprietors, and among the wilder or more uncivilized slaves, as in the north of Pemba, there were difficulties; but, where the refractory element was too obtrusive, a little judicious control, with the help of a military and police force, under Captain Goldie Taubman, was sufficient to repress lawlessness and preserve peace till, in the natural development of things, masters and men should, through the mere force of circumstances, be constrained to live together in harmony.

The process of manumission of slaves still proceeds. It is a very simple process. A slave appears before the Collector at his office and says-*Nataka kuandikwa*-I want to be written. His name, his master's name and place of residence; the slave's tribe, approximate age, height, marks and other details are all then entered in a book specially kept for the purpose; he is given a small brass counter, with a number stamped thereon, and at once dismissed, a free man. A few days afterwards his former master may appear and demand compensation, but before this can be awarded him he must furnish credible witnesses to prove that the freed person was his slave, lawfully held; and he must provide two guarantors, men of recognised standing, as surety against fraud. If it should turn out that the applicant has obtained compensation under false pretences, and that the freed person was not in reality his slave, the Government can recover from the guarantors.

A native has an abiding faith in being written down. If his name be in the book he knows that no man can touch him. When freed a native will often style himself -not a free man-but a slave of the Government or of the Consul. From thus describing himself he derives a sense of protection, which is no less sincere than convenient. "I want work; I am a slave of the Government," is not an infrequent demand. One of the most effective threats that can be used against an idle and good-for-nothing fellow is the threat to free him. When the question of the abolition of the legal status came up in 1897 the advocates of total abolition could never have realized the amount of hardship they would have inflicted upon many of the slaves of Zanzibar if they had had their way and compelled them, *nolentes volentes,* to be freed. The injustice to the Arabs would have been great, but the cruelty to the slaves would have been greater. Hundreds of people, who now contentedly live in their old homes, working only when they like, would have been turned out and become vagrants. Slavery, such as prevailed in the Southern

States, never existed in Zanzibar, and even that mild form of slavery which the leisure-loving Arabs could impose, has long since been dead. If the truth were known, I believe that the slaves, no less than the slave-owning classes, when first they observed the efforts of the British Government towards the suppression of slavery, looked upon the whole proceedings as a monstrous injustice. A slave, lawfully held according to Mohammedan law, rarely denied the fact. He never put in the plea that, according to all the laws of humanity and justice his master had no real right to him. According to his view his master had a right to him, and he himself, as soon as he could afford to do so, bought slaves of his own.

Natives come with the most amazing stories of how they were kidnapped and sold, but the most astonishing case that ever came under my notice was that of a youth named Makame, a native of Tumbatu, the large island on the north-west of Zanzibar Island. When a small boy, he was one day taken down to the beach, and *sold by one of his own slaves* to the owner of a dhow. He was taken to Pemba and in course of time obtained his freedom under the Decree of 1897. He was then sent to the Government plantation at Tundaua, under Mr. Lister, and put to the school which had been established there for the benefit of homeless children. One would have expected that when he grew up and came to realise the protection he could claim, Makame would have endeavoured to seek out and bring to justice the man who had wronged him. But nothing will induce Makame to go near Tumbatu; he is afraid he would be recognised by the slave who sold him, who, to escape the consequences of his act, would certainly make medicine on him, and bring upon him grievous trouble. The gullibility of the ordinary native is incredible. A native, whom I will call Juma, once complained to me that he had been the servant of a European, who lived some distance out of the town of Zanzibar. His employer one day sent him to the town on an errand. On the way he fell in with a man who had been his companion on a trading caravan to the Lakes, so they walked along together. When they had gone some way his companion invited Juma to go with him and see a friend who lived just off the road. When they arrived his companion introduced Juma as his slave and, to Juma's amazement, thereupon sold him to his friend. No doubt Juma protested and wildly gesticulated, but in the end he submitted and followed his new master; and probably his reflections were not those of indignation at being unjustly treated, but of regret at not being, beforehand with his betrayer.

All such doings are now at an end. In describing the efforts of our cruisers to destroy the slave trade, I have referred to several incidents of the chase. I will refer to one other, as it marks a contrast. About two years ago a report reached the Zanzibar Government that a girl had been kidnapped at a village on the northwest coast of Zanzibar Island. The First Minister kept the information as quiet as he could, and when darkness set in he despatched the Commanding Officer with a detachment of troops to march overland to the place. He himself at midnight, unknown to almost everyone in the town, proceeded up the coast in a launch. When he reached the spot he found there a British warship with lights out. Her Commander had also heard the report and, in order not to arouse suspicion, had appeared to pay no heed to it, till, under cover of darkness, he was able to creep out of the harbour. But they found no kidnapped girl, as there had been none to find.

The cruisers are still there, in and out of Zanzibar, in and out of Pemba, but the slave trader has gone.

CHAPTER XVI

ORGANISATION OF ZANZIBAR GOVERNMENT

THE year 1892 was an important one in the history of Zanzibar, as it was in that year that the reorganisation of the administration by Sir Gerald Portal came into operation, and with the form of government under which the island has since continued to thrive. The reorganisation dates from October 20, 1891, on which day General Mathews entered on his work as First Minister to the Sultan. On October 23, Portal arranged with the Seyyid Ali bin Said, that he should receive a fixed monthly sum for his own personal expenses; that proper accounts should be kept of all revenues and expenditure, and that various Departments of Government should be organised and placed under the control of British officials, who should be irremovable except by consent of the British Consul-General.

Before that date no organised Government really existed. The expenses of administration were small, as no works were carried out for the benefit of the public; the revenues, comparatively large, were for the most part appropriated by the Sultans, who were preyed upon by adventurers and retainers eager "to grasp as large a share as possible of the money which was poured into the Sultan's coffers." The advent of the German and English Companies, followed by the alienation to Germany of the maritime territories which now form the coast of German East Africa, and the lease to the English Company of the greater portion of the remainder of his continental dominions, resulted in the reduction of the Sultan's revenue to about one third of its former amount. But the Sultan did not on that account reduce his expenditure. Hence, on arriving at Zanzibar in the Autumn of 1891, Portal found that "the Sultan, and, indeed, the whole island of Zanzibar, were advancing towards a state of insolvency. Few accounts were kept, statistical returns were unknown, such moneys as could be collected by the Customs Officials were paid in to the Palace, and paid out again indiscriminately to a clamorous crowd of adherents who lived on the Sultan's bounty."

Sir Gerald Portal began his difficult task by abolishing the five per cent. import duty, which yielded 180,000 rupees a year. This was a bold step at such a time, but he considered it necessary if Zanzibar was to maintain its position as the chief port of transhipment, and the central market of East Africa. His choice of new sources of revenue was restricted by treaties which did not permit of an equable system of taxation; treaties which still hamper the administration, made as they were under conditions that have now altogether changed. Nevertheless, the range of taxation was extended and considerable revenue was derived from registration and from liquor licenses; at the same time rigid economy in expenditure was observed, and the host of Palace dependants, a source of trouble, as well as of expense, was weeded out, so that at the end of the year a satisfactory balance was carried forward. Many other improvements were effected; the port service, under Commander Hardinge, R.N., was organised, the registration of native vessels was enforced, the harbour approaches were buoyed and lighted, and other works for the improvement of wharves, roads, and sanitation were carried out. The military force numbering 860, all ranks, was taken over by General Hatch when General Mathews became First Minister, and in January 1892, it was supplemented by a police force. The first newspaper in the island made its appearance on February 1, 1892, under the title of *The Gazette for Zanzibar and East Africa*. It is of a semi-official character, and is the medium for the publication of information supplied by Government and by the British and Foreign Representatives. There are now in Zanzibar and in the British and German Protectorates several other newspapers, some official and some nonofficial.

Under Seyyid Said, Zanzibar had become the centre of East African trade, and its importance as such had been increased by subsequent Sultans, till at length all East African trade routes led to Zanzibar. Sir Gerald Portal saw that the prosperity of the island depended on the continuance of this commercial supremacy and, owing to his action, Zanzibar was on February 1, 1892, declared a free port. The wisdom of this step is shewn by the fact that the combined value of imports and exports, which in 1892 amounted to £2,093,370, steadiy increased till in 1899 it reached the value of £3,110,000. On October 1 of the latter year, the 5 per cent. *ad valorem* duty was, with certain modifications, re-imposed, a rebate being allowed on goods re-exported. From that date the trade began to decline. An exact comparison cannot be made, for, in 1900 and subsequent years, the trade with other ports of the islands was excluded from the Zanzibar commercial statistics; but since 1900, when the imports and exports amounted to the value of £2,283,835, there has been a decline, not continuous, but on the whole considerable, the total in 1903, having fallen to £2,087,980.

The direct trade of the German and British Protectorates with Europe will probably increase, and the trade of Zanzibar, both with Europe and East Africa, fall off for a time. It has been regarded as probable that the Uganda Railway will interfere with the commercial prosperity of the island, but, so far, there is little to support this belief. The railway will more probably injure German commerce by diverting to Mombasa the traffic between the interior and the coast towns of the German Protectorate. The depression of Zanzibar commerce will probably be neither serious nor long-continued. The island has advantages which, if rightly used, must secure her prosperity. She has a magnificent harbour which ships of all sizes can enter in any weather, and where they can ride securely at anchor; her rainfall is much higher and consequently her fertility is much greater than that of the continental coast, so that it is more convenient for ships to provision and water at Zanzibar than at any other port in the region. Moreover, Zanzibar is the favourite home of the Arab and the African, and where the people go the trade will follow. The clove industry established within the island has attracted an immense number of Indian merchants and traders, financiers and speculators, as well as members or representatives of several large European firms, and the presence of these men keeps the principal currents of trade flowing through Zanzibar.

Kilindini, near Mombasa, has a large harbour, but at the port of Mombasa, the terminus of the Uganda Railway, large vessels cannot be accommodated, and until the commercial interests of the British Protectorate are transferred to Kilindini, Zanzibar has little to fear.

On the German coast there are no ports where large vessels can lie conveniently, none to compare with the port of Zanzibar. The Germans made Dar es Salaam the capital of their new possession. They laid out a beautiful town and built commodious and substantial public buildings, and they provided magnificent steamship services which have been subsidised partly with a view to the fostering of trade at that port. Some of the, leading German houses transferred their head-quarters from Zanzibar to Dar es Salaam, but they have all gone back to Zanzibar, and Dar es Salaam, except for its official character, is only an unimportant coast town.

For German East Africa the way to prosperity lies rather through industrial than commercial enterprise. The Protectorate will flourish by the working of its plantations, the growing of cotton and textile plants, the development of such mineral resources as it possesses. Such enterprises will meet with no rivalry in Zanzibar, which seems destined to occupy on the African coast a position analogous to that held further east by Singapore and Hong Kong, both of which ports are, it may be observed, free ports.

The arteries of trade did not always converge on Zanzibar. There was a time when she was of no more account than Mafia is to-day, and, if the advantages she now possesses be not judiciously employed, prosperity may forsake her. She must maintain facilities for commerce; on no account ought she to fall behind in her harbour and shipping arrangements; above all she must keep her tariff low.

The Government of Zanzibar is administered by a First Minister, whose nomination is subject to the approval of the Foreign Office, and a staff of European officials. Great Britain is represented by an Agent and Consul-General who, in addition to being responsible for the liberties of British subjects, is the medium through whom communications between the Foreign Office and the Zanzibar Government pass.

Zanzibar and Pemba are divided into sub-districts, administered, under British officials, by Arab Governors or Walis, assisted by Arab judges or Kathis, who dispense justice to Zanzibaris in accordance with Mohammedan law. For Americans, Belgians, Germans, Italians, and Portuguese there are consular courts representing their respective countries. All other Christian foreigners, as well as British and British-protected subjects, are under the jurisdiction of the British Court. This court had its origin in 1866, when power was given to the British Consul to try disputes between British subjects, and to exercise the functions of a vice-admiralty court. As the judicial requirements of the island extended, authority was by degrees entrusted to professional lawyers till, in 1897, the British Consular jurisdiction was abolished and a separate British court of justice established. In this court the most conspicuous figure was that of judge Cracknall, who, having been successively legal adviser (1881), judicial assistant (1884), consular judge (1893), became (1897) the first judge in the new court, and retired in 1900. In 1902 this court was made the Appeal Court for the three Protectorates of British East Africa, Uganda, and British Central Africa. The

Indian Penal Code was made applicable to Zanzibar in 1867. The present court administers English, Anglo-Indian, Hindu, Parsi, and, since 1898, as delegated Court of the Sultan, Mohammedan law. The business of the court is at present conducted by judge Lindsey Smith with two assistant judges, a registrar, and a judicial officer for Pemba.

Since the year 1890 Zanzibar has been a British Protectorate but, as such, it holds a position widely different from that of the British East Africa Protectorate, or Uganda, or the Central Africa Protectorate. It would perhaps be more correct to say that Zanzibar is a protected State, or a Sultanate under British Protection. The island, so long as it occupies this position, is in a sense neutral territory where men of all nationalities may meet without mutual jealousy, and this state of things is vital to its welfare. The Pax Britannica rules there and, with brief intermission, has ruled since the sway of Great Britain was formally admitted.

A royal gathering in House of Wonders (Beit al Ajaib).

CHAPTER XVII

THE BOMBARDMENT

FOR a century Great Britain had maintained her influence with Oman and Zanzibar and had imposed her treaties upon their rulers without having to fire a shot; yet before reaching the goal of her patient and persistent policy in the Decree of 1897, she was compelled to resort to the humiliating expedient of a show of force. Born under the shadow of India, Seyyid Said, a much more powerful monarch than any of his successors, regarded his great neighbour as a friend whose protection might be sought, yet as a master whose wishes must be respected. With the death on March 5, 1893, of Seyyid Ali , the last of Seyyid Said's sons to occupy the throne of Zanzibar, the time-honoured relations of the two countries appear to have been forgotten. At that time there was some anxiety, as there were no fewer than three claimants to the succession. Of these the most energetic was Khaled bin Barghash, who at once seized the Palace, the others being Hamid bin Thuwaini and Hamoud bin Mohammed. When General Mathews heard of Khaled's proceedings, he occupied the square of the Palace, and by his personal influence held in check the supporters of the rival claimants. For an hour the situation was critical, but when the British Agent, Mr. Rennell Rodd and Captain Campbell, with 160 blue-jackets and a guard of marines from the *Philomel* and the *Blanche*, came on the scene, and, pointing a machine gun on the door, summoned the usurper to submit, Khaled opened the door and gave himself up. Hamid was placed on the throne, and after two days confinement Khaled was restored to his place of honour in the Sultan's court.

Hamid bin Thuwaini, though he owed his position to Great Britain, assumed an attitude of passive defiance towards his protector, and so successfully did he work on the prejudices of his subjects that, towards the close of his reign, Arabs began to jostle Englishmen in the streets. Khaled also was not idle, but was making ready to reassert his claim at the first opportunity which might arise. He was

171

regarded by a large section of the Arabs as the rightful heir to the throne, and since, according to their notions, might, coupled with election by the tribes, was right, he considered himself justified in his action. His hostility to the British was both the ground of his hope and the cause of his downfall. British influence seemed on the wane; the *laissez faire* policy was misinterpreted by the Arabs, and Khaled and his supporters thought that somehow, by a swift and sudden stroke the island might be restored to its former independence.

Thus it was that, when on August 25, 1896, Hamid bin Thuwaini suddenly died, Khaled again came to the front.

On the news of the Sultan's death Mr. Basil Cave, Acting British Agent and Consul-General, and Sir Lloyd Mathews, proceeded as quickly as they could to the Palace; but as they were mounting the steps Seyyid Khaled, with fifty armed followers, entered the Palace square, and entirely ignoring them, began an attack upon the door and windows. Mathews, who had known Khaled since he was a boy, endeavoured to reason with him, but the young Arab was now in no mind to be talked over as he had been in 1893, and within a very few minutes he, with a mob of 500 Arabs, entered the Palace and took possession.

Sir Lloyd's next impulse was to shoot Khaled on the spot, and had he done so he would probably have averted the bloodshed that followed; but he reflected that perhaps he was scarcely justified in taking upon himself this extreme step. There was nothing for it but to withdraw; so he and Mr. Cave, still covered by the rifles of the rebel horde, retraced their steps to the Agency.

The troops of the island were at that time divided into two forces: one commanded by a British officer under the orders of the Zanzibar Government, the other controlled by the Sultan. The Sultan's force originally consisted of 200 men, and was intended solely to provide a guard for the Palace, and an escort when the Sultan drove out. This force Hamid bin Thuwaini had on his own responsibility increased till it outnumbered the Government troops, and must at his death have been nearly a thousand strong. In addition to these troops and the armed corvette *Glasgow,* the Sultan possessed seven Hotchkiss and Krupp guns, two maxims, gifts from Queen Victoria, and a large number of old muzzle-loading cannon, which had been carried in the fleets of Seyyids Said and Majid.

Khaled increased his forces by the addition of about two thousand Persians, Comoro Islanders, and slaves whom he armed with weapons of every available kind, and disposed in the Palace, its approaches and adjoining houses. He ordered the *Glasgow* to fire a salute to announce his accession, and sent notices to the foreign Consuls demanding from them recognition of his claim. The Consuls, in reply, kept their flags at half-mast, declining to recognise him till the British authorities had first done so.

The European residents, meanwhile, had collected at the English club, from the roof of which a commanding view of the harbour, the Palace, and the town could be obtained. The southernmost watch-tower of the fort, which rises thirty feet landwards from the roof of the club, was occupied by a few decrepit Arab troops, who, with antiquated firelocks, prepared to despatch the assembled Wazungu (white men) when the appointed time should arrive. The *Philomel* and *Thrush* were the only two British warships in the harbour, but these lost no time in landing guards of marines and blue-jackets for the Agency and Custom House.

Outside, the *Sparrow*, on her way from the north, was carrying out evolutions, but on a signal from the *Philomel* she at once stood in and took up her position 150 yards from the shore, opposite the Palace. Following her example, the *Thrush* left her anchorage, and moored in line ahead of her. In the town all was confusion, and the European ladies who lived in isolated localities found refuge at the British Agency under the hospitable care of Mrs. Cave.

Thus Tuesday, August 25, drew to a close, Khaled having possession of the Palace quarter, and keeping the quickfiring and other guns trained on the approaches, the club, the Custom House, and the British warships; while the bridges and principal thoroughfares of the town were held by the Government troops under General Raikes.

The next morning the complexion of things underwent a change. First the *Racoon* steamed in from the south and took up her position opposite the Custom House, astern of the *Sparrow*; then at midday, to the surprise of everyone, as she was not expected for two days, the *St. George*, Rear-Admiral Rawson's flagship, was signalled from the south. Not knowing what was afoot she had prepared to salute the Sultan's flag but was happily warned in time.

The Admiral lost no time in increasing the forces ashore, strengthening the guards of marines and blue-jackets at the Agency and Custom House, and posting others in the thoroughfares leading to the European quarter. But in spite of renewed exertions to bring him to submit, Khaled still refused to quit the Palace, or to surrender the power he had usurped. Thus Wednesday, the 26th, passed and the city prepared for a second night of suspense. "Whether it was so or not, everyone the next day agreed that never had they known such a soundless night."

At seven in the morning Admiral Rawson sent an ultimatum to Seyyid Khaled, requiring him to haul down his flag, make his troops and followers pile their arms in the square and leave the Palace, and deliver himself up to him at the Custom House before nine o'clock, failing which he would open fire with the guns of his ships. At eight o'clock an envoy was despatched to Mr. Cave, who was at the Custom House, requesting a parley, but he was told by the British representative that no parley would be granted, and that salvation could only be found in fulfilment of the conditions of the ultimatum. With a parting defiance the envoy returned to his desperate master.

The English ladies and children in the town were taken off to the ships in the harbour; some to the *St. George*, others, as well as many British and Portuguese-Indian subjects, to the British India S.S. *Nowshera*, Captain Stone. On the first night of the rebellion the European and native members of the English Mission, both at Mkunazini in the town, and at the outlying stations to the south of the town, had remained at their posts, but on the morning of the 27th, when it was realised that a bombardment was inevitable, they were brought in.

The British forces on shore consisted of 330 seamen, 120 marines with five maxims and one 7-pounder, and 500 native troops of the Zanzibar Government. The seamen, with three maxims and the 7-Pounder, were at the Custom House; the marines guarded the British Agency and the approaches to the Palace square. It was thought that Khaled might endeavour to escape into the plantations, and to prevent this, as well as to turn back the looters who in the confusion would probably descend upon the town, the outskirts were held by General Raikes, with forty marines and two maxims, and a detachment of native troops.

The disposition of the ships was as follows: The *Thrush*, gunboat, Lieutenant and Commander Stoddart, *Sparrow,* gunboat, Lieutenant and Commander Wilkin, *Racoon*, third class cruiser, Commander Underwood, moored in line opposite the Palace and Custom House at pointblank range; the *St. George*, first-class cruiser, Captain Egerton, flagship of Rear-Admiral Sir Harry Rawson, anchored to the south of Shangani Point, a promontory which makes an entering angle into the harbour, and from which the coast falls away to the north-east towards the Palace and Mtoni and to the south-east towards Mbweni. The British Agency stands on this commanding site. The *Philomel* occupied a position between the *Racoon* and the *St. George*; and between the *Philomel* and *St.*

The Bombardment

George, and exposed to the stern guns of the latter, lay the *Glasgow*, sole surviving ship of the Zanzibar navy. Merchant vessels were warned to seek safe berths, a warning disregarded by some of them till the shot of the Palace guns began to whistle about their rigging, when, with more haste than dignity (in the case of one British steamer by the officers themselves heaving the anchor up, the crew having been scared below) they sought the shelter of Shangani Point.

On shore the Palace square bristled with cannon, manned by slaves, while the galleries of the Palace were thronged with Arabs. Crowds of natives lined the flanking shores, with the idea apparently that they were to witness a sort of fireworks display.

The Arabs themselves had no idea what was about to happen; they never reckoned on their houses being brought tumbling about their ears; the medicine men had foretold that the British guns would only discharge water, and at worst they anticipated that their fire would be confined to the wretched natives they had driven to the guns.

At five minutes to nine Admiral Rawson hoisted the signal to prepare for action; two bells struck and then followed a breathless three minutes of suspense till the Palace clock struck the hour.

A moment later the three bombarding ships discharged their batteries against the Palace guns. The *Thrush* opened the action, followed immediately by the *Racoon* and *Sparrow*. It is not necessary to describe the result in detail. In half-an-hour the Palace and clock tower were in flames, the middle palace was a ruin, the Arabs had fled, 500 dead and wounded lay in and about the square, and the *Glasgow* was at the bottom of the sea.

The Admiral had given orders that the *Glasgow* was not to be fired on unless she herself assumed the aggressive; but this she immediately did, and was only at length silenced by a six-inch from the *St. George* after repeated warning shots from the *Philomel* and *Racoon*. Nine of her crew were killed or drowned, the rest being brought to the *St. George*.

Thirty-seven minutes after the bombardment had begun the red flag was hauled down from the Palace flagstaff and the "cease fire" sounded. But Khaled had escaped. Horrified at the ruin that fell around him, he left the Palace and made his way through the main street of the town. Here he was stopped by a guard of marines, who, not knowing who he was, merely disarmed him and let him pass. A few yards brought him to the German Consulate, which he entered.

175

As soon as the preliminaries could be arranged Seyyid Hamoud bin Mahommed bin Said was conducted into the Custom House and proclaimed Sultan of Zanzibar amidst the salute of the ships.

Our casualties were mostly trifling, but one was serious, a bluejacket from the *Thrush* having been so severely wounded in the thigh that he subsequently died. The *Thrush* was hit over a hundred times, the *Philomel* only twice. The Italian man-of-war *Vulturno* was in harbour, and having declined the invitation to shift her moorings she received a shot into her companion which caused her to slip her cable and steam round behind Shangani Point.

A few houses in the town were struck by stray shots, but no serious damage was done. The wrecked Palace was the scene of much curiosity and interest. "To describe the interior is impossible. To produce a similar effect take chairs, tables, cabinets, clocks, vases, bookcases, an orchestra, an armoury, a manuscript library, a wardrobe, an instrument maker's, an electrician's, and an optician's store; lamp and perfume sellers' shops; spread the floor with choicest carpets; add all scraps of royal insignia procurable; put dynamite here and there, explode *ad lib.* and there you have it."* The Rev. J. P. Farler, writing in "Central Africa," thus described the scene at the Palace:" It was an awful sight; dead bodies lying everywhere, and such ruin and destruction! The looters had been at work; every drawer was opened and ransacked; valuables were lying all over the floors of the different rooms. I saw natives carrying off silver and other valuables. Money and jewels had disappeared, and soon nothing would have been left if an officer and a guard had not arrived and cleared the palace."

The Rev. K. Firminger, writing in the same paper, said: "After the 'cease fire,' leaving Mr. Lister to keep all our people within bounds, I set off to the Custom House to see what could be done for the wounded. Here I came in for two or three hours' work amidst a perfectly indescribable scene of horror-too terrible to strike one as a reality-more like the shambles than aught else. After a time the influx of wounded stopped, and hearing that our own hospital was full, I sent Mr. Prior off to assist and went up myself a bit later. There proved to be some interesting cases, and some especially sad ones. The captain of the usurper's guns, a Persian, was hopelessly wounded. Among the sad cases that turned up was a small boy, shot through the arm close to the shoulders. This boy was found in the street by Mr. Lister and brought in. Saddest of all was a mother and her baby boy,

* **The Gazelle for Zanzibar and East Africa.**

the bullet having passed through both legs of the latter into the mother's breast. This was not due to our people, but was the outcome of the recklessness of the rebel soldiers, who did as much damage as they could in their headlong flight through the streets when the Palace was destroyed."

The wounded, under the direction of Dr. G. A. MacDonald, were sent to the hospital of the Universities' Mission at Mkunazini, where they were received by the matron, Miss Brewerton, and Messrs. Faulkner and Saunderson, two lay members of the Mission, who had remained at Mkunazini during the bombardment with a native guard to defend the Cathedral and Church house. Others were sent to the Military Hospital, whither Pere Lutz and Father Smith, of the French Mission, had repaired to render what aid they could; and others again to Madame Chevalier and Sisters of the French Hospital.

The steps of the German Consulate give on to the beach, so Seyyid Khaled was able to get on board the German warship *Seeadler* without exposing himself to arrest. He was taken to Dar es Salaam and provided for by the Administration there.

He is there still.

It is idle to speculate upon what would have happened had the forces of disorder prevailed, but from one incident which occurred we may conclude that, if from any accident, such, for example, as the absence of warships, the state of anarchy had been prolonged, European residents would have been exposed to grave danger. Mr. Last, of the Zanzibar Government service, was at Chwaka, a village on the east coast of the island, when the rebellion broke out, and knew nothing of what was taking place. When the bombardment was over the chief of the village, who had witnessed in town the ruin of the rebel cause, made off to Chwaka with his armed followers, resolved that one European should suffer. But Mr. Last had received news of what was afoot, and had succeeded in joining his wife on the *St. George* some hours before the bombardment began.

Although the bombardment cannot be regarded as the direct outcome of England's attitude towards the slave trade, it proved a salutary prelude to the Decree abolishing the legal status of slavery; for the brief exhibition of power had the effect of clearing from the minds of the Arabs all doubt as to Great Britain's ability to compel its acceptance. No people are more loyal in defeat than the Arabs of Zanzibar, and their mutual relations having been determined both victors and vanquished settled down to work out the application of the Decree in as practical a way as they could.

Seyyid Hamoud reigned peacefully, prosperously, and in sympathy with the British policy respecting slavery. It was in his time that the Decree for the abolition of the legal status of slavery was issued, and so loyally did he cooperate with the British in carrying out the provisions of this Decree, that Queen Victoria marked her appreciation of his efforts by conferring on him the Grand Cross of the Most Distinguished Order of St. Michael and St. George.

Zanzibar, delivered from strife and slavery, was now about to lose the hand which, through many anxious years, had controlled her destinies.

After suffering from a prolonged attack of fever, Sir Lloyd Mathews, in February, 1900, went home to England for rest, returning to Zanzibar in November of the same year. The change, though it did him good, was of too short a duration to restore him to a normal condition of health. In October, 1901, he fell ill again, and on the 11th of that month died. I can convey no idea of the shock to the island the news of his death caused. His personality pervaded the remotest hamlets; not only wealthy Arabs but little children looked upon him as a personal friend and protector. Ragged urchins would waylay him in the street with their tales of woe, but he would never turn them away. Often after hearing their story he would take them to his house and give them food and clothing. On Christmas Eve he gave himself up to what was probably the happiest task of the year, arranging presents for the children. Every European child in Zanzibar received a present from him on Christmas Day. During the Boer war transports occasionally called at Zanzibar on their way from India. In one instance the troops were paraded on shore, marched to the golf ground and given liberty. They became thirsty and besieged the water-butts. Observing this, and knowing the injurious effects that often result from drinking water in Zanzibar, some residents, who were playing golf, began to get up a subscription to provide the troops with lager beer and lemonade, but before anything could be done word came that the General, as Sir Lloyd was usually called, had sent beer and lemonade on board the ship to suffice for all when they returned. Plutarch has told us that the secret of Caesar's power over his legions was his liberality towards them: the secret of the General's hold over the people of Zanzibar was his liberality and kindheartedness. No more liberal-handed man ever lived than Lloyd Mathews. But though he was loved, he was feared. No Arab dared to oppose his wishes; no native would rebel against his decision. During long residence in the country, being a man of great shrewdness, he had learned the arts and turns of African methods, and when once set upon his track, no man could escape him. He was personally acquainted with all the important Arab families, and knew the records of most of the village chiefs.

Men of strong personality have often marked failings, and Sir Lloyd Mathews was no exception to this rule. As might have been expected, he was too generous to be a good financier, and in some respects he was not a good administrator. One of the rules of life for a European in Zanzibar should be-never do yourself what you can get someone else to do for you. This sounds like a perversion of the good old maxim: If you want a thing done properly, do it yourself; but in a climate like that of Zanzibar a European should reserve his strength for things that he alone can do. He will probably find that as much as he can manage. Sir Lloyd Mathews tried to do everything himself. Surrounded in his early years by corruption and chaos, he discovered he could trust nobody, and he trained himself to see to the smallest detail. To these careful habits he owed, in no small measure, his success, but he never perceived that the newly-organised administration, which he himself had helped to establish, demanded from him considerable delegation of power. So he sank at last, literally fighting to the end with the cares of government which overwhelmed him. Sir Lloyd was a Welshman, born at Madeira in 1850. He entered the Navy in 1864, and served in the Ashantee war of 1873-4. He was made a C.M.G. on May 24, 1889; a K.C.M.G. on March 3, 1894; and he was the recipient of many foreign decorations. He was buried with full naval and military honours in the English Cemetery, just outside the town of Zanzibar. Mr. A. S. Rogers, Sub-Commissioner of the British East Africa Protectorate, and Resident at Witu, was, in January, 1902, appointed in his place, First Minister of the Zanzibar Government.

On July 18, 1902, scarcely a year after the death of Sir Lloyd Mathews, his friend and master, Seyyid Hamoud died also. Seyyid Hamoud was a wise ruler, who understood the attitude which circumstances required him to adopt towards the Protecting Power. Under him, for the first time in their history, no shadow of rebellion or strife fell across the lives of the people of Zanzibar. He was fond of Europeans, especially of the English, and took a delight in entertaining his officials and in having them near him. He inherited all the grace of manner and dignity of bearing that has never failed to impress strangers at the Zanzibar court, and, what is perhaps the chiefest indication of good breeding, he possessed the art of making his guests feel at home. He was a large man, very stout, and at his death was about fifty-four years of age.

Seyyid Hamoud was succeeded by his son, Seyyid Ali, the present ruler of Zanzibar. Seyyid Ali, at the time of his father's death, was on his way back from England, whither he had gone to represent his father at King Edward's Coronation. He had already spent several years of his boyhood in England, part of the time at Harrow, and thus speaks English fluently. He was proclaimed Sultan on July 20, 1902, but being under age, Mr. A. S. Rogers, the First Minister, was at the same time appointed Regent.

CHAPTER XVIII

MISSIONS

THE Christian missionaries working in Zanzibar represent the Universities' Mission, the Mission of the Holy Ghost, and the Society of Friends. A pioneer in their work was Dr. Krapf, who, with his wife, arrived in the island in January, 1844, having been compelled, after six years of effort, to abandon his labours in Abyssinia. He, however, only remained in Zanzibar till March of the same year, having selected Mombasa as his field of labour where, in June, 1846, he was joined by his famous colleague, Rebman.

The next missionary who appeared in Zanzibar was Livingstone, whose name- the greatest name connected with Africa-is indissolubly associated with the island. Though Zanzibar was the scene of few of his activities, he was virtually the founder of the Universities' Mission. The house where he dwelt still stands conspicuous before the traveller entering the harbour. It is not in the comparatively clean European quarter, but in the slums of Melindi, where Livingstone might have been expected to choose his dwelling; a square white house, towering above its neighbours as Livingstone towered above his contemporaries.

Bishop Tozer and Dr. Steere, the first representatives of the Universities' Mission, arrived in Zanzibar on August 31, 1864. The Bishop was received by the British Consul, Lieutenant-Colonel Playfair, and took up his quarters in a house that is now the British Consulate, "quite next to the Sultan's in appearance, and certainly superior in situation." I once heard a traveller, in comparing Zanzibar with Mombasa, say: "Zanzibar is the East; Mombasa is not the East" and so, as regards Zanzibar, Bishop Tozer found it- "you scarcely observe the crowd of huts which cover the surface like bees in front of a hive at swarming time, for all along the shore is a fringe of tall, and for the most part stately, flat-roofed houses, as Eastern as possible."

From the first the Mission has carried on its work in loyal co-operation with the constituted authorities and, no doubt for this reason, has enjoyed an immunity from local criticism probably enjoyed by missions in few countries. Its representatives witnessed the cruelties of the slave traffic, were grieved at the vexatious delay in its suppression, and yet restrained themselves in times when public opinion ran high. Nor is it less creditable to the Administration that through forty years of difficulty and anxiety they proved themselves worthy of the confidence and co-operation of these missionaries.

In January, 1871, St. Andrew's College, Kiungani, was founded. This is a school for the training of native teachers and clergy. It is situated about two miles out of the town, to the south, and contains from 80 to 100 pupils drawn from the preparatory school at Kilimani and from the schools of the mainland. The boys within the walls of Kiungani constitute the hope of the Universities' Mission.

The methods upon which the Universities' Mission works differ from those ordinarily followed by foreign missions. It may, I think, with truth be said that the aims are different, for whereas in the case of most missions the direct aim is to make converts to Christianity, to teach the people, and to train the children to useful crafts, that of the Universities' Mission is to found an African Church, whose work shall ultimately be carried on by a native Ministry. This involves the selection from the field in which they labour of the brightest and most promising youths and the devotion of the best energies of the Mission to the training of those youths. What I may term the ordinary educational and industrial side of mission work, is regarded as of secondary importance, and its interests, when they clash with those of the higher training, are made to give way before it.

It must be remembered that the Universities' Mission works in Equatorial and Tropical Africa; in climates where, for the most part, Europeans can never make for themselves permanent homes. In such countries the powers of Europeans are limited and they themselves will always be foreigners.

It should perhaps be mentioned that, in 1892, it was decided that Nyasaland should have its own Bishopric, and on December 21, of that year, the Rev. W. B. Hornby was consecrated first Bishop of Nyasaland. At the same time the Bishop of the Mission, who, since the first arrival of Bishop Tozer, had resided at Zanzibar, assumed the title of Bishop of Zanzibar.

The boys of Kiungani who do not seem fitted for the work of a teacher or for the Ministry, in time leave the Mission and seek employment in the town. They understand a little English, and act as interpreters to newly arrived Europeans, or as office boys or perhaps junior clerks, but when at length the effect of the school discipline wears off, they frequently develop habits of drink and become quite useless to serve in any capacity. The result is that mission boys as a class have, in Zanzibar, a bad name so that many residents of experience will not employ them and, what is far more serious, that the reputation of mission work itself is prejudiced. It is true that people not connected with the Mission come in contact as a rule only with the failures; that every institution must have failures, and that the work of the Mission must be judged, not by its failures, but by its successes; but it is equally true that people are accustomed to form impressions from what they see. It is certainly a fact, too, that a knowledge of English is often detrimental to a native. If he have brains and perseverance he can, of course, turn that knowledge to good account and procure advancement. Boys with these qualities, however, rarely leave the Mission. Natives who can speak a little English too frequently gravitate to the town beach and to the ships, where they meet with the roughest element that the human race can produce.

In addition to the school at Kiungani, the Universities' Mission in Zanzibar supports a Theological College at Mazazini, a children's school for the last 25 years under Miss Mills, at Kilimani, a girls' school at Mbweni, an Indian school and special town Mission at St. Monica's, a printing office at Mkunazini, and a hospital at Mkunazini. The principal residence of the Bishop, now Dr. Hine, is at Mkunazini. The girls' school at Mbweni was for many years presided over by Miss Thackeray, now one of the oldest residents in the island. The hospital is staffed by trained English nurses, and, since the year 1892, has been under the direction of Miss Brewerton, a nurse who has the reputation of being one of the best that ever went to Africa. Stations and schools are maintained in Pemba, and in the Rovuma district and Bondei country, German East Africa. It is in this territory that the principal work of the Mission is performed. The station at Wete, Pemba, founded by Bishop Richardson, was opened by Canon Sir John Key and Lady Key in 1897.

In describing mission work in Zanzibar the question not unnaturally arises:- What progress has Christianity made against Mohammedanism? The answer is that in Zanzibar Christianity has made little progress against Mohammedanism; perhaps it may even be said none whatever. The Mohammedan religion has its roots deep down in the people; its fatalistic doctrines are peculiarly adapted to their habits of thought and of life; its feastings and fastings appeal to their emotional character. Every educated Arab is in a sense a priest of Islam; a daily exponent of the formalities of his religion. The very language of the country breathes Islam. But perhaps more than to anything else the religion of the Prophet owes its power to the fact that it permits its devotees a plurality of wives and as many concubines as they can support. It is easier to overcome superstitious idolatry than to persuade people, who worship the same God as you do, that your way of worshipping Him is better than theirs; especially when you are compelled to admit, as I think most students of Mohammedanism would admit, that there is much about the letter and practice of their religion which is good. In religious matters the people follow the Arabs, and Christianity can never prevail against Islam by skirmishing on the outskirts. It must drive at the heart of it. But to be able to do this it must be provided with Arabic scholars, having a thorough knowledge of the language and the Koran.

The European members of the Universities' Mission staff receive no pay, though a nominal allowance of twenty pounds a year is made to them, if they should require it. They go out to Africa in the true spirit of Christ, who called upon His disciples to leave all and follow Him. The records of the Mission are rich in the names of men and women who have obeyed this call. It is a call to arduous labour, often to privation, sometimes to death.

With equal loyalty to the Government, and for an even longer period than the English Mission, the Black Fathers have laboured in the island. The Mission of the Holy Ghost, known locally as the French Mission, because its members are under the protection of the French Consul, was founded by Dr. Amand Manponit, Bishop of St. Denis, Réunion, who sent his Vicar-General to Zanzibar in 1860. The Rev. Father Horner was appointed Prefect Apostolic, and with him came the Rev. Father Etienne Baur, Père Etienne, as he is popularly called, now the doyen of the European communities, a witness, after more than 40 years' experience, of the amenities of the climate. The first Bishop of the Mission, Dr. de Courmont, was appointed in 1883. The principal branch of the Mission, that at Bagamoyo, has grown into a large home where carpentering, blacksmithing, building, shoemaking, vanilla-growing and other industries are taught by experienced Europeans. The new Roman Catholic Cathedral at Zanzibar was built by the Mission, largely with its own trained labour. The essentially practical character of the French Mission is one of its most marked features. On behalf of, and in cooperation with, the Zanzibar Government, it undertakes the care of lepers; and has control of a home for the sick and infirm at Walezo, about four miles from the town. Bishop Allgeyer, the present Bishop, established, in 1897, a station at Dongoni, near Chake Chake, Pemba, entrusting the founding of Roman Catholic missionary work in that island to the Rev. Father Smith.

In the same year the Society of Friends established under Mr. Theodore Burtt, a mission station at Chake Chake, Pemba, and subsequently another at Banani, where they maintain an industrial home.

Livingston's house, Zanzibar.

Forodhani customs area Zanzibar.

CHAPTER XIX

THE PEOPLE

IN a sketch of the people of Zanzibar and Pemba, the as the conquerors and landowners of the country, claim attention first. After a century of luxury in these balmy spice islands, where the fruits of the earth can be raised the minimum of effort, and where for generations slaves exerted this minimum, the Zanzibar Arabs have lost much of the vigorous temperament which distinguished their ancestors. The stoppage of the supply of slave has affected them very much as a perpetual strike would affect the mine-owners of Staffordshire: it has left them without any resources.

Nevertheless, though shaken by the ordeal through which they have passed, the Arabs of Zanzibar still possess most of the land, and carry on the clove-growing industry for which the two islands are far famed. They understand the natives, and the natives understand and like the Arabs, and accept their control more readily than that of any other race, except Europeans. It is, in many cases, easier to manage natives through an Arab than to treat with them directly, and plantations in Zanzibar can be more successfully worked by employing Arabs in subordinate responsible positions than any other people, not excepting Europeans. Europeans could not for long endure the sun, and are not fitted for active overseeing work in Zanzibar. Arabs enjoy the heat and can live on the fruits of the soil; to them travelling is no hardship or weariness. Indians always get ill in the shambas; they are bad riders and walkers; are often bullied and chaffed by the natives, in whom they seem to excite ridicule and contempt. Creoles drink, and never remain long in one place. The better-class natives make excellent overseers, but the best of them fall far short of the Arabs in intelligence. They have few wants and lack the stimulus of ambition, which can always be counted upon to keep an Arab up to a certain standard of efficiency.

Courteous and hospitable, Arabs exhibit the signs of national good breeding.

There is no more hospitable people. An Arab will not only set before you the best he has, but it will be a delight to him to see you eat and drink in his house. No men that I have ever met have such good manners as the Arabs. Their walk is slow and extremely graceful, *incessu Paluit Dea*; and, I suppose, save in warfare, no man in Zanzibar has ever seen an Arab run. Once a year, on the King's birthday, the Sultan and his court call on the British Consul-General. They drive up in carriages accompanied by mounted troopers carrying lances; but at one time it was the custom for the procession to arrive on foot, and the spectacle has suffered by the change, as all the charm of slow and dignified carriage, of which the Arab is master, and which on this occasion was seen to the best advantage, is now lost. The Arab receives his friend by lightly touching his own forehead and breast, and extending both hands; then follows a mutual exchange of greetings of a formal character, in which much repetition is used, and much concern is expressed by each as to the other's health and future happiness, though no reference is made to the household at home, except among very intimate friends. The whole bearing and manner of the Arab is indicative of leisure and an extreme regard for his own *heshima* and that of his guest or host. This word *heshima*, like many Arabic and Swahili words, cannot be literally rendered into English. It is usually translated as "honour" or "respect," but it means more than that. By our word honour we usually imply that such a man's honour is in his own keeping, but an Arab's *heshima* is in the keeping of his friends and fellow men. He values it above all else, for it belongs to his position, and it is in the observance of all the little courtesies which mark the appreciation of this fact, that the secret of successfully dealing with the Arab really lies.

The same dignified bearing is maintained at meals. Food is placed on the floor on mats, and eaten in silence with the fingers of the right hand. Alcohol is forbidden by his religion, and as a rule this veto is strictly observed; an Arab is either an abstainer from drink or a drunkard in private. His food consists chiefly of curry and rice, supplemented with vegetables and fruit; his drink is coffee and sherbet, and he loves all sweet things.

The Arab's character is influenced to a great extent by his religion, which he accepts literally as a little child. His unquestioning belief in the Almighty power and will of Allah, and the sense of his own importance, has given him the great quality of patience. Knowing that all things come to him who can wait, he is never in a hurry; he is learned in the Koran, and in the traditions of his own race; but of ordinary educational subjects-history, geography, mathematics, or scientific subjects of any sort-he is completely ignorant, and he is forbidden by the Koran to inquire too closely into such matters as being too high for him. Arabs calculate all distances by the time it takes to cover them, and their inability to understand a map or plan is as remarkable as it is at times inconvenient.

But though they have many excellent qualities, and, in many respects, are an agreeable people to have to do with, Arabs, like all other sons of earth, have their failings. Probably no European, with any extensive experience, ever thoroughly trusts an Arab, and, at the same time, it may be said that no Arab ever thoroughly trusts a European. Their ideals being different, and their conduct of life being regulated by different standards and religions, complete confidence between the races, or even between individual members of them, is impossible. "It may be observed," wrote Captain Hamerton in 1855, "that there are no people in the world from whom it is so difficult to get information as from Arabs. They have a religious dislike to talk of the past, they care little for the present, and for the future nothing at all.

I may perhaps best illustrate the intellectual position and the manner of life of the Arabs by a reference to an old Arab called Ali bin Mohammed, who lived near me at Dunga. Sheikh Ali was a doctor; that is to say, he had a good knowledge of native drugs; but he was shrewd enough to understand the value of the white man's medicine, and was always willing to give it a trial. He firmly believed in the efficacy of dieting, and prescribed a different menu for almost every ailment. He was a lawyer, a priest, and an indispensable agent in all local marriages and funerals. He was one of the few Arabs I have met who would discuss religious and metaphysical subjects, though most dogmatically, nor did I ever succeed in the smallest degree in shaking his convictions or altering his opinions. On one occasion I asked him how he explained the phenomenon of day and night. He said that the sun travelled across the heavens and was restored to its original position during the night by the Archangel Michael. It was true that the earth revolved on its axis, but only once a year, which accounted for the seasons.

This sheikh lived in a large mud house, thatched with palm leaves. Such houses have a framework of roughhewn mangrove wood, lashed together with coir rope; no nails are ever used in the construction of these houses, nor, it may be mentioned, in that of the locally-made dhows. It is wonderful what a tight job a native can make with his coir rope. The walls of Ali's house were mud and coral rubble, stuccoed with mortar made of slaked lime, sand and red earth.

The house was of the ordinary native type, but of a larger and more substantial build, and was raised on a plinth, three feet high. The compound at the back was enclosed by a stone wall, which concealed the women of the household, and permitted them to go about their domestic duties without fear of intrusion. At one corner of the courtyard stood the kitchen and under the eaves of the house an open stone tank, containing water green with slime, and full of the larvae of mosquitoes. Along the front of his house ran a stone bench or baraza, on which mats were spread for the accommodation of guests. One or two domestic slaves lived on the premises, all that remained of the host the sheikh at one time owned; but whether this faithful remnant was a curse or a comfort to him is doubtful. Sheikh Ali was fond of Wazungu (white men), but the injustice he considered he had suffered in being deprived of his slaves rankled in his soul. He, like all his countrymen, looked upon himself as a member of the chosen people of God, and the black man as specially created to serve him in slavery. No arguments had any effect on him whatever, and he for his part had but one argument for a recalcitrant slave, namely, a stick, which I have no doubt he used freely in days gone by. He complained bitterly of his helplessness in his old age, with no slaves to pick his cloves, or to weed his garden. The few that remained robbed him of his coconuts, and compelled him to keep every room in his house padlocked against them, and threatened him with "dismissal"; that is to say, with procuring their own freedom, if he became too rebellious. Sheikh Ali was very devout and said his prayers in his front porch, so that all men could behold him. If you happened to arrive at his house in the midst of his devotions he would take not the slightest notice of you till they were completed, nor abate one sentence from their length, but his welcome was no less warm afterwards. He would bring out his best and newest mats for you to sit upon and compel you to eat or drink something, were it but a draught of coconut milk. But he would never invite you into his house or courtyard unless you were on very intimate terms with him. His family consisted of a son, a smart lad, who, in contrast with his father, could neither read nor write, as he declined to go to school; and a daughter, who had made an unfortunate marriage, and was often forced to seek the protection of her father's house. He himself had married one of the concubines of the late Mwenyi Mkuu, but he informed me one day that he was about to marry again, which for a man over seventy was a courageous undertaking, especially as the bride was but fourteen years old.

In the treatment of dumb animals the Arab of Zanzibar is ahead of the people of this country. In place of bit and bridle he uses for his donkey a richly-adorned head-stall. The donkeys' mouths are, therefore, never tortured in the way horses' mouths are in this country. For a saddle he uses a set of brightly-coloured padded cloths raised in front to form a grip for the knees, but with no stirrups. He rides on the hind-quarters of his donkey, which he sends along at a rapid amble. The large white Muscat donkey of Zanzibar is of as much value as a horse, and will command 600 rupees, but the brown *jivu jivu* donkey, which is only used to carry loads, can be purchased for thirty or forty rupees.

The Arab's patience and powers of self-denial are illustrated by his endurance of the fast of Ramadan. Though not so important, from a religious point of view, as the festival of El Haji which occurs two months and ten days later, in Zanzibar, which sends but few pilgrims to Mecca at the El Haji, the Ramadan exercises a greater influence over the people, who count their months from its termination. Thus the Arab month of Shawal is called *Mfunguo wa mosi*, meaning the first from having left off fasting, the second *Mfunguo wa pili,* and so on. The Arabs keep strictly to the letter of the law and abstain from eating or drinking between the hours of 4 a.m. and sunset. Sick people are allowed to take sustenance, as well as those on a really laborious journey, though not on a mere ride of five or six hours. In the night time they gorge themselves to repletion, with the result that on the whole they get through far more food in the month of Ramadan than in ordinary times. Consequently, on the approach of the fast, servants and employees will come and demand a gratuity or advance to meet the extra consumption of food, the enhanced price of all market produce, and the open hospitality expected of them. Natives endeavour to follow the Arabs in their customs, not so much from religious convictions as from the heshima thus acquired; and as the natives are the labouring classes, serious interruption in all work and business is the result. But many natives, though they will begin the month with fasting, very soon drop it, while others, the majority, make no pretence of fasting at all. The month closes with the appearance of the new moon, which must be seen, unless the weather is very unfavourable, in which case, after a second unsuccessful attempt to detect the crescent, it is taken as having been seen, and the termination of the fast proclaimed. This ceremony takes place in the square in front of the Sultan's palace where all the troops are mustered with a battery of two guns and a company of rifles to fire a *feu de joie*. The signal is given by the Sultan from the palace; but if, after a period of watching, the new moon cannot be seen, the troops are marched back to the barracks and the attempt to see the moon renewed the following day. The prospect of another day's fast must be a disappointment to the people, yet they never betray any annoyance, but accept the result, as they do every reverse, with characteristic resignation as the will of God. At the close of the Ramadan bakshishi is lavishly distributed to all slaves and subordinates, the servants of Europeans also demanding it of their masters and of their master's friends.

THE SWAHILI.

The bulk of the Zanzibar population (apart from the ruling Arabs) consists of representatives of all the tribes of East Africa, intermingled with an Asiatic element. The name given to this mixed population is Waswahili, or, more usually, Swahili, a term formerly used to denote the coast tribes from Somaliland to Mozambique, "sahil," in Arabic, meaning coast. Among the early ancestors of the Swahili were refugees from the neighbourhood of the Persian Gulf, from Shiraz on the one side and Oman on the other. Burton speaks of conquest by Persians as well as by Arabs; Dr. Badger believed the conquerors to be Arabs, who, towards the end of the seventh century, having rebelled against Moslem tyranny, were vanquished and fled to "the land of the Zanj." The narrative of this event Dr. Badger regarded as "the most reliable record we possess of the first immigration of the Omani Arabs to the east coast of Africa." These Arabs were called the Emosaids (Ammu Said), the People of Said, and were so named from an Omani ruler, from whom their leader was descended. The Emosaids became the nobles and rulers of the Swahili, while in Zanzibar the great majority of this people were either descendants of the ancient possessors of the island or were of servile origin.

Tribal distinctions tend to disappear in the ordinary intercourse of Zanzibar life and, except in official documents, or for purposes of identification, the native classes are spoken of as Swahilis, just as the English, Scotch, Irish, Welsh, are often described as English. Socially and politically the Swahilis of Zanzibar may be conveniently divided into the porter class, which frequents the town and performs coolie labour, and the shamba people who live in the plantations and are the slaves or freed slaves of Arabs. Travellers and visitors seldom come in contact with the latter, their experience being limited to the "boys" who hang about the beach, for the most part wasters.

The character of the Waswahili has been the subject of much criticism by travellers. Burton,* speaking of the real Swahili, found that "from the Arab they derived shrewd thinking and practice in concealing thought; they will welcome a man with the determination to murder him; they have unusual confidence, self-esteem and complacency; fondness for praise, honours and distinctions; keenness, together with short-sightedness, in matters of business, and a nameless horror of responsibility and regular occupation . . . . their African languor upon doctrinal points prevents their becoming fanatics or proselytizers. African, also, is their eternal restless suspicion, the wisdom of serf and slave compensating for their sluggish imagination and small powers of concentration. They excel in negro duplicity . . . . honesty and candour are ignored even by name. When they assert, they probably lie; when they swear, they certainly lie."

Professor Drummond† wrote: "In Zanzibar these black villains, the porters, the necessity and despair of travellers, the scum of old slave gangs and fugitives from justice from every tribe, congregate for hire, and if there is one thing on which African travellers are for once agreed, it is that for laziness, ugliness, stupidity and wickedness these men are not to be matched on any continent in the world." Sir F. Lugard‡ in quoting this description of the Zanzibari by Drummond, after stating that it is fairly applicable to many individuals, remarks: "I know of no such raw material in the world; you can mould them as you will."

Some philanthropic people regard the native as a man and a brother; others look upon him as little better than an animal and treat him accordingly, but the majority of Europeans who go to East Africa take neither of these extreme views. It is plain that the African, intellectually, morally and physically, is not the equal of the European. Like a Waterbury watch, the Swahili of Zanzibar requires much winding-up, and will not go for any length of time. He is a great child, possessing many qualities of the Arab by whom he has been trained. There is no better houseservant than a boy who has been a slave. He has learnt obedience, silence; how to wait upon his master, how to receive and announce visitors; to keep himself clean, and to be loyal. The Swahili never betrays himself into disrespect towards his bwana (master), nor into talking of his bwana's affairs to strangers,

* "Zanzibar." † "Tropical Africa."
‡ "Rise and Fall of our East African Empire."

but, like a faithful dog, he will not always show respect towards others. To him his master is everything, and so long as he feels that he has his master's good opinion, the opinion of other men is of little moment; but it is well known that an ordinary native possesses no gratitude. No matter what services may be rendered him they are all taken as a matter of course and speedily forgotten.

I think it may be laid down that most natives are by nature thieves and liars. If, after long training, a native seem to have acquired honest habits, the explanation is that he has learned that, with Europeans, dishonesty does not succeed. The propensity of the natives to falsehood makes it difficult to deal with them, and sometimes renders the detection of crime almost impossible. But such faults are misfortunes resulting from the oppression of which for centuries the Swahili were the victims. Men who have themselves been stolen, who have had no means of redress for their wrongs except deception, cannot be expected to observe the precepts of a high standard of ethics, or to transmit to their successors a clear perception of distinctions between right and wrong.

In any statement he makes, a Swahili has always some undisclosed motive, some ulterior object, which perverts the truth, even if it be only the wish to gratify his interrogator. If, on a journey, he is questioned as to the distance of the destination, he will reply, "karibu" -it is near-and this he will repeat more and more emphatically, with kindly purpose, till the discouraged questioner carefully cross-examines him and finds that he has still half the road to travel. If a native has to give evidence in a court of justice, he will find the doors blockaded by door-keepers, messengers, and other trusty persons desirous of showing their interest in the case, and, even as the leopard cannot change his spots, so the Swahili cannot overcome his love of fingering a bribe.

In most cases of theft, especially in serious cases, the thieves are known to the people of the locality who can never be induced by our direct methods of investigation to give information against one another. Yet the thieves can be discovered by those who know how to proceed. Among the Swahili the denouncer of thieves is the medicine man, who, if he cannot always expose the culprit, will often at least indicate where the lost property has been concealed. These medicine men have a great hold on the superstitious people, and have secret agents who keep them informed of what takes place. Faith in medicine men is probably not entirely superstitious nor to be altogether despised.

A few years ago some men broke into my house at night and carried off my despatch-box, in which there were several articles of value, and, after much fruitless search had been made by detectives and police, I called in the local sheikh and requested him to make medicine and to inform me who the thieves were. There are numerous ways in which this is done, some of which are quite simple, and consist in compelling each member of the household, or anyone upon whom suspicion could possibly rest, to pass through some ordeal.

A favourite one is for two men to sit down on the ground opposite one another, and to hold four sticks in their hands horizontally, point to point. Each suspect is then required to place his hands between the four sticks, while a verse of the Koran is being recited by the sheikh, and to call the curse of God down upon himself if he should falsely protest his innocence. The sticks are supposed to be held quite lightly, and if they should incline inwards and catch the arm of the subject, he is denounced as the thief.

But this occasion demanded a more elaborate ceremony. The local sheikh took up his position under a large mango tree, sitting upon a mat on the ground facing the Kaaba,* and rocked himself to and fro, counting his beads and muttering prayers. The bystanders, who were collected in large numbers, and who were all greatly impressed with the solemnity of the ordeal about to be undergone, were instructed not to smoke or talk. The instrument of detection was to be a boy without physical blemish, and acquainted with the people in the neighbourhood, though not himself connected in any way with the house in which the robbery had occurred. While this boy was being sought for, the sheikh washed himself, divested himself of his *kilemba* (turban), rose upon his feet, and began to go through the form of mid-day prayer, prostrating himself at intervals towards the Kaaba. Presently a boy was produced, and the sheikh proceeded to wash him, and to clothe him in two pieces of new calico, one for his loins and the other to envelope his head and shoulders, leaving only the face exposed. He placed him on a low stool before him, and again washed his right hand and arm. Meanwhile he had called for fire to be placed at his side, and for incense to be dropped therein. He then took pen and ink and wrote upon the boy's hand, beginning upon the fingers, down the palm and across the wrist, then inked in the lines. This operation took some time, but when it was completed to his satisfaction the Sheikh covered up the boy with the calico, and resumed his prayers. After a

*The sacred shrine of Mohammedans, in the Great Mosque at Mecca, built over the miraculous stone, towards which all Mohammedans face when at prayer.

few minutes he asked the boy if he could see anybody in his hand and the boy replied yes, he saw a man. Instructions were then given by the Sheikh to the boy to be conveyed to the man in his hand, the Sheikh pausing now and again to inquire if his instructions were being carried out. "Tell him to pitch a tent, to sweep up, to carry water, to set a chair ready for the chief; now call the chief and hi guard, tell the man to kill a goat and cook it for the chief, and now tell the chief to wash his hands, to eat, and to drink some coffee, and give him my salaams and ask him to produce the thieves." The boy then said that the chief in his hand had produced the figures of my cook and his wife. The cook was a Goanese and a Christian, of whom I had entertained not the slightest suspicion, but the sequel proved that he was without a doubt the culprit.

A European always feels, when listening to an account of any affair, that only part of the story is being told to him, and probably the least important part; he knows that the native never at first betrays the real motive with which he has come; that however disinterested his story may appear, he has an axe of his own to grind, and, in all probability, somebody else's cabbage plot to spoil. There is an Arabic word, *fitina*, untranslatable into literal English, because the English people have not yet felt the want of such a word, though the word "intrigue" comes nearest to it. But with a native, the power of being able to make things uncomfortable for a troublesome friend, without telling clumsy falsehoods about him, is a valuable quality always to be reckoned with. A native seldom gives a direct answer to a question, or commits himself to a definite opinion upon any subject. This may be due to a natural disinclination to incur responsibility, or to a fear that his words, which are sure to be remembered and repeated, may be brought up against him later on. But a native is also a procrastinator. He dearly loves putting things off, and committing to Allah the responsibility for getting things done, by which means he often succeeds in leaving them undone. Never do to-day what can be put off till to-morrow is his motto. Kesho, inshallah: To-morrow, God willing, is as near as a native will ever go to committing himself to any undertaking; though this term is not meant to convey the impression that he will do the thing to-morrow or even the day after. General instructions are not sufficient in dealing with a native; they must be followed up with questions about the precise day on which he intends to begin, the manner in which he intends to start, the time his task will probably take; and after every detail has been arranged and understood, he must be pursued from time to time with inquiries as to the progress he is making, otherwise the matter in hand will not go forward.

A most unreliable creature, the Swahili can never be trusted to carry through even the simplest routine duties. He is like a broken reed, and for ever wants propping. Language is often characteristic of a people, and Swahili is no exception to this rule. One of the most valuable and frequently used words in the Swahili vocabulary is the word Bado. A native will never confess that he has failed to perform a particular duty, only that he has put it off, or rather that he has not yet completed it, but is going to do so after the lapse of an insignificant period of time. Hence his favourite bado- "not yet," or, as it is generally qualified, "bado kidogo" (kidogo-little). *Sijui* is another of his well used words; it means, "I know not," and it is on his lips in reply to every question that may involve either himself or his fellows in rebuke of punishment. *Siwezi* is another. This means, "I am not well," but also, "I cannot." An English youth's ambition is to be able to do anything, and he often deludes himself into the belief that he can do everything, but a Swahili will reply: "Bwana, I cannot; I am but a slave, a poor weak man. Look for some other man to do this work; do not give it to me, siwezi." The word *Shauri* signifies discussion. Nothing can ever be done without first having a shauri about it-the longer the better-and no man is more eloquent in pleading his cause, or in elaborating a statement from his own point of view than the Swahili. Shauri also means advice, and it is used as we used the word business in the expression It is not my business" - "Si shauri yangu." The native is plausible in the extreme, and no matter what scrape he may get into he will be provided with profuse excuses and explanations backed with a reassuring smile. His use of the word *jambo*, or, as it is sometimes used, *Si jambo*- "I am well"-is very characteristic of his nature, which is extremely optimistic and fatalistic. He may be in great suffering, yet, in answer to an enquiry, he will always begin with "Si jambo" - "I am well," or, "It is well with me" -and then go on to describe his complaint. His social life is governed by *Dasturi*-Custom, in the observance of which he is most conservative and strict, especially in all relating to his domestic arrangements, to the manner of eating and drinking, and to the performance of his duties towards his master. Often there is no more effective rebuke than to ask him if such-and-such a thing is dasturi. No one ever thinks of entering another man's house without first shouting "Hodi" -an untranslatable word used to announce the visitor's approach-nor enters till he has received the invitation, "Karibu" - "Come near," or " Come in. "Natives never stand up when they are drinking, but always squat upon their heels or sit on the ground, and, in eating, the right hand only is used. They seldom or never eat singly, there being always at least two or three gathered round the dish; and no matter how hungry or how poor they may be there is never any haste in eating, or any endeavour on the part of one to get more than his share, while strangers are always welcome. In Zanzibar there is no poverty or privation, as we know these things in England.

The Swahili language is easy enough to acquire. Its vowels are pronounced as in Italian, and it is spelt phonetically, an advantage it owes to its great philologist Bishop Steere, third Bishop to the Universities' Mission to Central Africa. The Swahili manner of putting things is often puzzling to the newcomer; for instance, in answer to such a remark as, "There is no water in the bucket," the Swahili will say *Ndio*-Yes, or truly, meaning, Truly, it is as you say, there is no water in the bucket" or, "You did not go to the plantation yesterday as I told you. "Ndio," "Truly, I did not go. "To a direct question he will reply by an assertion, not by yes or no as we do. "Did you go to the plantation yesterday? I went there." "Have you planted those nuts yet? I have planted them." If he had not planted them he would say, "Bado." Upon receiving a present a native never says thank you, unless he has been taught to say so at a Mission, but he is most punctilious with his *Sabalkheri*, a corruption of the Arabic "Saba al kheir," or "Subalkh Allah bilkheir," which answers to our "Good morning," or "Good day," and he will never enter on his business until he has first delivered himself of this salutation. The more humble folks say *Shikamu*, an abbreviation of *Shika mguu-*" I catch or kiss your feet," to which the great man replies, "Marahaba". It is well, or Welcome. Both Arabs and natives are long-winded folk and consume much time in coming to the point. They always come provided with an elaborate and plausible story of their antecedents, their forbearance, their integrity, before coming to their tale of woe, and in order that the threads of the case may be kept distinct, and due emphasis be bestowed upon each point as it is made, each period is closed with the ejaculation, Basi, as we might say, "Do you see?" or, "Very well, now." Basi, or Bas, is also used to cut short and dismiss a person, as in the expressions, "That will do," "That is enough, you can go now." Like many others in the Swahili language, Basi is a most useful and indispensable word, though it cannot be literally rendered. "Is there nothing but weeds growing on that plantation?" "Weeds; Bass," "Weeds, nothing else." "How many rupees will you give me for this mat?" "I will give you five rupees." "Bas?" "Bas." Natives have a delicate appreciation of letting bygones be bygones, and do not like reopening old wounds. The headmaster of my school once told me that in a "row" between a master and a boy the odds were ten to one that the boy was in the wrong. And so with a native; the odds are ten to one that in a dispute with a European he is in the wrong. Certainly he generally comes out worsted, and his way of acknowledging defeat is to exclaim, "Basi," which means, Enough. I give in, and I don't want to hear any more about it."

The plantations of Zanzibar are traversed by a maze of footpaths, which wind about like the brook of Philip's farm, and in order to come by the nearest road it is necessary to have a local guide. Any lounger who happens to be at his doorway as you pass will cheerfully conduct you on your way, and hand you over to a neighbour when the road becomes no longer familiar to him. Though he may receive he does not ask for, and probably does not expect, a reward for his services. "Kwaheri rafiki," "Eewallah, bwana;" "Marahaba"- "Good-bye, friend;" "So be it, master" "It is well, and so he retraces his steps.

At the close of the month Ramadan comes the Siku Kuu, or Great Day, which for the Swahili takes the place of our Christmas time. It is the great day of giving and receiving presents, of putting on new clothes, of feasting and dancing, and the festivity will continue for a week. The crowds that assemble at the Nazi Moja, the Grand Boulevard and golf-ground, just outside the town, at this festival never fail to excite the admiration of all who behold the order and good behaviour which distinguish them. The administration of the island has complete control over the inhabitants, and exercises its power with tact and efficiency.

Thousands of people come together for five or six days, some in groups of tribes, each tribe dancing its own especial *Ngoma*, some patronising the cranky hurdy-gurdies of the various peep shows, but the vast majority merely wandering about. In England, drinking booths would be scattered about, and around them would be collected noisy or excited knots of people. But in Zanzibar no drunken man is ever seen on the Nazi Moja at the Siku Kuu, while small children could be trusted to amuse themselves in the crowd without danger of offence.

The Waswahili of Zanzibar have complete confidence in the judgment, integrity, and, above all, the justice of the European; the same confidence that a well-trained horse has in his rider. This happy effect is due in no small degree to the fact that they come in contact with the educated classes, and have little to do with the lower orders. A friend of mine once related a story which shows that the

Swahili, though he looks upon the Wazungu as in every way his superior, understands that all Wazungu are, nevertheless, not like those with whom he is most familiar. Some of his boys were discussing outside his room what it was that constituted a *pukka bwana*, or, as we should put it, a real gentleman; and after various solutions had been offered the following was accepted as the simplest test: that a *Pukka bwana* had a bath every day. Thus cleanliness was goodness. The instinct of order in the Swahili is closely allied to the quality of patience, which he possesses in a marked degree. He will endure without complaining the most loathsome sores, and suffer in silence the most unjust treatment, because he knows how to wait, and never loses hope. A friend of mine in Pemba had a cook called Ambali, and when one evening dinner was late, and he asked his houseboys the reason, he was told that Ambali was not well. He went into the kitchen, and finding the dinner almost ready to dish up, he asked Ambali what was wrong with him. "I have small-pox," he said. "Then go to bed at once. "I will finish cooking your dinner first," said Ambali. Some years ago I happened to be suffering from an attack of fever, during which my head boy, Sadallah, nursed me, and when I was getting better I pointed to his arm, and asked him what the spots upon it were. He replied, "Small-pox." It was but a very slight attack, and it is not often that a native would display such devotion as to nurse his master under such circumstances, but the point that struck me at the time was the patience that this boy exhibited in saying nothing about his complaint, notwithstanding my irritability of which he must have been the victim.

Natives are most particular in their clothing. The idea that anything is good enough for the African is, I suppose, exploded; and it may be presumed that the English manufacturer has come to realise that the African knows what he wants, and will insist upon having it. He loves colour, pleasing patterns, and something new. Durability is with him a secondary consideration, sometimes even an objection, and coarse fabrics he will have none of. For a loincloth he uses unbleached calico, locally known as *Amerikani*, as it was originally introduced from America; or, if he can afford it, a *kikoi*, a rather finer white calico cloth, with a native-spun coloured border. His body is clothed with an ordinary cotton singlet, costing half a rupee, while over all he will wear a sort of ecclesiastical alb, called a *kanzu*, a white gown, descending to his heels, made of fine linen, Indian muslin, or, more rarely, tussore silk. He pays little attention to the quality of his singlet, but is particular about his *kikoi*, and still more about his *kanzu*, which is hemmed and stitched round the neck and shoulders with red silk, and finished off in tassels and loops down the back. For attending upon his master on public occasions, or at table, or to gratify his lust for fine clothes, one of his main delights, he is provided, or provides himself, with a coloured waistcoat, called a *kisibau*, adorned with fancy work. Arabs wear a *joho* over their kanzu. A joho is a robe, usually of black cloth, faced with gold braid. The head is covered with a white linen skull-cap, beautifully embroidered, or, in the case of natives, generally a red fez. Arabs and well-to-do natives wear a turban, though only out of doors, or in strangers' houses. Members of the Sultan's family have the prefix Seyyid attached to their name, and gather the front of their turban into a peak. Around his waist the Arab buckles his *jambia*, a richly mounted dagger, with a hooked point, and when attending the Sultan's court will carry a sword. The sword, generally a curved sabre, though provided with a sling is never fastened to the waist, but is carried in the hand; the sling being arranged so that when travelling it may be hung upon the shoulder. In the days of Seyyids Said and Majid, Arabs never went out without spear and shield, but these warlike implements are now never seen in the hands of Arabs of Zanzibar.

 Women are simply clad in two square cloths of coloured calico, one of which is tucked under the arms, and the other thrown over the shoulders. They are very particular about the patterns of the prints, the fashions of which change every few months. The fashions of the men's clothes never change, but the women, as in other countries, are the slaves of fashion; and I have no doubt Zanzibar sets the fashion for all that part of the world, as Paris does for Europe. The people of Zanzibar are in more prosperous circumstances than those on the mainland, and dress better. Over their heads the women twist a brightly-coloured cotton or silk turban cloth, resembling a large handkerchief. The native women never veil, but Arab women either veil or wear a mask covering the eyes and nose. Arab women are of course kept in close confinement, and are never seen, except in the evening, when, masked and attended by their women, and a man with a lamp, they issue forth to visit their friends. They wear brightly-coloured frilled trousers; they walk upon wooden clogs or leathern sandals. All classes in Zanzibar that can afford to do so, wear sandals which are left at the bottom of the stairs on entering a house. Women pierce their ears and nostrils with large holes, and stuff in rolls of coloured paper, which can be purchased ready made up at the shops. Silver rings sometimes hang from the cartilage of the nose and lobes of the ears.

The neck and wrists are adorned with beads or silver chains and bangles, accumulated savings being invested in large silver anklets. Arabs are very fond of scent, especially attar of roses, of which they sometimes reek. In morals the natives of Zanzibar fall far below the standards of Christendom. Arab boys are provided by their fathers with concubines to keep them at home; the Swahili youths exercise no restraint upon themselves, nor is any imposed upon them by their parents. Maternal responsibilities do not include the "bringing up" of daughters, who enjoy complete liberty with their lovers, while the only qualification expected of a suitor is the possession of a stated quantity of rupees, to be delivered to the bride at the wedding.

Swahilis do not shut up their wives, but they never trust them, and are always ready to listen to and investigate charges of infidelity against them. Husbands resent infidelity in their wives, but not to the extent that they do neglect of domestic obligations, especially cooking. The native is but a big child, whose first consideration is his stomach; he loves to think that when he gets home his evening meal will be ready for him, cooked as only a woman can cook it. Europeans employ men cooks, but a native's first care on arriving at a village is to seek out a woman who will cook for him. A full stomach, a woman waiting and cooking for him at home, seclusion and independence in his home (be it but of palm leaves), fine clothes-these include the sum of his desires and will satisfy all his needs. For the intense love and devotion between man and wife exhibited by the cultivated and civilised races of Europe, and lasting throughout long periods of married life, the natives of Zanzibar have no capacity.

Not that they are deficient in family affection, as every European who has had natives in his employment knows too well. It is a remarkable thing that when a native gets new employment his relations begin to die off one by one, beginning with his mother. Each successive bereavement involves a loan or gratuity, and one or two days' leave to join in the feast that is prepared to commemorate the virtues of the deceased and afford relief to his mourners. Apart, however, from this humbug, which a native always rehearses when he breaks fresh ground, ties of kith and kin count for a good deal with him, though they manifest themselves in tribal loyalty rather than in family affection. The terms mother, father, brother, have not the restricted meanings that they have with us; a man may claim another as a brother if he belongs to the same tribe; he succours him in trouble or sickness, and if he dies lays claim to his effects. It is never safe to accept a native's description of relationship; if, for instance, he claims brotherhood with a person he must be made to state whether he is of the same father and mother; if he announces himself a son of a "mama," did she actually bear him. "Mamangu," my mother, is a distinction conferred upon anyone who may have acted as a mother towards a child; and we not infrequently hear of "mama mkubwa," and "mama mdogo," my great mother that is, my mother, and my little mother, or my guardian or aunt. Every family has an *Mzee*, or elder, who is the oldest male representative of the senior branch. He acts as its protector, arbitrator, executor in the case of death of one of its members. His hospitality is always at the disposal of any of the family, who from time to time contribute small sums of money towards his expenses, treat him with respect and deference, accept his ruling in family disputes and loyally support him if he become involved in litigation.

A volume might be written about *sheitani*, the devil; *mapepo*, spirits, good and evil, though mostly evil; charms, magic, exorcisms; all profound realities to the Swahili. A not uncommon sight in Zanzibar is a troop of men and women, faces whitened with chalk or flour, feathers on their heads, a profusion of beads about their necks and arms, rattles in their hands, parading the streets, singing, or rather chanting as they go; making a hideous din, and looking hideous objects. These are they who, possessed of evil spirits, are under treatment by mganga, or witch-doctor. Nothing can be done, of course, without an *ngoma*, or dance, and the prolonged beating of drums; but inasmuch as there are many Varieties or tribes of spirits, so there are many sorts of dances and witch-doctors, each of whom is a specialist. 'Some spirits inhabit the sea or the mountains; others live in large pits, or caves, or in trees; beneath great rocks or in large rivers. A man may be passing under a large baobab tree, and the spirit therefrom enter into his head and give him malignant fever or violent toothache. There are wachawi, or wizards, who possess mysterious powers over the affections and actions of the people and even over their lives. A man who may be crossed in love seeks the services of an mchawi, who makes medicine to influence the affections of his charmer; a suitor at law provides himself with a prescription from an mchawi to enable him to plead his cause with advantage. The wizards are the keepers of the people's customs and traditions; they use potent poisons and understand the stars.

But the European can have no part or lot in all this witchcraft, which to some will seem to be absurdities. Yet it cannot all be explained away; and though the native may assimilate many of the habits of the European, especially his vices, and even embrace his religion, he will secretly cling to the mystic lore of his own people, and in his extremity turn to the medicine man.

The descendants of the early settlers of the Island of Zanzibar are called Wahadimu, and live principally on the eastern portion of the island, especially on the east coast, where there are a number of fairly large fishing villages. Each village is presided over by a *sheha*, or chief (from the Persian word Shah), who is usually the eldest male representative of the ruling family. An Mhadimu is literally a servant, a term bestowed upon them by northern tribes when they conquered the country; but the latter, though they exacted taxes and corvee from Wahadimu, never enslaved them. No written records exist of the Wahadimu, but the traditions of the ruling families have been preserved, extending, however, no further back than the fifth generation. In the times of Seyyid Said and Seyyid Majid the Wahadimu were governed by the Mwenyi Mkuu, a great chief of the Shirazi, who lived at Dunga. His real name was Mohammed bin Ahmed, but he was sometimes called Sultan Hamadi. He succeeded his brother Sultan Hasani, who lived at Bweni, a village joining Dunga.

Sultan Hasani came from the coast, probably Pangani, in the time of Seyyid Said, settled at Bweni, and built himself a stone house there, the ruins of which may now be seen. Though of a good family he appears to have been a person of no great consequence, but he obtained from the *serkali* (government) some position of power with the Wahadimu, over whom he exercised a limited influence. His brother Hamadi was at that time living with the principal sheha of Dunga, one Kimemeta bin Mgwa Mchenga, the most noted sheha of the tribe of the Wamchangani. On succeeding his brother he began to extend his influence, and soon was able to reduce the Wahadimu to the most absolute subjection. He built himself a stone palace at Dunga with a mosque, bath-rooms, and houses for his retainers. Fifty armed slaves kept guard at each of the many doors of the palace.

On approaching him the Wahadimu fell on their knees, and crawled up to him, cap in hand, saying, "Shikamu! Shikamu! and when he went out everyone in his vicinity who happened to be up a tree gathering coconuts or picking cloves descended to the ground, as it was not considered etiquette for anyone to be above the chief. In addition to possessing thousands of slaves and owning all the rich land in the neighbourhood, which at that time, before the hurricane, was covered with clove trees, he levied taxes in kind upon the Wahadimu for the supply of all his wants.

His principal official function was to collect the poll-tax from the Wahadimu for the Seyyid, and in the season to send them to his plantations to pick his cloves or perform other special service.

The tax was two dollars per head, one of which went to the Seyyid and the other to the Mwenyi Mkuu. The tax was abolished by Barghash, but reimposed by Hamoud. Barghash, to break the influence of the chiefs, placed the Wahadimu under ordinary Arab law, administered by Kathis of the Sunni sect.

About the year 1846 the Mwenyi Mkuu began to build the present palace at Dunga, which took ten years to complete, but it was finished some time before he could bring himself to leave his old residence, and when he had lived in it four years, he died. Various legends attach to this building. It was supposed that to consecrate its foundations many slaves were slaughtered, but this is not correct, though the house is haunted, according to the natives, by the Sheitani, and according to the testimony of several Europeans, by an Arab lady, or an Arab man with a black dog. The sacred horn of the Swahili was supposed to be buried somewhere in the walls, the identical spot being known by only one man, who kept the secret till, on the point of death, he handed it down to another man. The sound of this horn would carry a great distance, and if blown all the Wahadimu would rally to its call. This legend of the buried horn may be traced to the great Siwa, a huge wooden horn five feet in length, which belonged to the Mwenyi Mkuu, and which at his death was most jealously guarded by the natives and kept in close concealment. It came from Utondui, a place on the mainland, and was used only on great occasions. With it was a smaller Siwa, and two great war drums beautifully carved. These relics are now in the possession of residents in Zanzibar. The last time the Siwa was blown was three days after the Mwenyi Mkuu died in 1865. He was rather a small man, with a fringe of white beard, but he possessed the qualities of a great ruler; his memory is still cherished by a few of the old inhabitants of Dunga who served him. Still those were by no means peaceful times. Human life was held cheap, and it was scarcely safe for a man to venture along the highway at night. Near the ruins of his first palace there is a deep pit, avoided by the natives as the place where slaves convicted of drunkenness and other crimes were slaughtered and then thrown in. The Mwenyi Mkuu left a son, who though receiving the same heshima that his father had enjoyed, exercised no power over the people, as he lived in the town. The great chief as ruler of the Wahadimu had no real predecessor, and no successor, and the Wahadimu since his time have been left pretty much to themselves.

They are not great tillers of the soil, and seldom enter the labour market. They get their living as carpenters, builders, sawyers, blacksmiths, tailors, chilli or copra merchants, fish hawkers, pedlars, small shopkeepers, fishermen, pig hunters, game snarers; and in days gone by they also carried on slave traffic with the mainland.

Wahadimu are the principal cattle breeders of the island, and hold their stock for high prices, a bullock selling for eighty or one hundred rupees, and a good cow sometimes for three hundred. The cattle are extremely quiet, docile creatures, and have a hump on their withers, which serves as a reserve store of energy when grass is deficient. Cattle from the coast will not live in Zanzibar, and are purchased for no other purpose than to kill for beef. Goats are also bred by the Wahadimu, though to a greater extent by the slaves and others who live among the clove plantations of the western portion of the island.

The large island of Tumbatu, on the north-west coast of Zanzibar, is inhabited by the Watumbatu, who for the most part follow a seafaring life, either in the coasting dhows or as fishermen and pilots. Tumbatu is a coral island with little cultivable land and building space; consequently, the houses of the villages, instead of being strung out, as in Zanzibar, are packed close together. Colonies of the Watumbatu settle behind Mkokotoni on the main island, and in Pemba. They are great clove pickers and migrate to Pemba in large numbers during the season, just as the Irish come across to England for the harvest.

The natives of Pemba are called Wapemba; they do not live in such seclusion as the Wahadimu on the larger island, but are mixed up more with the Arabs and Waswahili. Their chiefs are called shehas and also wazee (elders), a term often applied to the native chiefs throughout both islands. The Waswahili from Zanzibar laugh at the Wapemba; they call them foolish and regard them in very much the same way as cockneys regard Hodge. Like the Wahadimu, the Wapemba were conquered by the Arabs, but not enslaved.

The Wapemba of the south of the island are darker than those in the north, and claim descent from the Wamakua and other southern tribes brought over by the Portuguese.

Banyans, Khojahs, Borahs Hindus, Parsees, Goanese, possess the trade of the island, either as shopkeepers, money-lenders, merchants, small traders or skilled mechanics. Goanese run the European stores and provide the cooks and clerks in European houses, though many clerks are Parsee. If we look upon the Arabs as the aristocracy, or landed class, and the African races as the lower orders, then the Indians may be compared to the middle classes of England.

The town swarms with beachcombers, guide-boys, carriers and camel drivers from Baluchistan, gold and silver workers from Ceylon, Persians, Greeks, Egyptians, Levantines, Japanese, Somalis, Creoles, Indians and Arabs of all descriptions, making a teeming throng of life, industry and idleness.

A few words may be said on the wages paid in Zanzibar, as Europeans usually employ a large number of servants, and are the wage-paying class. Houseboys get from five to twenty-five rupees a month, according to their work as punkah boys, body servants, or head stewards. The latter positions are often filled by Comoro boys, who are more intelligent than Swahili, but are very clannish, and when they once get a footing in a household, often succeed in turning out the Swahilis from the higher positions and replacing them with their own countrymen. Goanese cooks receive from forty to fifty rupees a month, supplemented by small change and commissions from bazaaring or marketing. There appears to be a sort of ring or union among the Goanese cooks in Zanzibar, as, however inferior his qualifications may be, it is impossible to get a man for less than forty rupees. They spend their money in drink, and are often to be found intoxicated on the night of a dinner party. Swahili cooks receive from fifteen to twenty five rupees a month, and though on safari they are far superior to the Goanese, who cannot travel, they never seem able to rise to their level as cooks. Indian syces, who are also much addicted to the bottle, can be obtained for thirty rupees a month. The Waswahili are excellent donkey boys and good grooms, but they are unable to concentrate their attention sufficiently to make good drivers. On the other hand, as boat boys they are superior to the Indians. They are good oarsmen, and on a long pull will always accompany their swing with a song or rather a chant, the soloist improvising verses as he goes along, not infrequently about his master in the stern sheets, the remainder of the crew lustily responding with the refrain. Head boat boys are paid from fifteen to eighteen rupees, the others ten to twelve. Coolies and town porters make from twenty pice to a rupee a day; Swahili masons and carpenters, forty pice to a rupee; Banyan carpenters, two to three rupees; town labourers, twenty pice to a half-rupee; plantation labourers, twelve to twenty pice; Goanese and Parsee clerks, thirty to two hundred rupees a month; Arab overseers, fifteen to fifty rupees. Food is not as a rule given, though the master will sometimes keep a bag of rice in the house for the use of the boys. Laundry expenses amount to twelve or thirteen rupees a month per head.

No European should in Zanzibar receive less than 250 rupees a month, if he has to feed himself. In order successfully to resist fever and the general debilitating effects of the climate, he must live well, have at least two servants, a cook and a boy, and be provided with a well-stocked wardrobe of tropical clothing. All the world over it is recognised to be false economy to under-pay employees, and if this applies to England it applies with much greater force to a country like Zanzibar, where by the time he has arrived at the scene of his labours a European will have cost his employers a considerable outlay in passage money alone, if he is engaged from Europe. It is worthwhile, therefore, to treat him well.

There are no statistics as to the population of the islands. The town of Zanzibar is believed to contain 100,000 inhabitants, and the plantations another 100,000, making 200,000 for the larger island. Pemba has probably between 50,000 and 60,000. There are over 10,000 Indians in the islands, and nearly 400 Europeans, half of whom are English.

CHAPTER XX

THE PLANTATIONS

THE clove-growing industry is by far the most important industry in Zanzibar, representing an annual value to the country of £200,000. The clove tree (*Eugenia caryophyllus, natural order Myrtacea*) came originally from the Moluccas and was first introduced into Zanzibar from Reunion by, it is said, an Arab called Saleh bin Huremil.

Burton says they were introduced in 1818. Captain Smee visited Zanzibar in 1811, but in his account of the industries of the island makes no mention of cloves, so it may be presumed there were no bearing plantations in his time. Seyyid Said first visited Zanzibar in the year 1829 and built the Mtoni palace (now a ruin) where, local tradition asserts, cloves were first planted, though the first regular plantations were laid out at Kizimbani, Seyyid Said's country residence, now a well-known centre of the clove industry. Whether or not the plant was introduced before Seyyid Said's arrival, to him must ascribed the credit of establishing the industry, for without his support it could certainly never have taken root and flourished as it has done. No little credit, too, belongs to the Arabs, who introduced the plant from Reunion who planted large areas, and replanted them when the trees were blown down in Zanzibar Island; who recognise the wonderful adaptability of the islands for the growth of the spice, and who succeeded where other countries had failed.

The seed, unless it be planted fresh, will not germinate. It can only be transported in water, and this fact has no doubt operated against its cultivation in other countries. The plants are of very slow growth, and are not ready to set out in plantations until they are at least two years old. Arabs prefer them four or five years old and even older. They allow young nurseries of self-sown seed to collect round trees in plantations, and plant several seedlings in a hole, sometimes as many as seven. Experience has shown that this is by no means such a crude method as it might appear to be, for the young clove plants suffer severely from the dry weather, which almost invariably follows upon the rainy season, and large numbers of them die. But the Arab will let the whole collection of young trees that he has planted grow up together without thinning them, a process he apparently does not understand.

The returns from a plantation will, of course, depend upon the market. Within the last eight years prices in London have varied between $2\frac{1}{4}$d. and 6d. a pound; 4d. a pound in London is equal to about 7 rupees a *frasila* (35 lbs.) in Zanzibar, and at this rate clove plantations there will give a gross return of about 5 annas per tree, or about 4 annas net. In Pemba the trees will net about 6 annas. From these figures a 25 per cent. export duty exacted by the Government must be deducted. Experiments at the Government's experimental plantation at Dunga have shown that by good cultivation, manuring and pruning, i.e. topping, clove trees can be made to produce regularly about 5 lbs. a tree, as against from 2 to 3 lbs. a tree under Arab methods, which consist in merely weeding the plantations once or twice a year. In exceptionally prolific years, such as occur at rare intervals, clove trees in Pemba have yielded considerably over a *frasila* a tree, and I have known a single tree, not specially selected, give six *frasilas* -210 lbs.- of dried cloves. Seven or eight years elapse before the young tree begins to bear, and ten years before it brings any real returns. Young trees are planted 18 to 30 feet apart according to the soil, and are shaded by a little *banda*, which consists of a palm leaf, or a few tufts of dried grass, suspended upon sticks.

Clove trees in Zanzibar may be said to grow wild, and will withstand drought, fire, and even the axe. I have known plantations converted into bare white poles from the effects of drought, and after remaining so for two years, slowly begin to bud again. When the plantations are ill-kept and weedy, the trees become covered with *maji ya moto* ants, which are very injurious, and the natives light fires beneath the trees to smoke them out. It often happens that the fire rushes up through the branches and destroys the foliage. There are clove trees in Zanzibar which have not had a hoe near them for fifteen years; the weeds and scrub, fifteen or twenty feet high, completely smothering them, yet they continue to grow and bear fruit. These facts show that the Zanzibar Islands are eminently suited for the production of this spice; better probably than any other country in the world. Pemba is even more suitable for the clove plant than Zanzibar; the trees there grow to 60 feet in height. The soil has more clay and body in it, and can resist the effects of drought very much better than the lighter and more sandy soil of Zanzibar. Cloves like a deep sandy-clay soil, with good drainage.

The trees begin to bud about January or February, which corresponds with our English summer, and clove picking may begin any time between July and November. The clove of commerce is the unexpanded flower bud. Just before the imbricated petals of the "head" fall off and release the stamens, the tube of the bud begins to turn pink and then red. It is in this stage that it should be picked. If the buds are left till the flowers are opened and then picked, a greatly inferior sample of clove will be obtained. Arabs never begin to pick, however, until there is a good show upon the trees, enough to make it worth their while to take an interest in the proceedings. They send their people out in small groups under headmen. Women are the best pickers, they climb the trees, and bunch off the cloves and stems in handfuls, putting them in a piece of blue calico cloth, hung from the neck; or they will stand on the ground and bend the boughs down with a crooked stick, often breaking the branches. About one o'clock they assemble at the homestead, sit down under a shady mango tree, or in an open shed, and stalk (*chumbua*) the cloves, which are then measured over by the overseer. The measure is called *pishi*, a wooden bowl containing usually four or five pounds. The pickers receive three or four pice, or more according to market (1 pice farthing) for every pishi of green cloves they bring in. A good picker will gather ten, some even twenty pishi a day, though the average is about six. Next day the cloves are spread out on mats (majamvi) in the sun, and in four or six days of good weather they will be dry enough to store. When dry they are almost black and the stem cannot be bent about, but is brittle and breaks off. The stems are generally left to heat in a corner of the yard, to be afterwards collected and sold; but if properly dried, stems sell at one-seventh the current value of the cloves. Arabs measure their cloves into bags by a wooden oblong box called a lara, which contains about forty pounds.

The clove market is the Custom House in the town of Zanzibar. All cloves whether in Zanzibar or Pemba must be collected at the Custom House for export. They are conveyed thither by donkeys or on the heads of porters, or, if they come from coast plantations or from Pemba, in dhows. In the latter case they often arrive in a damaged condition, through exposure, or from having been conveyed in leaky vessels. For this reason Pemba cloves command a lower price than those of Zanzibar, and also because they are smaller. The bulk of the cloves are bought up for export by German, French and Indian firms, and are sent to Bombay, Rotterdam, Marseilles, New York and London. They are largely used for the distillation of oil of cloves which is employed in the manufacture of drugs, perfumes and confectioneries.

The spice is generally considered a speculative market, and for this reason the industry is looked upon as in a more or less precarious condition. But in its clove industry Zanzibar has a unique and valuable asset. The islands yield seven-eights of the world's clove produce, which is estimated at about 90,000 bales, or 12,600,000 lbs.

The result has falsified Burton's opinion of the industry. In his book on Zanzibar, written in 1872, before the hurricane, he said: "The people would do well to follow the example of Mauritius, whence the clove has long departed in favour of sugar. For the latter Zanzibar is admirably adapted: when factories shall everywhere be established, the island will have then found her proper profession, and will soon attain the height of her prosperity."

Much uncertainty, as a rule, prevails in the European market, in the early months of the year, as to the abundance of the coming clove crop. Reports from Zanzibar are not to be relied on, for the simple reason that no one there can estimate the amount of the yield till some time after the trees begin to bud. Much depends on the rainfall, and the crop of the previous year. Very large crops, such as those of 1898-9, 1902-3, and 1904-5, are apt to exhaust the trees, though it does not always follow that a poor crop will be succeeded by a large one or *vice versa*. The Pemba crop varies much less than that of Zanzibar, and as it produces three-quarters of the total output, this fact exercises a steadying influence on the production. Clove trees suffer if the rainfall is considerably below or above the average, though the influence of a season's rain does not appear to manifest itself in the trees till the year next but one following. Much rain inclines the trees to run to leaf at first, though heavy crops may be expected subsequently. With a short rainfall in the latter part of the year trees will sometimes be unable to ripen the crop, and the immature buds will fall to the ground. Such buds are swept up by the natives, and sold in the market as koka cloves, or, as they are usually called in the plantations, *peta* cloves, from the fact that they are sifted out from the dead leaves and rubbish beneath the trees (*Kupeta*-to sift).

Coconuts grow in Zanzibar without any cultivation whatever, and yield about thirty nuts per tree per annum, that is to say, the owner's share will come to about that. The Arab has to provide portions for others besides himself. One-third of the produce of coconut trees is stolen by the plantation people; one-third is "annexed" by the overseer and the proceeds of the remaining third are all the master can count his own. No amount of vigilance ever prevents theft. The trees, except in a few instances, are not set in regular plantations, but are scattered about among mango trees, orange trees, jack fruit, bananas and even clove trees. They are used to mark boundaries, a double row being always planted, half of which belong to the one owner and half to his neighbour. Arabs do not understand a common boundary line, there must always be two lines with a strip of neutral ground between.

Coconut trees are planted at all times of the year, though principally in the rainy season, about April. Very little care is taken about the selection of seed. Nuts are placed end to end on their sides in trenches about six inches deep, just deep enough to allow of their being covered. The spot selected for the nursery must be in the vicinity of an overseer's or head-man's house, else the nuts will soon be dug up and disappear. Prowlers will even dig up the young plants when they have been set out in a plantation. After about six months, when they should be eighteen inches to two feet high, they are roughly chopped out with a hoe, and are set out in small shallow holes just large enough to receive the nut. Here they are left to grow as best they can, receiving perhaps an occasional weeding, till they are eight years old, when they may be expected to bear their first crop. They continue to grow and to bear for sixty or seventy years. In most countries the trees are allowed to shed their nuts, which are collected and brought in every day; but in Zanzibar, trees are not allowed to shed their nuts. Once in three months the overseer collects his people for a gathering; boys and young men are sent up the trees to cut down the ripe nuts, which the women collect in heaps in the long grass. The nuts are sold on the spot to local copra-makers, who are always at hand, at prices varying from fifteen to thirty shillings per thousand, according to market, locality, state of the weather and size of the nuts. These local manufacturers, or *wachuruzi*, as they are called, purchase on the credit system, paying by instalments as they sell their copra, and seldom or never default. They split the nuts and spread them out in the sun for three or four days. There is a prejudice against drying the nuts too thoroughly; in fact the natives would not dry them at all but for the Government regulations. The small native manufacturers sell to Indian traders, who are scattered over the island, and are to be found in the early mornings with weights and scales posted at the junctions of the principal thoroughfares. These traders sell again to large exporting firms in the town.

No use is made of the husk fibre, which is thrown away. Ten years ago a European firm had a fibre factory at Bububu, five miles north of Zanzibar town, on the coast, but was soon compelled to close the works. Under present conditions of labour, transport, and market, the manufacture of coir fibre in Zanzibar does not pay. The fact of the trees being promiscuously scattered about, makes, the collection and transport of the husks expensive. European supervision is costly; native supervision more costly still, and the prices obtainable for the fibre are low. Natives, however, work up the coir fibre and produce a very serviceable rope, which is used for building and thatching, though not in sufficient quantity to supply the demand of the island.

There are few coconut trees in Pemba. Except at Masuka, in the north and at various spots on the coast, the soil of Pemba is too sticky for coconut trees, which like a loose sandy soil. Several varieties of coconuts are cultivated, which may be distinguished by the colour of their nuts, some of which are brown, some green, others a rich cream colour, but no attention is paid to their selection. A small species, called Pemba coconut (though as it is common in both Zanzibar and Pemba the reason of the name is not obvious), is grown only for the milk of the young nuts, which provides a very refreshing drink.

Chillies are grown principally on the coral country in the eastern part of Zanzibar Island, though they are to be found in almost every native garden. The plants are for the most part self-sown, or grow from seed scattered about by birds. It is very difficult to rear them in a nursery, but when they have once got a good hold of the land they grow rapidly, and in favourable weather will bear in a few months. The bushes grow to about four feet in height, and in the second or third year die down. Natives sometimes prune back the dead wood, and the stock shoots out again. The chilli industry is in the first place entirely in the hands of the natives, principally Wahadimu, who set up as small traders, and buy the green or dry chillies brought to them by women and boys, at the rate of about a penny a pound. They are spread out on the ground or sometimes on mats to dry and are sold to the Indian middlemen, who re-sell to European firms. The Indian of course cheats the native trader whenever he can, whether in the purchase of chillies or copra, yet it is a curious fact that the latter would rather be cheated by the Indian than take his produce direct to the European firms. There is an export duty of 10 per cent. levied at the Custom House. The bulk of the Zanzibar chillies go to London, though New York exercises a controlling influence in the market. Zanzibar chillies have the reputation of being the hottest in the world, and any anticipated shortage in the crop sends up the price. The annual value of the trade is about £10,000.

Chillies are very troublesome to pick, as they make the fingers and eyes smart. A woman will pick a pishi (2 lbs.) or more per diem, which in value just about covers her wages; hence it is impossible for the large planter to grow chillies profitably. The season begins generally about February and continues until September or October.

The rubber of Zanzibar is the product of a creeper, or "vine" (*Landolphia Kirkii*). It is found growing in the forests of Pemba. Compared with the rubber industry of the mainland, that of Zanzibar or rather Pemba is a very small affair. Nevertheless a few words about the way it is collected will not be out of place. The rubber forests of Pemba lie in the north of the island where the population is sparse, and where there are few Arabs and few clove plantations. The forests are Government property, and the collection of the rubber is regulated by Government officials. Native rangers or overseers are appointed, whose duty it is to see that the creepers are not destroyed by the collectors, and to purchase the rubber from them, on behalf of the Government. The collector sets out in the morning provided with a knife and a calabash of salt water, and having fixed upon a favourable spot with plenty of creepers about, he proceeds to slice off the bark in little chips here and there, beginning at the bottom of the creeper and working up as high as he can reach. He immediately dabs salt water on the wounds and then goes on to tap two or three other vines in like manner. In about half an hour he returns to the first creeper to find the rubber coagulated by the salt water into a rich, white, sticky mass which can be peeled off quite cleanly from the wounds. He begins with a very small ball which keeps growing and growing as each successive vine is visited. Sometimes, instead of dabbing the wounds with salt water, he will smear the liquid latex upon his arm as it comes fresh from the cut, when the saline exudations of the skin soon coagulate it. In the course of a day an expert collector will have accumulated a ball of rubber the size of a large orange, which will weigh, in its green state, about a pound. This is placed in the scales against pice. A pound of rubber will weigh down a rupee's worth of pice.

It would be obviously easy to roll the rubber round a nucleus of stone or to adulterate it with sand, and this was formerly sometimes done; but the Government regulations now require that all rubber balls shall be cut in half before being received into the Custom House for export.

The first account of the rubber vine we have is that by Captain Owen, of H.M.S. *Leven,* who, in describing Lieutenant Reitz's journey from Mombasa to Pangani wrote: "Some of the few trees that grew upon this island [? Tanga] are entwined with the convolvulus, from which exudes a species of india-rubber, which is only collected by the children to amuse themselves in imitating the report of a pistol. They make an incision in the bark, and, as the juice runs out, collect it on a leaf, wherein it remains until it begins to acquire a glutinous quality; it is then moulded by the fingers into the shape of a tube, with one end closed; in the other they introduce a reed, through which the caoutchouc is blown into a globe of the size of a bullock's bladder; on striking this it bursts, and yields the desired report."

The development of the india-rubber trade of Zanzibar and the East Coast, is due to the energy of Sir John Kirk who, in 1868, began to induce the natives of Dar es Salaam to collect the produce of the vine which before that time was not an article of trade in Zanzibar. Sir John Kirk's endeavours bore fruit only after the lapse of several years owing to the absorbing interests of the slave trade.

Landolphia florida grows more profusely than *Landolphia Kirkii* but is not tapped. The latter will not coagulate.

The foregoing include all the products of Zanzibar that find their way to the European markets with the exception of nutmegs and vanilla, which as yet are grown in but very small quantities. Nutmegs, though of very slow growth, thrive wonderfully on the richer soils. The cultivation of vanilla has been comprised within the experimental work which has been carried out by the Government.

A great variety of fruit, vegetable, oil and fibre products common to most tropical countries find a congenial home, and a ready local sale in the islands.

Of the fruits, the most important are the plantain and banana, which, as they differ only in size and flavour, are in Zanzibar both included under the former term.

Bananas are not cultivated in large plantations but in small groves round native houses. Arabs and natives, while they will leave coconuts and cloves to struggle with the weeds as best they may, keep their bananas clean. The bunches of fruit exhibited daily for sale in the market would compare favourably with those in any part of the world. Very little trouble is taken with the actual planting of the banana boles, as with the planting of other trees of whatever kind. There are over twenty sorts of bananas and plantains. The sweetest and best are known locally as *sukari* (sugar); and the largest is called *mkono wa tembo* from its size and resemblance in shape to an elephant's trunk. It is also known as *mkono mmoja* from its measuring one hand, *i.e.*, a cubit.

Lest they should be stolen the bunches of bananas are never left to ripen fully on the trees, but are cut green and hung up in the houses for ten days to mature. To hasten this process they are sometimes buried in a hole in the earth previously heated with cinders, whence they will emerge in three days rich and mellow. The bunches sell in the town for anything up to a rupee according to their variety, condition and size; and are retailed in the shops at three or four pice a hand. The trees carry their first bunch of fruit twelve months after planting. The stem is cut down when the bunch is gathered, but by this time other young shoots are on their way up. In a few years, if not thinned out, the clumps would meet and occupy all the ground. The cooking varieties are more in favour with -the natives than those for the table. They are cooked in various ways as a vegetable or in some form of meal.

No care is bestowed on mango trees, which are to be found everywhere growing to an enormous size, even on poor soil. They are often planted in avenues and round houses. There are, in Zanzibar and Pemba, about twenty-four varieties, and consequently their flowering season, beginning in June, extends over several months during the southwest monsoon. The crop, which is ripe in the hot season, December to April, depends to a great extent on the weather in the flowering months. The natives attribute certain ailments, including ophthalmia, prevalent in June, which is the most unhealthy month in the year, to the influence of the young mango flowers. The trees are a source of very little profit to their owners, unless they happen to be natives, with the time to sit and watch the fruit. The fruit on the trees can sometimes be sold for three or four rupees per tree, the purchaser taking all risks. The latter, however, is wary, and does not conclude a bargain till the mangoes are nearly full grown, and ready for plucking. The fruit is gathered in the roughest manner possible, by throwing up sticks or stones, or by climbing the trees and shaking or knocking it off. The wind, however, does the greatest part of this work, and those who live in the neighbourhood of bearing trees make it their business, every morning at the dawn of day, to kick about in the grass for windfalls, whether the trees belong to them or not. One of the best varieties is the *dodo*, a large and rather fibrous fruit; the *bourbon* is also much sought after; it has a pink skin, and hangs to the tree by a very long stem. The *Bombay* is however the choicest kind, but this is rarely found in the market, there being but a limited number of trees on the island and these growing principally in the Sultan's plantation at Marahubi. In a good season thousands of mango fruit fall and rot on the ground, or are stolen, and it is usual to let the plantation people have the run of the trees. The proceeds of a load of fruit sold in the town market does not cover the cost of carriage, and this applies to nearly all the minor products of a plantation.

Jack fruit trees begin to ripen their fruit in November and go on till March. Four or five pice are obtained in the plantation for one jack fruit. Both the fruit itself and the seeds, which are cooked, are eaten with avidity by the natives, but by Europeans never. The trees, as in the case of mangoes, are sometimes sold for a few rupees for the season's crop. No attention is paid to their cultivation. The bread fruit is found here and there, but is by no means common, though it grows luxuriantly. The durian tree grows to very large proportions equalling the mango tree in size, and its fruit is much prized by the Arabs, who pay fancy prices for it; but the crop is very uncertain, and is liable to destruction by high winds. The fruit emits such an atrocious and searching odour that the presence of even one in the house is sufficient to make every room uninhabitable.

Orange trees abound everywhere, and though quantities of the fruit find their way into the market, the waste in the plantations in a good season is enormous. The trees ripen their fruit from March to July. The ordinary orange is known as the *Mchungwa wa kipemba*, of which there are two varieties, the thick and the thin skinned, the latter being considered the sweetest. The Mandarin orange and the Tangerine are both common, the former being an especial favourite with Europeans. The Zanzibar orange has a good reputation, but in comparison with carefully selected varieties now cultivated in other parts of the world it is doubtful whether it really deserves the reputation it has acquired. Small quantities are exported to Mombasa and other mainland ports, but the coast trade in Zanzibar fruit is very small in comparison with what it might be if properly organised. Large quantities are sold to passing ships, which, in the orange season, are crowded with home-going passengers, and to the fleet, which usually pays its annual visit to Zanzibar in June or July.

The Seville or bitter orange grows freely, its fruit being used as a condiment in curries; but it has no market value. Several varieties of sweet and sour limes, two varieties of citron, and two or three of lemon are found. Lemon trees bear from May to June, but they are seldom used by Europeans, the sour lime taking its place in the manufacture of lemon-squash. Limes can be obtained all the year round. Citrons are very rarely seen in the market. Two varieties of the pumelo or shaddock (forbidden fruit), the large and the small, are grown in Zanzibar, though more abundantly in Pemba.

Two varieties of pineapple-the green-skinned and the pink-skinned-are grown in Zanzibar. The former is the better of the two, though they are both small and fibrous. Pineapples are not a favourite fruit with the natives, who will scarcely take the trouble to steal them. In the season, which begins in December, they can be purchased in the town at an anna each.

The papaw tree may be said to grow wild, as it takes root easily and grows rapidly with little care. It is found everywhere and lasts for four or five years. Luscious fruit can be purchased for a pice or two each. Other fruits more or less common are the rambutan, litchi, pomegranate, guava, rose-apple, Malay-apple, *zambarao* (*Eugenia jambolana*), sweetsop, soursop, custard apple, sapodilla plum, Chinese date (*zizyphus jujuba*), Otaheite apple (Spondias dulcis), granadilla, loquat, musk melon, water melon, tamarind, date. Dates do not grow well in Zanzibar, nor is the fruit so good as that which comes from the drier climates of Egypt and Arabia. At his plantation at Sherif Msa, Dr. Andrade has made some valuable experiments with tropical and sub-tropical fruits, and has succeeded in introducing many improved varieties into the island.

Natives pay a considerable amount of attention to the cultivation of their vegetables, and exhibit much judgment in the observance of times and seasons, and in the selection of varieties. Planting times are counted from the *mwaka*, a fixed season of the year occurring on or about August 14. Thus *mtama* (sorghum) may be planted 150 to 180 days after mwaka, namely, from January 11 to the first week in February. The planting seasons are arranged in decades of days from the mwaka, thus the 116th day from mwaka would be referred to as in the *mia wa ishirini* (the 120), just as in stating the hour of the day, a native would call a quarter to four *saa tano* (the fifth hour), or if correctness were required *saa tano kasa robo* (less a quarter).

The staple food of the native is cassava or manioc, of which there are two main species-the sweet and the bitter each having three or four varieties. The bitter is the favourite with the native, though it takes longer to grow. Cassava is planted any time in the year, and in all sorts of soils, from deep rich loams to light sands and gravels, though in the latter case only poor crops are obtained. Cuttings six inches long are stuck in the ground in the most casual manner, about eighteen inches or two feet apart. At first the garden is kept fairly clear of weeds, but after the plants have grown to three or four feet high, it is left to itself. In six months the plants are ready to pull. Cassava can be bought at almost every cottage, and in every local market-place, where it is displayed in small heaps of three or four roots and sold for two pice a heap. In one form or other it forms the daily food of all people in the plantation, and of the bulk of those in the town.

The sweet potato belongs to the natural order *Convolvulacea*, and is propagated by planting slips or cuttings of the stem. Five varieties are grown. Natives plant them at all times of the year, when rain serves, though the principal season is the *Masika*, or big rains, in April and May. The earth is moulded up in long tortuous beds, two or three feet high, and three or four feet wide, and the cuttings crowded indiscriminately all over the surface. They rapidly creep over the beds, nearly hiding the soil. In two to five months, according to season and variety, the crop is ready to dig. When digging the potatoes, the natives may frequently be observed sticking in the tops again behind them, for a second crop, and in well-made beds this process may be repeated several times. No manure is ever applied for this or any other crop; natives do not seem to understand its use; hence large crops of potatoes are seldom obtained. They are sold in the local markets in little heaps like cassava, and occupy an important place in the economy of the household. Sweet potatoes are boiled with salt and sometimes mixed with coconut or syrup. In Tumbatu the haulms are trained up poles, evidently to economise space, land available for planting being scarce there.

Rice is grown in the low swampy flats, and is usually planted from about the middle of December to the middle of January. There are at least seventeen kinds of rice grown in Zanzibar. The seed is lightly dibbled in, the method pursued in this as in every case where seed has to be sown, being for one man to go ahead with a hoe chopping little holes in the ground all around him, and a second to follow with the seed which he lets fall into the holes and covers with his foot. Natives pay great attention to their rice fields, and as the harvest approaches devote the whole of their time to keeping the birds off. Crude arrangements of tin cans are often employed for this purpose. Harvesting, which takes place in June or July, is conducted in the most primitive manner, by plucking the ears singly. In dry weather the grain is sometimes threshed out on the spot. Compared with its yearly consumption the island produces very little rice; hence large shipments arrive from Rangoon. The sweltering, swampy valleys of Pemba could produce abundant crops of rice, and in the time of Seyyid Said rice was an article of export from that island to Zanzibar.

In every native garden Indian corn is to be found, usually among beds of pulse. It is dibbled into the ground in the same way as rice. The natives state that it is a mistake to cover up the seed, except perhaps very lightly, or to press it down, as we should do by using a roller. It is left lightly resting in the soil and sufficiently exposed to benefit by the action of the heavy dews, which fall nightly. There are at least three kinds of Indian corn, but they are all very poor compared with the splendid samples produced in sub-tropical and temperate climates. It is sown before the rains, to allow the plants to be a few inches above the ground when the rains arrive. The ears must be closely watched, as they ripen or they will most certainly share the fate common to most food products, and be stolen by the first wayfarer who catches sight of them.

Sorghum is chiefly grown by the Wahadimu upon the rich shallow soils of their coral country. About every third year fresh ground is cleared of its scrub, and seed dibbled in. Plants grow to twelve feet in height and are really a beautiful sight, especially in the early morning, when the nodding pinnacles glisten with dew. It is planted from the second week in January to the first week in February and harvested in August. At harvest time the owner with his family often migrates to his plantation, if it is some way from his village, and erects a temporary house with sorghum stems and palm leaves. Wild pigs, if they are not watched, make great havoc with the clearings. There are three varieties grown, with seeds of white, pink and red colour. Sorghum is very largely used as a meal or porridge in cases of sickness, and as food for donkeys.

African millet (*Penisetum typhoideum*), a small gramineous plant, is sometimes found in native gardens, though not in large quantities. It may be planted at all times of the year. Both sorghum and millet are imported from India.

In the time of Seyyids Said, Majid and Barghash, sugar was quite an important industry, and even so late as 1897 molasses was still made at one factory.

Natives used wooden crushing mills of their own manufacture, but these have passed into disuse. The cane is now grown in all parts of the island, in the deep soil, but only in small patches and for household consumption. The sticks sell from a halfpenny to a penny each in the market.

Many years ago Zanzibar exported a large amount of indigo, but the industry was presumably killed by the fall in prices. The plant grows wild in great profusion, but is now entirely neglected.

A variety of pulses are cultivated by the natives, the chief of which is the pigeon pea (*Cajanus Indicus*), which is very common in their native gardens. This plant is perhaps found at its best on the edge of the coral country, where the soil is deep enough to accommodate its roots, and at the same time the coral sufficiently near the surface to provide a rich Store of lime. The bushes bear in about a year, growing to a height of eight feet or more, and will stand three or four years. When systematically cultivated, a crop of cassava is taken off the ground before the peas are planted, and, while the latter are in occupation, ground nuts, beans, or some other low-growing crops may be obtained.

Pigeon peas are often followed by sessamum, or as it is commonly called simsim, and by the natives ufuta (oil). It is planted in September, harvested in January and February; but the bushes ripen their seed very irregularly, and go on flowering at their terminals after the lower branches have begun to ripen their seed. Hence branches have to be cut out as they ripen. The native method of threshing is to take a sheaf of the simsim and tap it with a stick or the back of a knife, when the small clover-like seed falls into a mat below. The sheaf is then put back in the store and taken out again the next day when another crop of ripe seed will fall, and so on. The bushes grow to about seven feet in height, spreading in proportion. There are two varieties of simsim, so-called black and white, from the colour of their seed. The oil is expressed by wooden mills made from a section of the trunk of a mango tree set on end and hollowed out at the top. The seed is put into the cavity and crushed by a wood pestle, weighted down, and worked round by a camel.

Ground nuts are a favourite crop with the natives, but yield very poorly, and cannot be profitably grown when hired labour has to be employed. Unlike many annuals they cannot rise above the weeds, which, in Zanzibar, grow with amazing vigour and speed. They must be kept clean by weeding every fortnight or three weeks. Ground nuts are planted in December or January and occupy the

THE PLANTATION

ground three or four months.

The bambarra ground nut (*Voandzeia subteryanea*) is also common and can be planted at any time of the year.

Quite a number of dwarf peas and beans are cultivated in Zanzibar; they fill an indispensable place in the daily menu, though they are generally grown in the gardens as subsidiary crops.

The yam, called in Swahili *Kiazi kikuu* (large potato), is seldom to be seen except isolated and trailed up the garden fence. The tubers grow to a great size: from two to three feet long and over twelve pounds in weight. They are propagated by large sets buried to a few inches in the ground, either in trenches or in holes, and grow very rapidly.

The betel leaf (*Tambuu*) industry is almost entirely in the hands of the Wahadimu and the Watumbatu. The latter devote a good deal of attention to their plantations, which are set out in groups of clumps, each clump belonging to a different owner, though the whole presents the appearance of one plantation. The Watumbatu are the only natives I have ever come across who do not steal growing crops from one another; in the management of their betel plantations this honest behaviour is strictly adhered to. The vines are trained up stout supports. In the hot season, that is to say in the north-east monsoon, which blows in January and February, or in dry weather, the plants produce very few leaves. Only young leaves are plucked, old leaves not being saleable. The leaves are ready to pluck twenty-five days after budding, and retail at a pice (a farthing) each. All Arabs and natives chew betel-leaf, mixed with betelnut and lime, a supply of which is always carried on the person.

Tobacco is often planted after sorghum, in the rocky coral country, but it is also extensively cultivated on the light soils in the north of Zanzibar island. Plants are generally set in August, in raised beds, three feet apart. A considerable trade in tobacco is carried on by the Wahadimu on the east coast, who send their produce into Zanzibar town.

Two or three varieties of brinjal and at least three varieties of tomatoes are grown in Zanzibar, and several varieties of large capsicums. Of cucurbitous plants, the principal are the large gourd, snake gourd (*Momordica charantia*), luffa (two varieties), cucumber, musk- and watermelons. Other cultivated plants are lady's finger, a species of radish, garlick-which is an invariable ingredient in curries-turmeric, tanias, ginger (very rarely grown).

Among other economic products to which more or less attention is given is the cotton tree (*Eriodendron anfractuosum*), which crops in October and November. Indian cotton, castor oil (very common but neglected), the large hollow bamboo, cashew nut tree, the soap berry tree, two varieties of cardamum, the physic nut tree used as a hedge plant and to mark boundaries, lemon grass, the leaves of which are brewed with tea and are supposed to be good for fever, the areca nut palm, the oil palm, growing extensively in Pemba. The natives eat the fruit of the Borassuspalm raw, having first scraped off the outside of the husk. Seeds are sometimes planted and allowed to sprout, and the young tender plant then plucked for food. The full-grown trees are too large to climb, but the leaves of the smaller and more accessible trees are used for making mats and rice bags. The Raphia palm is also found in Pemba, and provides material for mat making, but mats are more frequently made from a species of wild date found on the mainland. Anatto grows vigorously, but natives pay no attention to it. Liberian coffee may be met with here and there near Arab houses. A variety of plants provide cordage, namely, *Triumfetta rhomboidea*, the bark of the Baobab, the midrib of the coconut leaf, the stem of the banana, the leaves of the pineapple.

The mangrove is the principal timber tree of the country. It grows in profusion in the shallow inlets of the sea, both in Zanzibar and Pemba. There are at least three species, the largest of which, *mzimzi,* grows to a height of sixty feet. The mangrove provides beams for the roofs of stone houses, and lathes and rafters for the walls and roofs of mud houses. The best timber in Zanzibar comes from the Chedju creek, the export village of which is Chwaka on the east coast. A considerable trade is done in Pemba, where the trees are somewhat larger than in Zanzibar. The mangrove is also cut down for its bark, largely so in Pemba, which provides the principal supply. The trees are first felled, the bark then stripped off and filled into sacks or baskets. The trade is in the hands of a few Indians who buy from the native collectors at the rate of about eight annas a bag, which, in Zanzibar, is worth about a rupee. The bulk of the bark is exported, but some is used locally for tanning. The bark is cut into small pieces, put into a cask and covered with water. Ox hides are then steeped in the liquor for from 18 to 20 days; goat and sheep skins for six days, and afterwards pegged out in the sun to dry. The lack fruit tree, mango tree, coconut palm, *mzambarau* (*Eugenia jambolana*) provide timber for rough doors.

Gum copal, *sandarusi*, is found in Zanzibar, but only to a limited extent.

Traces of an old gum field are to be found at Bomani, north of Chuini. The soil is poor and sandy, the coconut trees in the vicinity thin, carrying but very small crops of nuts. Natives dig large holes in the ground, but they state that it is little use digging in the dry weather, the proper season being in the rains. I can offer no explanation of this, or affirm whether it really be true, as very little attention is paid to gum; and though I have myself dug for it, I have never succeeded in finding any. Most of the gum copal exported from Zanzibar comes from the mainland.

The following account of gum copal is taken from Doctor Kirk's researches, communicated to the Linnaean Society in 1868, 1870 and 1873. Dr. Kirk described three distinct kinds of copal in the Zanzibar trade, subdivided by merchants into many classes. First the tree copal or *Sandarusi ya mti,* an excretion from the trunk and branches of the *Trachylobium Hornemannianum*, a large tree of the natural order Leguminosum, and distinguished by its rounded head of glossy leaves, with white groups of flowers projecting from the points of the branches. The gum solidifies, but drops to the ground in solid brittle lumps. This is an inferior sort, and goes chiefly to India. The tree is found along the mainland coast from Mozambique to near Lamu, chiefly between Cape Delgado and Mombasa, though only to a short distance inland, becoming very rare, and finally disappearing when removed from the influence of the sea. The second sort of copal is known as *Chakazi*, and is found in the ground at the roots of the trees, or in the country where these exist. It is of modern origin, having remained but a short time in the soil after the death of the tree which produced it. In value it is about equal to the *Sandarusi ya mti.*

The third, the valuable animi of the English markets, is found all along the ancient sea beach of the maritime plain which fringes the continent to a depth of from 20 to 40 miles. This is the true *Sandarusi*-a semi-fossil or bituminized resin, which, in Dr. Kirk's opinion, is the product of extinct forests of the identical *Trachylobium Hornemannianum*, now found growing at the coast.

The great produce market of the island is that in the town. It used to occupy an open space outside the fort, but is now at Mkunazini, where a large and convenient building, called the Estella market, has been put up by the Government, who levy a 10 per cent. duty on all produce sold therein. In return they protect the natives from the rapacity and extortion of the Indian, and compel the latter, when produce is being taken to his shop, to pay the price agreed upon in the market, which is registered at the time by officials appointed for that purpose. Nearly three thousand loads of produce, all borne upon the head, enter the Estella market daily, the statistics showing a marked rise during the month of Ramadan, during which all followers of Islam are supposed to fast, but in reality feast, though only in the night time. The scene in the Estella market in the morning is, as may be imagined, a busy one, and extremely hot. There is no yelling or advertising of goods, but each man squats on the ground with his neatly-arranged basket of fruit or vegetables, or spreads his wares in front of him. All varieties of tropical fruits and vegetables are on view as well as goats, sheep, poultry, foddergrass, while, in an enclosed building, stalls are fitted up for the display of clothing and house furniture. In the country the local market-place is often under a mango tree or a large spreading African almond tree, and it is the favourite meeting place where the villagers gather and exchange their gossip.

For cultivating the ground, the native uses a hoe called a *jembe*, which serves the purpose of weeding, digging and shovelling. It is made of wrought iron, hammered out by the local blacksmith into a pear-shaped outline, contracting at the head into a spike to fit a hole in the handle. The handles are made of rough-hewn brush-wood; they are from two feet to two feet six inches in length and may be fixed by the owner himself. The hoe costs from 4d. to 6d., according to size and quality, and is much to be preferred to the foreign imitations which may be purchased in the bazaar. In spite of many enterprising attempts to introduce something more modern and up-to-date, the native still clings to his homely implement, which is cheap and strong. He can use it with one hand, while with the other he picks out the weeds. He has a rough, light axe, with a very narrow edge, for felling timber, while for staking or fencing he employs a large hooked bush knife of wrought iron. In the museum at Naples there are axes and bush knives, found in the ruins of Pompeii, which very much resemble those now in use in Zanzibar. In one of the houses at Pompeii a kitchen is shown, which has been left exactly as it was found, and among other relics there are some iron cooking-pots, with expanded bases, identical in shape with the cooking pots in common use in Zanzibar.

In Appendix VII. will be found the analysis of two samples of soils of Zanzibar Island, made by Dr. Welker, Consulting Chemist to the Royal Agricultural Society of England. They are fairly typical of the lighter and richer soils of the island. Judged by the standards of this country, the soils are both of inferior quality, especially No. 1, but in Zanzibar, as in other equatorial countries, as much or more depends upon the rainfall as upon the richness of the soil. A soil like No. 1 would be deemed a very poor soil in England, yet in Zanzibar it supports a rich vegetation, and coconut and clove trees thrive upon it. Even No. 3 would not rank as a rich soil; but at Dunga, where the sample was taken, the growth upon it is most luxuriant. The whole of the eastern part of Zanzibar, with the exception of a fringe round the coast, is coral rag. The line which marks the division between this and the deep soils begins roughly at Kidote to the north of Mkokotoni, makes a curve inwards behind Dunga, meeting the sea again below Chukwani. This coral country sometimes takes on an open park-like appearance, with rock outcropping only here and there, and with a deposit of rich vegetable loam, from six inches to a foot deep. In other places it is very rough; broken coral covers the surface with spurs projecting in every direction, flanked sometimes by great holes worn out by water. A rich black mould is lodged in the pockets and supports a dense, though stunted, forest vegetation. The open park-like expanses were no doubt at one time covered with thick forest growth, and in some previous age, when the Wahadimu were more populous, were regularly cultivated by them, the scrub upon them having at last been killed by repeated clearing. The greater part of the coral country is uninhabited and uncultivated. It will not support large trees except the *mzambarau* and the *baobab,* and coconut trees, if planted upon it, bear no nuts, but fall a prey to the rhinoceros beetle, which ravages the leaves and growing points. Clove and coconut plantations are found upon the deep soils on the western portions of the island.

Three low ranges of hills traverse the greater part of the island in a longitudinal direction, the highest point being Masingini, 420 feet.

The soil on the tops of the ranges is a red clayey loam, passing into a brown sandy loam in the valleys. The richest part of the island is from about Mangapwani on the coast, ten miles north of Zanzibar town, to Mbweni in the south, and extending to about ten miles inland from this base. The soil in the north of the island is generally lighter in character than that in the middle.

In contrast with the gentle undulations of the surface of the larger island, Pemba is cut up into a succession of steep low hills and valleys. Travelling is laborious, and in wet weather difficult, as the valleys are then converted into swamps, and the small rivulets, which are far more numerous than in Zanzibar, become torrents.

As in Zanzibar, the west part of the island is the cultivated part, though the proportion of waste coral country is far less in Pemba, and is confined to a flat strip a few miles wide along the east coast, inhabited by Wapemba. The soil is generally a sandy clay, sufficiently tenacious to enable it to retain moisture in dry weather. The clove trees clothe the hill tops and sides, but neither cloves nor coconuts will grow in the valleys, which are principally devoted to the cultivation of rice. At Wete are some enormous clove trees, probably the largest in the world. The soil in the north of Pemba is much lighter and more sandy than that in the south, and the surface of the land more even. It is covered in places with primeval forest, in which the *Landolphia* rubber thrives. There are evidences that the whole of the north and east of Pemba was at one time covered with forest, which no doubt supported the rubber vine, and even to within a few years ago the Wapemba were in the habit of cutting down forest to make themselves fresh gardens.

Land in Zanzibar and Pemba is owned principally by Arabs, though large numbers of small plantations are owned by freed slaves and by Wahadimu and Wapemba. The land is held in freehold, and there is always considerable demand for plantations that may be in the market, as this and house property are the only form of investment open to small capitalists. Plantations are valued according to the number of coconut and clove trees they carry, though a complete list of every sort of tree growing is generally included in the inventory. Values run from two to six rupees per tree, according to locality, condition of the plantation, and prevailing prices. The people do not understand acreage.

Many of the Arabs have mortgaged their plantations, and are now in the power of the Indians, who exact interest at the rate of 20 per cent. per annum and upwards. The system adopted is somewhat as follows: an Indian will lend an Arab, say, 5,000 rupees, the latter signing a deed stating that he has received 8,000 and undertaking to pay the interest on that amount. If valued according to European standards, the estate would probably be worth 4,000 rupees as an investment.

In dealing with the Indian, the Arab gets a larger advance than he would from a European, while the probability of the former foreclosing is remote, as he could never recover the face value of his mortgage; though it must be confessed that the Arab pays dearly for these privileges.

Some attempts have been made by European capitalists to supplant the

Indian, but they have not been successful; the former are too cautious and will not risk enough. If after investigation, a European capitalist does not consider the investment satisfactory and rejects it, the Arab is liable to lose *heshima* (respect), and is exposed to the suspicion among his fellows that his affairs are not altogether as he represented them to be. An Indian money-lender on the other hand is generally also a trader, and if he cannot meet the Arab in one way, will compromise with him in another. It is not easy to see how the Arabs are to be rescued from the financial tangle in which they have become involved.

The abolition of the legal status of slavery in 1897 was thought at the time to be full of danger to the landed industries of the island, yet it is a remarkable fact that since that date plantations in Zanzibar have steadily risen in value. Improved markets for both cloves and coconuts have enhanced the value of trees, but at the same time there is, I think, little doubt that the releasing of slave labour has brought about an improvement, multiplying the number of small holders and making it possible for Indians who, a few years ago, were in the position of absentee mortgagees, to obtain labour and work plantations themselves.

Coconut plantation administered by Beit al-Mal.

Cattle fodder being brought to town over one of the bridges.

CHAPTER XXI

THE CLIMATE

ZANZIBAR has a terrible record of death, and for the men who first went out there in the 60's and 70's it must have been anything but a nice place to live in, and might even have justified the description of it attributed to Mr. Gordon Bennet by Vizetelli in his book "From Cyprus to Zanzibar." Mr. Bennet was explaining to Mr. Nizetelli that he wanted him to go to Zanzibar to find Stanley: "It's an awful place, you know; you get the fever there, and die in a week." The foreshore at that time reeked with carrion and garbage from the town, which polluted the atmosphere, and even now the odour of Melindi Spit, the east-end of Zanzibar city, can be detected some distance out at sea. Captain Hamerton, writing in 1842, stated that he had seen at one time fifty dead bodies of slaves, which had been thrown on the shore, being devoured by the dogs of the town, but in consequence of his representations on this shameful practice, the Imam had caused such bodies to be buried. It was the habit all over the town to bury the dead amongst the houses, commonly under a tree, close to the deceased person's habitation. Arabs and the wealthy were properly interred, but the poor were wrapped in a mat and placed in such shallow holes as scarcely to be concealed from view, while slaves were left to putrefy on the beach.

The country has improved since those days, and Europeans, from experience and tradition, have got to understand it better. The town is now supplied with good water, which is led in pipes from a spring about two miles and a half to the north. It is swept daily and cleared of its refuse. Communication with Europe is frequent and regular, whereas in the 70's, the island was left sometimes for six months without a mail. The houses are better; in every way the conditions of life have improved, and they continue to improve. While therefore the climate of Zanzibar cannot perhaps be described as good, it is certainly not so bad as it is sometimes said to be.

The malaria-bearing *Anopheles* mosquito had not till quite recently been discovered in the town, though its existence was detected some years ago at Bunga, but the harmless *Culex* is very prevalent. No systematic measures are taken for its extermination, though this would not be an impossible task, at least in the European quarter of the town. Nor has the now approved method of living in mosquito-proof houses been adopted, except in the case of one or two residents who have made themselves mosquito-proof bedrooms.

In Pemba mosquitoes are more numerous, and in parts when in camp it is necessary to retire into the mosquito curtains at sundown. The species in Pemba seem to be more vicious, as they will bite through ordinary drill trousers. Mosquitoes attack the ankles, wrists, and backs of the hands, or wherever the veins are near the skin; but their bite is not very serious unless the place be scratched. Acute irritation is set up, for a few minutes but soon passes off.

Probably everyone who goes to Zanzibar and resides there any length of time contracts malaria, which manifests itself sooner or later in one form or another. The type commonly met with is ordinary benign, which may be brought on by chills, exposure to the sun and disordered digestion; the three most exciting causes of fever. The prevailing symptoms of an approaching attack of fever are a feeling of languor with an inclination to yawn and stretch, irritability, loss of appetite, headache and aching limbs. It is an old saying that at forty a man is either a physician or a fool, and it is equally true that with experience each man should in time find out the treatment that suits him best in an attack of fever. Some endeavour to carry on their daily work and to fight it; others go to bed immediately and physic themselves. The treatment that suits one man may not necessarily suit another, but once having got rid of the fever in whatever manner, it is universally acknowledged to be a dangerous thing to dispense too quickly with precautions and tonics, and to run the risk of a relapse. Dr. Hine, Bishop of Zanzibar, in some notes addressed in 1904 to the members of the Universities' Mission of his diocese on the subject of the treatment of fever in the absence of a doctor, mainly cautioning them what to avoid doing, condemns among other things the use by new comers of "that rather dangerous instrument," a pocket clinical thermometer. "I well remember," he writes, "one youth lying in bed with his thermometer in his mouth for at least half an hour and being quite distressed because, as he said, "I am sure I have fever coming on, but I can't make this thing go up." With those people who look upon the doctor and nurse as natural ene-

The Climate

mies engaged in a conspiracy to keep them in bed; with the fidgety patient who is nervous if his temperature reaches 101 and seriously alarmed when it is "subnormal"; and others who are haunted with fancies about parasites and big spleens, or who quote "what Dr. Manson told me," and experiment upon themselves and their brethren who are weak enough to submit, with the whole gamut of the presentation medicine chest, the Bishop, has no sympathy; though, as he explains, no one would be more surprised than Dr. Manson himself to hear what strange utterances he is credited with.

Natives frequently get fever, often acutely, but it does not last long with them, nor does it leave them weak and helpless as it does a European. Both natives and Arabs live in closely-confined houses, and shut all doors and windows at night. Some years ago a philanthropist went to Zanzibar, visited one of the country prisons and came back to England and denounced the authorities for confining prisoners in rooms with no windows in them. But he did not explain, and possibly did not know, that native houses seldom or never have windows, or, if they have, that they are only small squares of glass not meant to open. The native at night shuts the whole house up, however hot the weather, and sleeps in a confined atmosphere. This is of course contrary to our ideas of fresh air, and, in fact, we could not endure such conditions, yet there is something to be said for them. A cool breeze blowing through the bedroom is very pleasant, but if the bed be in a draught so that the chill night air can strike the heated body, which is always but lightly covered, then no doubt there is risk of a chill. It is related by Captain Owen that in 1824, four of a boat's crew of the *Andromache*, who, from unavoidable circumstances, were not able to return on board for the night, landed and lay round a large fire on shore instead of sleeping in their boat. For nearly a fortnight no ill effects were visible, but at the end of that time three died and the fourth was invalided home in a broken down condition.

"Is Zanzibar itself unhealthy?" was a question put to Major-General C. P. Rigby by the Chairman of the Select Committee of the House of Commons appointed in 1871 to enquire into the slave trade of East Africa. "The town is not," was the reply, "but it is almost certain death for any white man to sleep in the plantations. Some years ago the commodore went with several officers and a boat's crew to one of the Sultan's country houses in the interior of the island, a distance of about fifteen miles; they only slept one night in the interior, and a few days afterwards the only one of the whole party alive was the one who had slept in the boat, the vegetation is so dense and rank." The house here referred to (Doonger) is probably Dunga. That this lamentable result was not due solely to the unhealthiness of the interior of the island is proved by the fact that many Europeans have since that time stayed at Dunga and other parts of the interior without suffering ill effects therefrom, and that the author lived at Dunga five years.

Until quite recent years it was thought that Zanzibar was free from blackwater fever. Cases of blackwater fever have occurred, but in every instance it was discovered, or thought to be discovered, that the patient had contracted the disease on the mainland. Since the year 1901 several cases have occurred in Zanzibar and Pemba, namely at Dunga, Mtoni and Wete, affecting people who never resided on the mainland. I am not aware if scientific research has yet determined the special microbe to which blackwater fever is due; but the predisposing causes of an attack have been shown to be a succession of low fevers, which at the time may be thought little of, and an injudicious application of drugs, especially quinine. Two cases of blackwater fever which came under my notice appear to me to illustrate the danger of chills. There were living with me at Dunga two Europeans; one a guest, the other an official. In July, 1901, I had occasion to go to Pemba, and returning in ten days I found one of the men dead from blackwater fever, and the other in hospital from the same disease. They had lived in the same house for months and were struck down within half an hour of each other. I had left both in excellent spirits, and apparently in fairly good health, though I recalled afterwards that one at any rate had been for some time subject to slight attacks of fever, a rise in temperature of only a degree or two, for which he did not think it necessary to lay up, and that he used to get up early in the mornings and take strong doses of quinine. But these men had been in the habit of sitting out in the open air after sunset, and enjoying a cool pipe in their shirtsleeves, after a hot walk round the plantations.

Dysentery is now seldom contracted in Zanzibar, thanks to the excellent water supply and the soda-water factories that have been established. Small-pox is endemic among the natives, and sometimes takes an epidemic form. This occurred in the years 1898 and 1901 when thousands in the two islands perished. In the latter year several thousand natives were vaccinated by the Government, and this checked the disease. Natives, especially Wahadimu, display a curious antipathy to vaccination, which arises from their fear of the witch-doctors and medicine men in whose power they have a most abiding faith. The medicine men threaten them with the direst penalties if they submit to the treatment of the white man; so that instead of the subject, as in this country, being required to pay a fee, he will in Zanzibar demand bakshishi for allowing himself to be operated upon. In the efficacy of the remedy, the Wahadimu have not the smallest belief, or if in some cases they may have, they prefer to submit themselves to their predestined fate than to the lancet of the white man. This curious prejudice against vaccination was observed by Captain Smee so long ago as 1811, when the island had just recovered from a devastating wave -of the disease, which carried off 15,000 people in the town alone. Nevertheless the people would not consent to be vaccinated. Although not ignorant of the danger from infection, they are extremely careless about it, especially the Wapemba, who will sit round the houses of sick friends and scramble for their clothes when they are dead.

Zanzibar, though geographically in the very centre of an affected area, has hitherto escaped the plague. Within the last eight years plague has broken out in Bombay, Mauritius, Madagascar, Durban, Delagoa Bay, Nairobi and Aden, all in direct communication with Zanzibar. In 1899 a British - India ship arrived at Mombasa with coolies for the Uganda Railway, among whom plague had appeared. The ship was sent to Zanzibar where facilities for provisioning and watering are greater than at Mombasa; she was anchored outside the reef, and in the course of about three weeks or a month the disease had disappeared and the ship was given a clean bill of health. That Zanzibar should have escaped while her neighbours one after another became affected is all the more remarkable when it is remembered that it is the great transhipping port of East Africa, at which all vessels proceeding north or south call. In the north-east monsoon hundreds of dhows come from Bombay and the Persian Gulf, and in the south-west monsoon hundreds more come from Madagascar and the neighbouring islands. Admirable precautions for protecting the port were instituted and carried out by the late Sir Lloyd Mathews and Doctor A. H. Spurrier, special plague officer of Zanzibar and British East Africa. It has been pointed out that ships arriving in Zanzibar do not lie up at the wharf but discharge their cargo by means of lighters, which greatly reduces the risk of infection through rats. But when every allowance is made for this and every credit given for skilful and vigilant precautions, it is impossible to believe that the germs of plague have not found their way into the port even if they have not penetrated the town. In March 1902 plague broke out in Nairobi, and the infection was subsequently traced to the presence of plague germs, which were discovered in some sugary foodstuffs imported from Bombay. These germs must have passed through Mombasa, but had lain dormant till they reached the cool altitudes of the interior. Bombay has a much larger trade with Zanzibar than with Mombasa, and it may be assumed that as plague germs have been conveyed to Mombasa they have probably also been conveyed to Zanzibar, but have been kept dormant by the even and elevated temperature of the island. If this assumption is correct, then it is probable that Zanzibar will never become the scene of a great outbreak of plague. I believe there is no record of an epidemic of plague on the littoral of the equatorial belt. There is a huge bazaar in Zanzibar in which the Indians live in full liberty of filth, so that if an outbreak occurred it would make terrible ravages.

A few years ago "jiggers" were common in Zanzibar, having come across Africa from the West coast, but they are now much less prevalent. Isolated cases of sleeping sickness have reached the coast, but the species of tetse fly which plays the part in the spread of this disease, corresponding with that of anopheles in malaria, has not yet been discovered in Zanzibar, though search for it has been made. The natives of Zanzibar suffer from elephan tiasis, leprosy, ophthalmia, consumption, beri-beri, terrible sores, and other prevailing complaints of Africa. The lepers, both in Zanzibar and Pemba, are segregated in homes supported by the Government. Europeans, apart from fever and its complications, enjoy singular immunity from disease.

A few words may be said of the life usually led in Zanzibar, though there may be little to add to what has been already written on this subject by travellers and others. Europeans live in the Arab stone houses, which are large, white, rectangular, flat - roofed buildings, two or three stories high with an open courtyard in the middle. The rooms are long and narrow, their width being regulated by the beams of mangrove wood which span them and support the ceilings. The flat concrete roof is the best style of roof for the country, affording ample protection from the sun and rain. Residents in Zanzibar have in East Africa the reputation of keeping a good table, the principle that the system should be well nourished being thoroughly believed in and practised. Most people rise at seven or half-past; office hours are from eight to four, with an interval for lunch, and at half-past four everybody turns out for a ride or drive, cricket, tennis, golf, or a sail in the harbour. There are admirable links and tennis courts; the Zanzibar cricket team is acknowledged to be the best in those parts, being only defeated when the combined strength of the fleet is once a year pitted against it, and not always then. Dinner is announced at eight o'clock every evening by a gun fired from the saluting battery to call Mohammedans to prayer. The fixing of the time at sunset every day is quite an interesting ceremony. The Arab whose duty it is to determine the exact moment which is to be called six o'clock takes up his position at the Sultan's landing pier, watch in hand, and observes the sun slowing sink into the horizon. A few seconds before he gives the signal he gets up from his seat and advances a few paces, so that the man in the clock-tower, and the corporal of the guard which is to fire the volley, may more accurately observe his movements. He holds up his stick, the guard discharge their rifles, the bugle sounds a royal salute, the band plays the Sultan's anthem and His Highness, who is supposed to have really given the signal, bows his acknowledgments from one of the windows of the palace. There are of course two systems of time reckoning, the European and the Mohammedan, the latter being from six to six, so that Saa tatu, the third hour, is equivalent to our nine o'clock. In all dealings with Arabs or natives, Mohammedan time is kept.

The Moslem year consists of twelve lunar months of 29 or 30 days each, making altogether 354 days. Eleven times in every cycle of thirty years a day is added to the last month of the year, which then contains 30 instead of 29 days and the year is stretched to 355 days. In official and business transactions, which are controlled by Europeans, the Gregorian calendar is used, Sunday being the *dies non*, when all offices are closed, but Friday is the Moslem holy day and day of rest. I suppose no one is more tolerant of other people's religious beliefs and observances than an Englishman, and in Zanzibar scrupulous regard is paid to the susceptibilities of Mohammedans, whose religion is recognised to be that of the country and whose laws are as far as possible administered. Nevertheless, while he leaves the Arabs to arrange their week as they like, respects their day of rest and will even date his letters to them according to the traditions of Islam, yet the Englishman declines to open his office for them on Sunday. He is not perhaps considered very religious, still he insists on his Sunday and on his church, though he may not attend it very often.

The ordinary native of Zanzibar takes little heed of the course of years and has but the vaguest notion of periods of time beyond a year or two. I never met a native who could accurately state his age nor heard of anyone celebrating a birthday. In Zanzibar events are referred to the reign of the Sultan who happened to occupy the throne at the time of their occurrence. A man will state for instance that he was born in the time of Seyyid Majid; another that he was freed in the time of Seyyid Khalifa.

The temperature in which one lives in the house in Zanzibar averages about 80° F. In the shade in the town, it ranges from a minimum of 69° to a maximum of 93°, and from 60° to 98° at Dunga. Thus there is an extreme range during the year of 24° in the town and of about 38° in the country. The average for a number of years would work out at a little less than these figures. Captain Hamerton in 1855 found the thermometer ranged from 71° to 90° and estimated the rainfall at from 84 to 100 inches.

Meteorological observations have for some years been kept in Zanzibar by Doctor Charlesworth; since 1898 by the staff of the Agricultural Department at Dunga; and since 1898 by the Friends' Industrial Mission at Banani, Pemba.

The mass of masonry in the town stores up the heat of the day, and releasing it at night prevents the temperature in the town falling to the extent that it does in the country, where radiation can proceed unchecked. The proximity of the sea also tends to moderate the temperature of the town. No records have been taken of the maximum temperature in the sun. The condition in the narrow white streets of Zanzibar at midday in the hot season resembles that of a furnace, and is even greater than the choking heat experienced in the clove plantations. The hottest months are January, February and March; November, December and the early part of April before the rains have set in are often trying, as at these times the monsoons may have ceased to blow. Pemba is supposed to be hotter than Zanzibar, but the records at Banani do not confirm this view. Their extremes and means are both within the limits of those recorded at Dunga. Pemba is a degree nearer the equator, but on the other hand it is a small island much indented, so that no part of it is very far from the sea. The temperature of both islands, it will be observed by reference to the tables in the appendix, is very even and regular, but the heat is aggravated by the extreme humidity of the air which, in the rainy season, will register over 95 per cent. The difference between the temperature of the hot and cool seasons is slight, and it is only after a year or two's residence that it comes to be fully appreciated. To the newcomer both are trying, but the old resident who knows how to dress and to take advantage of the breeze which is nearly always blowing, and understands the importance of keeping out of the sun, enjoys the cool months from June to September, and gets through the hot season without much discomfort. Newcomers are apt to think lightly of the power of the sun, but the Zanzibar sun is a terrible enemy to the European. Its rays seem to fall all round him like a cataract. Cork helmets are not sufficient protection to the head; nothing in fact except pith is really safe; and there are some men who never go out in the sun without their "life preservers," as white umbrellas are sometimes called. An old African will not even allow a ray of sunshine to fall into the room anywhere near where he may be sitting. No European could stand a regular outdoor life in Zanzibar. If his occupation should be in the country, he should contrive to get through his outdoor work by nine in the morning, and keep indoors till three. If he makes a practice of keeping out till eleven or twelve, he will not last long.

The average rainfall in the town may be set down at about 60 inches per annum. The lowest fall on record was the year 1898, when only 27.49 inches were registered. In 1900, 74.05 inches were recorded, the highest for twenty years of observation. At Dunga 97.94 inches fell in 1899, 87.60 in 1901; at Banani 105.24 inches were recorded in 1899, and 92.78 in 1901. The greatest fall in one month was that of May 1899, when 60.68 inches were measured by Sir John Key at Wete, Pemba. On May 2 of that year 11.12 inches fell at Wete, which is the record, I believe, for East Africa. April is the wettest month, then May, then December; June and August are the driest months, but no month ever goes by without a little rain. There is often a shower between three and four o'clock in the morning, when the temperature is at its lowest. A reference to the tables will show that rain falls on nearly half the number of days in the year. There are two rainy seasons, the most important being in April and May, when the northeast monsoon has ceased to blow and the south-west is setting in. The rains may begin any time after the beginning of March, though usually not till the middle or close of that month. They come down in terrific floods, and penetrate windows and walls; iron roofs will not keep them out, and mackintoshes and umbrellas are practically of no use. The land, being very porous, quickly dries, and a few hours' not sun is generally sufficient, except in flood-time, to restore the roads to their normal condition. In 1899 all the bridges in the island were washed away, and many houses were unroofed. There was scarcely a house in the town in which, on the worst nights of April, the residents were not flooded out of their bedrooms. The lesser rains occur in November and December, rarely at the latter end of October; but they are very uncertain and sometimes do not arrive until

January. The rainy season in Pemba is often a month later than in Zanzibar. The big rains travel in a northerly direction, following the course of the sun, and arrive at Mombasa in May and at Kismayu in June. The rainfall is less in the northern coast ports than in the southern; Dar es Salaam, for example, having greater rainfall than Mombasa, and Mombasa again than Kismayu. But no place on the coast equals Zanzibar either in amount or distribution of its rainfall. The great commercial and industrial prosperity of Zanzibar must be traced to this, and it will help to keep her in the future the chief centre of activity in East Africa.

Heavy dews fall nightly and saturate all vegetation. The dew not only provides the soil with a light draught of moisture, but it enables plants to ward off for a considerable time in the morning the withering effect of the sun's heat. Dews are dangerous for Europeans, especially in the plantations where they begin to fall immediately after sunset. The sun sinks so rapidly that there is no intervening twilight between daylight and darkness to allow for the gradual cooling of the air. In the town the heat from the houses postpones the fall of dew till halfpast seven or eight o'clock. Next to exposure to the sun, probably more mischief has been caused through the effect of dews than from anything else in Zanzibar.

Not that there is anything intrinsically injurious in the dew itself; but with the conditions under which its influence is felt, it is mischievous. Sunset is the time when one generally returns heated from a walk, a ride, or a game of tennis, and to sit down in the dew and rapidly falling temperature is a certain way to invite a chill.

The breeze which is always blowing in Zanzibar, except in brief intervals between the monsoons, has an average rate of six miles, in the height of the monsoon ten or fifteen miles an hour. The northeast monsoon begins to blow about December and goes on till March. It is known locally as the Kaskas. The Kusi, or the southwest monsoon, begins with the rains of April and continues till October. Though violent squalls often sweep down upon the island, such a thing as a really heavy gale of wind is very rare. Zanzibar fortunately lies out of the track of cyclones. The only occasion on record on which Zanzibar has ever been visited by a hurricane was on August 15, 1872. It began to blow at eleven o'clock on the night of the 14th from the south or south-west, and continued until 1.30 P.M. the next day, when there was a lull of half an hour. The storm then suddenly burst upon the island in greater fury from the north, and raged for about three hours. Every ship and dhow in the harbour was driven ashore save one, an English steamship, the *Abydos*, Captain Cumming, which by steaming at full speed was able to keep her moorings. The town was wrecked, the clove and coconut plantations levelled, and many people were killed and drowned. The interior of the island must have presented a curious sight; as when one travels in it now, it is difficult to see more than a few yards in any direction, because of the abundant tree growth. Natives who remember the cyclone, declare that when the hurricane was over they could see for miles, as everything was blown flat. The storm seems to have been preceded by about a month of heavy rain and thunder storms, violent weather continuing for some time afterwards. It did not visit Pemba, so the clove trees on that island were not blown down. This partly accounts for their large size. On December 10, 1903, a severe storm from the west burst upon Zanzibar, but it was not nearly of such violence as that of 1872. It resembled the tornadoes of the west coast, and occurred just as the northeast monsoon was setting in. It may possibly be accounted for by the accumulation of a curtain of moisture in the channel between the island and the coast, formed by a deadlock between the westerly winds from the mainland and the newly-arrived north-east monsoon from the Indian Ocean, the former at length bursting through the obstruction. The storm was local, about seven miles wide, its centre striking the town, where much damage was done. Fifty dhows were driven ashore, but most of them were got off again. The plantations suffered little damage; the clove trees none at all; one boy appears to have been killed by a falling tree. The storm occurred at five o'clock in the morning, when the fishermen had not as yet gone out. Its effects were not felt on the mainland or in Pemba.

Summer lightning is almost a daily occurrence in the hot months, and the heavy rains are often accompanied by heavy thunderstorms. Yet as a general rule thunderstorms are far less severe in Zanzibar than they are in England. On September 14, 1903, a meteor of great brilliancy passed over Zanzibar about 7.30 P.M. It came out of the west and travelled almost due east, lighting up the sky like a full moon, and descended into the Indian Ocean with a loud report. It was observed in Pemba and upon the mainland, but few Europeans in Zanzibar saw it, as at that time of the day most people were in their houses. The medicine men divined, doubtless from the direction whence it came, that in the coming year trade would undergo a great stimulus; many people would come over from the mainland to trade, while in Zanzibar everyone would enjoy special freedom from epidemic diseases. Arabs with whom I have conversed, describe a magnificent display of shooting stars which they remember to have seen years ago, which I have little doubt refers to the Leonids of 1866.

Waterspouts are seen in the harbour and the channel during the stormy weather in the early part of the southwest monsoon and must often cause destruction to the small dug-outs in which the fishermen will venture for miles out to sea, even to Pemba and the mainland.

No account of the climate in Zanzibar would be complete without reference to the glorious moonlight effects that may be observed. The intensity of the moon's light at the equator, compared with that in temperate climates, is probably known to astronomers, but however it may be mathematically expressed it is certainly considerable. The nights are generally still save for the hum of insect life, the croaking of frogs in stagnant pools in the valleys, and the occasional thud of a falling palm leaf. Palm trees are for the moonlight, and all tropical vegetation seems to enjoy its cool and mellow beams, which, while they conceal the blemishes and irregularities of growth revealed by the searching and brilliant light of the sun, accentuate the grace and outline of form. No scenic effect at Earl's Court could reproduce the sweet influences of moonlight upon the harbour, with the sea like a sheet of glass; to the north the dhows, herded together within a few yards of the shore; a sailing ship or two; the mail boats each with its brood of barges and coal lighters; a war ship off Shangani, and a multitude of boats at the beach, or hurrying to and from the ships. Yellow lights glitter in the town, though feeble compared with the brilliant electric light of the Sultan's palace.

Stars, too, shine much more brilliantly at the equator than in higher latitudes, appearing within half an hour after sunset. As the nights are nearly always clear, opportunities for the study of the heavenly bodies are exceptionally favourable. The faint column of the zodiacal light, projected into the evening sky as it follows the sun through the seasons; the grand procession of the planets; the rise of the constellations are all so clearly defined, so near and so real, as to intensify the awful silence of the celestial depths.

APPENDIX I

RULERS OF ZANZIBAR

NAME.	DATE.			
Said bin Sultan	November 20,	1804	to	October 19, 1856
Majid bin Said	October 28,	1856,	"	October 7, 1870
Barghash bin Said	October 7,	1870	"	March 27, 1888
Khalifa bin Said	March 29,	1888	"	February 14, 1890
Ali bin Said	February 14,	1890	"	March 5, 1893
Hamed bin Thuwaini	March 7,	1893	"	August 25, 1896
Hamoud bin Mohammed	August 27,	1896	"	July 18, 1902
Ali bin Hamoud	July 20,	1902	Whom God preserve	

APPENDIX II

METEOROLOGICAL observations recorded by the Agricultural Department at Dunga, Dr. F. Charlesworth at Zanzibar Town, and the Friends' Industrial Mission, Banani, Pemba.

1899.

	Mean Pressure of Atmosphere	MEAN TEMPERATURES							RAIN	
		Dry Bulb	Wet Bulb	Maximum	Minimum	Daily Range	Highest	Lowest	Inches	Number of Days
Zanzibar	30.155	78.9	73.6	84.2	76.2	8.0	90.2	69.0	66.69	144
Dunga	30.023	77.9	74.0	87.3	70.7	16.6	98.1	61.5	97.94	183
Banani	...	...	...	83.3	70.2	13.1	92.0	65.0	105.24	149
Wete	...	...	...	...	...	...	...	...	96.69	47

APPENDIX II

DUNGA, 1901.

MONTHS	Mean Pressure of Atmosphere	Hygrometer Mean		Mean Temperature			Extreme Temperature			Wind Average. Miles per Hour	Cloud Amount Mean.	Rainfall		No. of Days Rain
		Dry Bulb	Wet Bulb	Maximum	Minimum Dry †	Mean Range	Highest Reed	Lowest Reed	Extreme Range		0-10	Ins.		
January	29.999	81.3	77.8	91.2	72.7	18.5	96.6	69.8	26.8	7.240	5	3.01		11
February	29.990	78.9	76.6	86.9	71.4	15.5	91.6	67.0	24.6	7.535	7	9.73		17
March	29.968	80.2	77.8	90.1	71.4	17.7	93.8	68.0	25.8	4.560	5	5.21		18
April	29.986	77.2	75.7	85.7	70.4	15.3	90.8	66.0	24.8	3.875	6	19.01		23
May	29.728	75.6	76.3	82.6	69.7	12.9	89.0	64.5	25.5	7.442	7	19.90		29
June	30.145	71.7	70.0	82.6	64.7	17.9	85.4	61.0	24.4	7.399	4	2.60		13
July	30.132	72.9	71.2	82.8	64.4	18.4	85.2	60.0	25.2	6.626	4	3.61		14
August	30.141	72.0	70.0	83.1	64.4	18.7	86.0	58.8	27.2	5.098	6	3.01		14
September	30.146	71.6	70.0	83.3	64.0	19.3	87.5	61.3	26.2	5.682	4	4.50		16
October	30.091	74.5	72.5	85.6	65.2	20.4	89.9	61.5	28.4	5.246	5	3.77		21
November	30.013	76.6	74.9	86.1	67.5	18.6	90.5	64.5	26.0	4.975	5	7.44		19
December	30.035	79.4	76.8	89.8	70.6	19.2	90.8	67.4	23.4	6.949	5	5.81		16
12 months	30.031	75.9	74.1	85.8	68.0	17.8	96.6	58.8	37.8	6.052	5.25	87.60		211

† The Minimum dry Thermometer recorded about 4 degrees too low during 1901

ZANZIBAR TOWN, 1901.

Months	Mean Pressure of Atmosphere 8 a.m.	Temperatures in the Shade							Rain			Prevailing Winds
		Means.					Extremes					
		Dry Bulb 8 a.m.	Wet Bulb 8 a.m.	Maximum 24 Hours	Minimum 24 Hours	Range 24 Hours	Highest for Month	Lowest for Month	No. of Days	Amount in Inches	Average Amount for 18 years	
January	30.073	83.2	77.7	88.0	80.8	7.2	89.7	76.8	9	3.87	3.60	North Easterly.
February	30.064	81.6	77.3	86.5	79.1	7.4	88.4	73.2	12	9.08	3.11	Do. do.
March	30.068	82.9	78.0	88.3	80.8	7.5	90.7	76.0	14	4.67	6.70	Variable.
April	30.064	80.7	76.9	85.6	78.2	7.4	89.2	71.9	17	17.97	13.64	South Westerly.
May	30.126	78.5	75.3	84.4	76.4	8.0	87.7	72.1	22	17.47	9.45	Do. do.
June	30.207	74.8	71.3	81.3	72.9	9.4	83.8	71.1	10	2.06	1.38	Do. do.
July	30.194	74.6	71.2	81.5	72.7	8.8	82.6	71.0	7	1.63	3.80	Do. do.
August	30.212	74.8	71.2	81.2	72.5	8.7	83.3	70.8	10	1.20	1.51	Do. do.
September	30.245	75.3	71.5	81.3	72.1	9.2	85.0	69.7	13	2.87	2.71	South Easterly
October	30.152	78.2	74.1	83.5	74.7	8.8	87.2	72.8	16	2.16	3.06	Variable.
November	30.119	80.4	75.5	85.0	76.4	8.6	87.2	74.3	22	6.60	7.78	Do.
December	30.075	82.5	77.2	86.3	79.0	7.3	88.6	77.2	17	4.07	8.18	North Easterly.
	30.133	79.0	74.8	84.4	74.6	8.2	86.9	73.1	169	73.65	64.92	

The *Temperatures* generally were somewhat below the average throughout the year. The lowest recorded was 69.7 on September 1st, and the highest 90.7 On March 22nd.
The *Rainfall* was about 9 inches above the average, mostly accounted for by the heavy rains of April and May. The heaviest rainfall in any 24 hours was that of April 13th-14th, which measured 4.47 inches. Rain fell on 169 days, being some 50 days above the average.
The *South monsoon* set in on the night of April 8th-9th, about the same date as last year.
The *North monsoon* blew steadily from December 5th and has been stronger and accompanied by more squalls than for some years.

BANANI, PEMBA, 1901.

1901.	Mean max.	Mean min.	Absolute max.	Absolute min.	Rainy days.	Rain-fall.
January...	84-S6	73-80	90.0	70.0	13	4.00
February...	82-50	71-90	85-0	68.0	13	12.09
March...	85-80	74.23	90-5	72-5	12	6-54
April...	81.90	70.62	87.0	70.0	23	20.79
May...	80.22	70-05	84.0	68.0	25	27.40
June...	78-90	68. 10	830	66.0	16	3.23
July...	78-46	67-10	80-0	66.0	14	3-06
August...	79.16	67.26	82.0	66.0	11	0.93
September...	80-53	67-38	83.0	65-0	5	0.90
October...	83-18	69.50	86.0	67.0	8	2.73
November...	82-93	71-48	87.0	70.0	13	7-50
December...	83-50	73-00	87.0	71-0	13	3.61
Year...	81-80	70-37	90. 5	650	166	92-78

HIGHEST TEMPERATURE TAKEN IN SUN 175°.

Years.	Mean max.	Mean min.	Absolute max.	Absolute min.	Rainy days.	Rain-fall.
1899...	83.30	70.20	92-00	65: 00	149	105.24
1900...	83.50	71-30	95-00	66	160	90-35
1901...	81.80	70-37	90-50	65-00	166	92-78

DUNGA, 1902.

MONTH	Mean Pressure of Atmosphere	Hydrometer Mean		Temperature Mean			Temperature Extreme			Wind average miles per hour	Cloud amount mean	Rainfall	No. of days rain
		Dry Bulb.	Wet Bulb	Maximum	Minimum	Mean Range	Highest Record	Lowest Record	Extreme Range			Inches.	
		o	o	o	o	o	o	o	o				
January...	29.981	80.3	75.7	91.4	75.0	16.4	94.3	70.5	23.8	8.817	6.5	0.23	6
February...	30.038	80.4	75.5	92.4	74.9	17.5	95.5	71.2	24.3	9.114	6.2	8.20	8
March...		80.2	77.3	90.0	72.8	17.2	94.1	66.0	28.1			11.66	20
April...	29.998	78.6	76.8	86.6	73.5	13.1	90.2	70.6	19.6	9.317	6.4	14.80	27
May...	30.078	76.6	75.3	85.4	70.3	15.1	89.1	67.8	21.3	6.287	6.3	17.04	18
June...	30.853	73.1	71.8	84.3	67.2	17.1	87.0	64.4	22.6	5.520	5.5	2.80	13
July...	30.119	73.7	72.2	83.8	66.7	17.1	87.1	62.3	24.8	6.726	4.5	3.04	12
August...	30.112	74.9	74.8	84.7	65.1	19.6	88.8	62.0	26.8	5.648	6.7	0.87	11
September...	30.127	76.7	73.7	85.4	66.2	19.2	89.4	64.2	25.2	5.260	6.6	2.13	11
October...	30.027	77.9	74.3	86.0	67.4	18.6	89.8	64.8	25.0	5.356		5.95	15
November...	31.700	75.2	73.2	87.5	72.8	14.7	93.0	69.0	26.0	3.757		9.38	20
December...	30.160	79.7	77.1	87.8	73.7	14.1	92.0	71.2	20.8	5.260		9.51	14
12 Months...	30.290	77.2	74.8	87.1	70.4	16.6	95.5	62.0	33.3	6.460	6.0	85.61	1.175

ZANZIBAR TOWN, 1902.

MONTH	Mean pressure of Atmosphere 8 a.m.	Temperature in shade — Means					Temperature in shade — Extremes			Rain			Prevailing winds
		Dry bulb 8 a.m.	Wet bulb 8 a.m.	Maximum 24 hrs	Minimum 24 hrs	Range 24 hrs	Highest for month	Lowest for month	Range	No. of days	Amount in inches	Average amount for 18 years	
January...	30.056	81.5	76.4	87.5	79.4	8.1	87.9	78.0	9.8	6	0.22	3.60	N.E.
February...	30.113	81.3	76.4	86.8	79.0	7.8	89.1	76.0	13.1	9	3.83	3.11	N.E.
March...	30.042	82.5	78.0	87.4	79.7	7.7	89.7	76.5	13.2	17	6.25	6.70	Variable
April...	30.065	80.7	76.9	86.1	78.0	8.1	89.0	74.8	14.2	26	9.79	13.64	Variable to 13th S.W. Monsoon April 14th.
May...	30.128	78.7	75.4	84.5	77.0	7.5	87.8	72.2	15.6	16	13.23	9.45	S.W.
June...	30.164	77.1	73.4	83.5	75.1	8.4	85.3	73.6	11.7	5	0.66	1.38	S.W.
July...	30.194	76.0	72.5	85.7	73.9	11.8	84.1	71.2	12.9	9	4.94	3.80	S.W.
August	30.170	76.1	72.0	83.2	73.7	9.5	85.0	72.0	13.0	5	0.61	1.51	S.W.
September	30.181	77.0	74.0	84.6	75.1	9.5	86.8	73.0	13.8	17	2.63	2.71	Southerly.
October	30.150	79.0	74.8	83.9	75.1	8.8	87.0	72.0	15.0	21	6.38	3.06	S.E.
November	30.160	81.0	76.8	85.8	78.0	7.8	91.6	73.4	18.2	18	7.33	7.78	Variable.
December	30.058	81.1	77.1	87.3	78.7	8.6	93.0	74.8	18.2	17	10.43	8.18	N. Monsoon 3rd N.E.
12 months...	30.123	79.3	75.3	85.5	76.8	8.6	93.0	71.2	21.8	166	66.30	64.92	

BANANI, PEMBA, 1902.

1902.	Mean max. 0	Mean min. 0	Absolute max. 0	Absolute min. 0	Wet days	Rain-fall.
January	83.39	72.24	87.00	70.00	2	0.05
February	83.23	72.17	88.00	70.50	8	3.31
March	86.00	74.00	91.00	71.50	17	6.35
April...	84.25	73.66	87.00	72.00	21	11.16
May...	82.00	72.23	85.00	70.00	20	8.97
June...	81.07	70.00	83.50	68.00	7	2.69
July...	79.67	68.69	82.00	67.00	8	3.06
August	80.14	68.70	82.00	67.00	3	0.13
September	82.18	69.40	85.50	67.00	4	0.76
October	83.34	70.20	86.50	68.00	10	4.18
November	83.50	72.10	88.00	70.00	21	23.00
December	84.71	73.43	89.00	70.00	11	5.06
For the year.	82.79	71.40	91.00	67.00	132	68.72

RAINFALL.

	Zanzibar.	Dunga.	Banani.
1898	27.49 ...	14.98 (7 months)	
1899	66.69 ...	97.94 ...	105.24
1900	74.05 ...	(79.09) ...	90.35
1901	73.65 ...	87.60 ...	92.78
1902	66.30 ...	85.61 ...	68.72

APPENDIX II

DUNGA. 1903.

MONTHS	Mean pressure of atmosphere	Hygrometer Mean		Temperature Mean			Temperature Extreme			Wind average Miles per hour	Cloud amount mean	Rainfall	Number of days
		Dry bulb	Wet Bulb	Maximum	Minimum	Mean Average	Highest Recorded	Lowest Recorded	Extreme Range				
January...	30.009	80.6	77.9	90.5	74.7	15.8	93.2	72.4	20.8	6.012	-	3·07	10
February...	30.033	80.1	77.2	89.3	73.8	15.5	93.8	71.2	22.6	6.012	-	5.67	9
March...	29.969	80.5	78.6	88.6	74.4	12.2	91.0	71.0	20.0	4.509	-	10.22	17
April...	29.986	77.7	76.7	85.9	73.3	12.6	92.1	70.4	21.7	4.508	-	12.05	21
May ...	30.040	75.8	74.8	83.8	71.9	11.9	85.4	66.9	19.5	6.012	-	9.15	16
June...	30.086	74.3	73.2	84.2	70.1	14.1	86.5	65.4	21.1	6.001	-	0.76	5
July ...	30.122	73.5	71.5	83.4	70.3	13.1	92.0	65.0	27.0	6.764	-	2.92	11
August	30.121	73.3	71.6	83.4	68.4	15.0	87.0	62.4	24.6	6.012	-	5.77	14
September	30.139	74.2	72.4	83.1	68.4	14.7	86.0	66.0	20.0	6.012	-	3.40	16
October	-	75.8	73.9	86.3	68.7	17.6	94.0	65.4	28.6	5.261	-	4.41	10
November	-	81.8	76.4	87.8	72.9	14.9	94.0	69.0	25.0	6.012	-	4.74	4
December	29.999	79.2	75.9	88.8	74.7	14.1	93.5	68.5	25.0	5.260	-	12.82	5
Year	30.050	77.2	75.0	86.2	71.8	14.4	94.0	62.4	31.6	5.697	-	74.98	138

251

ZANZIBAR TOWN, 1903.

MONTHS	Mean pressure of atmosphere	Temperature in shade						Extremes			Rain	
		Means										
		Dry bulb 8 a.m.	Wet bulb 8 a.m.	Maximum 24 hrs	Minimum 24 hrs	Range 24 hrs		Highest for month	Lowest for month	Range	Number of days	Amount in inches
January...	30.072	85.8	81.1	93.1	83.0	10.1		90.7	76.0	14.7	13	2.17
February	30.098	82.6	77.7	86.8	79.5	7.3		89.4	75.4	14.0	9	3.87
March...	30.303	83.8	71.9	89.1	79.1	10.0		91.4	75.4	16.0	13	4.37
April...	30.345	81.0	77.0	85.8	78.4	7.4		90.0	76.0	14.0	19	8.56
May...	30.109	78.3	75.3	84.0	76.0	8.0		87.0	72.3	14.7	19	11.92
June...	30.156	76.9	73.7	84.2	78.0	6.2		85.9	73.0	12.9	4	0.87
July...	30.196	75.6	71.9	83.0	73.8	11.2		84.6	72.1	12.5	8	1.25
August...	30.179	76.2	73.6	82.8	73.4	9.4		85.0	72.1	13.5	11	2.72
September	30.212	77.3	73.4	83.1	74.2	8.9		86.0	70.9	15.1	7	2.17
October	30.135	79.2	75.2	85.1	75.4	9.7		88.0	73.9	14.1	9	3.02
November	30.124	81.2	76.0	85.6	77.5	8.1		89.4	77.2	12.2	16	6.12
December	30.040	81.7	77.3	86.0	78.8	7.2		88.7	69.7	19.0	13	6.77
Year	30.164	79.9	75.3	85.7	77.4	8.3		88.0	73.7	14.3	141	52.81

APPENDIX II

BANANI, PEMBA, 1903

1903-	Mean Max.	Mean Min.	Absolute Max.	Absolute Min.	Rainy Days.	Rainfall.
January...	84.60	73.90	90.00	70.50	5	4.90
February...	84.60	73.12	89.50	71.00	4	2.00
March...	86.70	75.19	91.50	71.50	5	1.40
April...	83.10	72.50	86.50	70.00	24	13.09
May...	80.30	71.00	85.00	68.50	24	17.93
June...	81.35	70.48	83.00	69.00	13	5.22
July...	79.37	69.04	82.00	66.00	15	3.15
August...	79.51	68.45	84.00	67.00	14	1.14
September.	80.90	68.6o	84.00	67.50	6	0.52
October...	82.83	70.01	86.00	68.00	2	1.91
Novembe...	80.90	71.68	86.00	70.00	11	2.65
December	83.16	72.26	87.00	70.00	15	9.33
Yea...	82.28	71.43	86.21	69.08	138	63.24

Months	Mean elastic force of vapour	Temperature of air						Mean temperature of		Mean weight of water in a cubic foot of air	Mean additional weight of water required to saturate a cubic foot of air	Mean degree of humidity (Saturation = 1)	Mean weight of a cubic foot of air	Wind		Rain		Mean amount of clouds
		Highest	Lowest	Mean of all the Highest	Mean of all the lowest	Mean daily range	Mean	Evaporation	Dew point					Duration	Strength	Number of days if it fell	Amount fallen	
	in.	°	°	°	°	°	°	°	°	grs	grs		grs		lbs		in.	
January	0.995	87	80	85.7	81.2	4.5	83.3	79.9	78.2	9.95	0.88	0.91	No barometer observed in Zanzibar	N.E.	0-4	2	2.70	4-6
February	0.791	88	79	86.2	80.7	5.5	83.4	76.4	72.9	8.27	1.53	0.87		N.E.	0-4	1	2.10	4-6
March	0.968	88	79.5	85.9	80.7	5.2	82.5	79.8	78.4	10.00	0.78	0.91		Easterly Variable	0-2	10	6.31	4-6
April	1.042	86	78	83	80	3.0	81.5	80.5	79.3	10.35	0.60	0.96		S. to S.W.	2-4	16	16.30	5-6
May	0.928	83	70.5	79.5	77.6	1.9	78.0	77.7	77.3	9.80	0.16	0.99		S.W. to S.S.W.	4-6	15	9.18	5-6
June	0.879	82.5	75.5	80	76.8	3.2	78.4	76.8	76.0	9.44	0.10	0.96		S.W. to Variable	2-4	3	0.55	5-6
July	0.913	81.5	74	79	75.3	3.7	77.1	77.0	77.0	9.89	...	1.00		Variable / S.W to S.S.E	2-4	9	3.42	5-6
August	0.891	81.5	74.5	18.8	15.8	3.0	77.3	76.8	76.6	9.70	0.10	0.99		Variable / S.W. to S.S.E.	2-5	6	3.12	4-6
September	0.834	82	73.5	79.5	75.3	4.2	77.4	75.2	73.1	8.49	0.91	0.91		S.W. to E.S.E.	2-4	12	3.80	4-6
October	0.855	83	75	81.2	77.1	4.1	79.1	76.4	74.5	9.74	0.85	0.91		S.W. to E.S.E	1-3	15	11.83	4-6
November	0.844	84.5	76	80.8	78.8	2.0	79.8	78.5	77.8	10.01	0.35	0.97		S.W. to E.S.S.	1-4	14	8.39	4-6
December	(No observations for December, the person who tookthem being obliged to quit the place on account of ill-health.)																	

APPENDIX III
FINANCE

THE revenues of Zanzibar are derived chiefly from import and export duties, shipping dues, registration and market fees, a tax of two dollars on each hut, and from the Post Office and Crown property. There are also considerable revenues from the continental territories; the British East Africa Administration pays £11,000 annually for the ten mile wide coast strip of that Protectorate; the interest on the £200,000 received from Germany amounts annually to £6,000, and the rent paid by the Italian Benadir Company amounted to £8,000 a year. Under the arrangement made in January, 1905, the Italian Government takes over from the company the administration of the Benadir Territory, having acquired from Zanzibar sovereign rights on payment of the sum of £ 144,000 at once, instead of an annual rent.

The revenue from customs, the total revenue (exclusive of loans) and the total expenditure in twelve years are shown as follows:-

| Years | REVENUE ||||| EXPENDITURE |
| | From Customs |||| Total Revenue | |
	Import Duties	Export Duties	Other sources	Total customs		
£	£	£	£	£	£	£
1892	3,880	32,030	10,740	46,650	72,113	70,980
1893	1500	32,746	5,567	39,813	74,336	72,706
1894	317	33,118	6,605	40,040	96,770	94,693
1895	1,487	39,863	7,793	49,143	113,404	101,623
1896	1,529	25,927	7,571	35,027	102,594	142,029
1897	1,978	25,155	8,601	35,734	105,363	117,479
1898	7,382	44,338	10,420	62,140	127,528	121,335
1899	12,673	46,866	11,565	71,104	118,249	133,374
1900	25,104	31,719	11,033	67,856	114,565	131,892
1901	23,490	40,007	11,528	75,025	123,328	121,581
1902	22,916	36,614	10,869	70,399	148,112	140,119
1903	24,592	40,418	9,062	74,072	148,590	121,429

The outstanding debt of Zanzibar, at the end of 1894, and subsequent years, was:-

Years.	Debt.	Years.	Debt.
	£		£
1894	35,000	1899	83,000
1895	35,000	1900	83,000
1896	35,000	1901	96,000
1897	35,000	1902	100,000
1898	48,000	1903	95,333

APPENDIX IV
COMMERCE

TOTAL VALUE OF IMPORTS AND EXPORTS into and from the PORT Of ZANZIBAR during each of the Years ended December 31, 1892 to 1903.

Years	IMPORTS			EXPORTS		
	Total imports including bullion and specie	Imports of bullion and specie	Imports from the United Kingdom including bullion and specie	Total exports including bullion and specie	Exports of bullion and specie	Exports to the United Kingdom including bullion and specie
	£	£	£	£	£	£
1892	1,185,330	No stated	102,338	908,036	Not stated	105,028
1893	1,146,759	74,740	93,793	1,002,035	119,233	111,806
1894	1,197,681	69,804	96,296	1,096,240	125,109	167,913
1895	1,293,646	132,488	91,163	1,199,841	Not stated	152,594
1896	1,275,470	80,003	118,022	1,158,806	137,557	129,199
1897	1,399,078	118,592	159,894	1,189,668	150,952	162,422
1898	1,555,070	115,619	121,211	1.497,883	205,730	114,716
1899	1,596,606	100,163	146.143	1,513,407	176,438	116,964
1900 (a)	1,116,041	94,715	106,400	1,167,794	137,817	106,165
1901	196,831	166,048	107,205	1,168,518	149,355	83,095
1902	1,106,247	48,206	156,503	1,080,277	108,194	90,852
1903	1,033,135	89,601	114,846	1,054,846	89,149	88,777

NOTE. -Conversions into £ sterling have been made at the rate of 1s. 3d. per rupee in 1892 and 1893; 1s. 11/4d in 1894 and 1895; 1s. 21/3d. in 1896; 1s. 31/2d. in 1897, and 1s. 4d. in later years.

(a) The trade carried on with other portions of the Sultan's dominions is excluded after the year 1899.

The value of the imports and exports at the port of Zanzibar from and to each country in 1900 and subsequent years was as follows:-

From or to	Imports				Exports			
	1900. £	1901. £	1902. £	1903. £	1900. £	1901. £	1902. £	1903. £
United Kingdom	106,400	107,205	156,503	114,088	106,165	83,095	90,852	88,777
British India	405,902	401,528	301,806	379,924	123,123	1311311	120,238	159,563
British East Africa	72,507	82,469	78,423	73,327	101,520	129,748	153,367	82,567
Other British Possessions	25,494	39,998	30,388	20,792	18,727	16,979	13,918	16,138
Germany	67,331	62,974	75,158	57,891	35,592	45,200	63,672	56,879
German East Africa	180,628	223,878	202,797	176,796	437,811	406,398	295,516	332,929
Holland	4,944	58,096	59,617	39,023	37,673	31,513	33,168	10,450
Belgium	51,066	11,368	2,700	–	–	–	–	–
France	23,560	17,016	17,724	15,050	55,907	124,521	132,929	117,446
Benadir Coast	44,115	34,894	39,513	36,725	38,508	38,54	46,869	37,758
Southern ports of Africa	32,995	30,239	21,673	16,286	113,503	63,564	53,586	54,108
United States	60,781	67,126	80,480	48,993	81,477	76,765	59,680	67,631
Austria-Hungary	3,438	6,704	5,240	–	1,802	700	5,671	–
Italy		5,095	3,130	*				–
Norway	40,318	6,690	4,288	*	117,788	19,108	–	2,162
Arabia		44,817	17,959	18,168			9,079	23,795
Other foreign countries			7,384	30,832			6,073	
Total	1,116,04	11,196,831	1,106,247	1,033,135	1,167,794	1,168,518	1,080,277	1,054,846

* Included in "Other Foreign Countries."

APPENDIX V
RATES OF CUSTOMS DUTIES ON IMPORTS AND EXPORTS

ARTICLES.	RATES.
Import Duties.	
Beeswax, coal, coins, Colombo root, copal, copra, gum arabic, gunny bags, hides, hippopotamus teeth, ivory, orchella weed, rhinoceros horns, rubber, shells, skins, sim-sim, and tortoiseshell	Free.
Distilled liquors, at 50° Gay Lussac alcoholometer at 15°C.	per gallon 2 rupees.
All other goods	ad valorem 5 per cent.
Export Duties.	
Ebony, shells, tobacco	ad valorem 5 per cent.
Orchella weed, borities (Zanzibar poles and rafters), chillies, hippopotamus teeth, hides, rhinoceros horns, and tortoiseshell ...	ad valorem 10 per cent.
Ground nuts and sim-sim ...	12 "
Copal, ivory, and rubber ...	15 "
Cloves, stems, and mother of cloves...	25 "
Grain ... ... per 360 lbs	35 cents.
Rice in husks	25 "
Chiroko beans	1 dollar 10c
Camels ... ... each	2 dollars.
Cattle and donkeys...	1 dollar.
Horses	10 dollars.
Sheep and goats	25 cents.

Importation of alcoholic liquors for consumption by natives is not permitted.

APPENDIX VI
SHIPPING

The port of Zanzibar is visited by the vessels of the British India Steam Navigation Company, the German East Africa line, and the Messageries Maritimes. In 1903 the Austrian Lloyd Company began a service between Trieste and Durban, the vessels calling at Zanzibar. The number and tonnage of vessels engaged in the foreign trade that entered the port in twelve calendar years are given as follows:-

Year.	British.		Foreign.		Total.	
	No.	Tons.	No.	Tons.	No.	Tons.
1892	44	48,677	105	167,769	149	216,446
1893	45	58,483	84	129,299	129	187,782
1894	44	71,235	82	122,251	126	193,486
1895	70	99,175	100	144,467	170	243,642
1896	64	98,273	96	145,993	160	244,266
1897	48	75,013	102	170,355	150	245,368
1898	62	91,269	121	194,940	183	286,209
1899	69	103,457	129	221,504	198	324,961
1900	62	107,983	145	240,422	207	348,405
1901	55	92,504	113	205,236	168	297,740
1902	70	123,275	123	229,630	193	352,905
1903	83	162,466	143	278,250	226	440,716

APPENDIX VI

The nationality of the vessels which entered in 1902 and 1903 was as follows:-

Nationality.	1902.		1903.	
	No.	Tons.	No.	Tons.
British ...	70	123,275	83	162,466
Austro-Hungarian	4	6,962	12	26,344
French ...	25	48,602	24	49,349
German ...	89	168,075	100	196,602
Norwegian ...	4	5073	6	4259
Others ...	1	818	1	1,696
Total ...	193	352,905	226	440,716

The increase in the number and tonnage of the vessels which entered in 1903 was due partly to re-arrangement of the traffic by the British India and German East Africa lines, their vessels having visited the port more frequently, and partly to the inauguration of the Austrian Lloyd service.

APPENDIX VII

Fairly representative samples of the soils of Zanzibar Island were in January, 1897, sent home to Dr. Augustus Voelker, consulting chemist to the Royal Agricultural Society of England. The following are the figures of the Analyses:-

No. 1.

	Dried at 212° F.
*Organic matter and loss on heating	3.83
Oxide of Iron	2.28
Alumina	5.34
Lime	0.23
Magnesia	0.33
Potash	0.15
Soda	0.07
Phosphoric Acid	0.05
Sulphuric Acid	0.02
Insoluble Silicates and Sand	87.70
	100.00
*Containing Nitrogen	0.09

No- 3-

Dried at 212° F.

*Organic matter and loss on beating	8.20
Oxide of Iron	6.49
Alumina	15.06
Lime	0.40
Magnesia	0.37
Potash	0.29
Soda	0.10

APPENDIX VII

Phosphoric Acid	0.26
Sulpburic Acid	0.03
Insoluble Silicates and Sand... ...	68.83
	100.00
*Containing Nitrogen	0. 16

263

BIBLIOGRAPHY
FEBRUARY 21, 1853

A Bill for carrying into effect the Engagement between Her Majesty and Syed Syf bin Hamood.

A.D. 1869.

A Bill to regulate and extend the jurisdiction of Her Majesty's Consul at Zanzibar.

January 24, 1870.

Report addressed to the Earl of Clarendon by the Committee on the East African Slave Trade.

January 1 to December 31, 1870.

Class B, East Coast of Africa. Correspondence respecting the Slave Trade and other matters.

August 4, 1871

Report Slave Trade (East Coast of Africa).

1872-73.

Correspondence respecting Sir Bartle Frere's Mission to East Coast of Africa. Slave Trade, No. 2 (1874).

Treaty between Her Majesty and the Sultan of Zanzibar for the suppression of the Slave Trade. Signed at Zanzibar, June 5, 1873.

Slave Trade, NO. 5 (1874).

Reports on the present state of the East African Slave Trade.

Slave Trade, No- 7 (1874).

Further reports on East African Slave Trade. (In continuation of Slave Trade, NO. 5, 1874.)

Slave Trade, No. 8 (1874).

Correspondence with British Representatives and Agents, and reports from Naval Officers, relative to the East African Slave Trade. From January 1 to December 31, 1873.

1873-74.

Administration report of Zanzibar and its Dominions for the years 1873-74.

Slave Trade, No. 9 (1874).
Papers relating to the emancipation of the Negroes of Puerto Rico.
Slave Trade, June 1, 1875.
Return to an Order of the Honourable House of Commons.
Slave Trade, No. 1 (1875).
Correspondence with British Representatives and Agents abroad and reports from Naval Officers, relative to the African Slave Trade.
Zanzibar, No. 1 (1876).
Treaty between Her Malesty and the Sultan of Zanzibar, supplementary to the Treaty for the suppression of the Slave Trade of June 5, 1873. Signed at London, July 14, 1875.
Slave Trade, No. 3 (1876).
Communications from Dr. Kirk, respecting the suppression of the land slave traffic in the dominions of the Sultan of Zanzibar.
Slave Trade, NO. 4 (1876).
Correspondence with British Representatives and Agents abroad, and reports from Naval Officers, relating to the Slave Trade.
Slave Trade, No. 5 (1876).
Instructions respecting reception of fugitive slaves on board Her Majesty's ships.
Slave Trade, No. 2 (1877).
Correspondence with British Representatives and Agents abroad, and reports from Naval Officers relating to the Slave Trade.
Slave Trade, NO. 3 (1878).
Correspondence with British Representatives and Agents abroad, and reports from Naval Officers, relating to the Slave Trade.
Slave Trade, NO. 4 (1878)-
Annual reports of the Commander-in-Chief in the East Indies on the Slave Trade,
Slave Trade, No. 1 (1879)-
Correspondence with British Representatives and Agents abroad, and reports from Naval Officers, relating to the Slave Trade.
Slave Trade, No. 5 (1880).
Correspondence with British Representatives and Agents abroad, and reports from Naval Officers and the Treasury, relative to the Slave Trade.

Slave Trade, No. 1 (18k).
Correspondence with British Representatives and Agents abroad, and reports from Naval Officers and the Treasury, relative to the Slave Trade.

Slave Trade, No. 1 (1882).
Correspondence with British Representatives and Agents abroad, and reports from Naval Officers and the Treasury, relative to the Slave Trade.

Slave Trade, No. 1 (1883).
Correspondence with British Representatives and Agents abroad, and reports from Naval Officers and the Treasury, relative to the Slave Trade, 1882-83.

Slave Trade, No. 1 (1884).
Correspondence with British Representatives and Agents abroad, and reports from Naval Officers and the Treasury, relative to the Slave Trade, 1883-84.

Slave Trade, No. 1 (1885).
Correspondence with British Representatives and Agents abroad, and reports from Naval Officers and the Treasury, relative to the Slave Trade, 1884-85

Slave Trade, No. 1 (1886).
Correspondence with British Representatives and Agents abroad, and reports from Naval Officers and the Treasury relative to the Slave Trade, 1885.

Africa, No. 1 (1886).
Correspondence relating to Zanzibar.

Africa, No. 1 (1887)
Treaty of Friendship, Commerce, and Navigation between Her Majesty and His Highness the Sultan of Zanzibar. *Signed at Zanzibar, April 30, 1886.*

Africa, No. 3 (IS87).
Further correspondence relating to Zanzibar. (In continuation of "Africa, No. 1, 1886." C, 4,6og.)

Slave Trade, No. 1 (1887).
Correspondence relative to the Slave Trade, 1886.

Slave Trade, No. 1 (1888).
Correspondence relative to the Slave Trade, 1887.

Africa, No. 6 (1888).
Correspondence respecting suppression of Slave Trade in East African Waters.

Africa, No. 7 (1888).
Reports on Slave Trade on the East Coast of Africa, 1887-88.

Africa, No. 10 (1888).
Further correspondence respecting Germany on Zanzibar.
Slave Trade, No. 1 (1889).
Correspondence relative to the Slave Trade, 1888-89.
Africa, No. 1 (1889).
Further correspondence respecting Germany and Zanzibar.
Africa, No. 1 (1890-91).
Anti-Slavery decree issued by the Sultan of Zanzibar, dated August 1, 1890.
Africa, NO. 3 (1890-91).
Correspondence respecting the Punitive Expedition against Witu, of November, 1890
Africa, No. 5 (1890).
Despatch to Sir E. Malet respecting the affairs of East Africa.
Africa, No. 4 (1891).
Declaration between Great Britain and Zanzibar, relative to the Exercise of judicial Powers in Zanzibar.
Africa, No. 6 (1892).
Papers relative to Slave Trade and Slavery in Zanzibar.
Treaty Series, No. 7, 1892.
General Act of the Brussels Conference relative to the African Slave Trade.
Treaty Series, No. 3 4893).
Declaration between Great Britain and Zanzibar respecting the exercise of judicial Powers in Zanzibar.
Africa, No. 4 (1893)
Reports on Zanzibar Protectorate.
Africa, No. 6 4893).
Paper respecting the Traffic in Slaves in Zanzibar.
Africa, No. 9 (1893).
Correspondence relating to Witu.
Treaty Series, No. 10 (1893).
Agreement between Great Britain and Portugal relative to Spheres of Influence North of the Zambesi.
Africa, No. 12 4893).
Returns of Slaves freed in Zanzibar Waters through Her Majesty's Ships, 1892-93.

Treaty Series, No. 14 (1893).
Arrangement between Great Britain and Germany respecting the Boundaries in East Africa.
Treaty Series, No. 17 (1893).
Agreement between Great Britain and Germany respecting Boundaries in Africa.
Treaty Series, No. 17 4894).
Protocol between Great Britain and Italy respecting the Demarcation of their respective Spheres of Influence in Eastern Africa.
Zanzibar Indemnity, A.D. 1894
A Bill for authorising the Treasury to indemnify the Bank of England with respect to the Transfer of Consolidated Bank Annuities standing in the name of the late Sultan of Zanzibar.
Africa, No. 6 (1895).
Correspondence respecting Slavery in Zanzibar.
Zanzibar, No. 1765.
Report for the year 1895 on the Trade of Zanzibar.
Treaty Series, No. 3 (1896).
Agreement between Great Britain and Portugal.
Africa, No. 6 (1896).
Correspondence respecting the recent Rebellion in British East Africa.
Africa, No. 7 (1896).
Correspondence respecting Slavery in the Zanzibar Dominions.
Africa, No. 1 4897).
Instructions to Mr. Hardinge respecting the Abolition of Legal Status of Slavery in the Islands, of Zanzibar and Pemba.
Africa, No. 2 (1897).
Abolition of the Legal Status of Slavery in Zanzibar and Pemba.
Africa, No. 7 (1897).
Report by Sir A. Hardinge on the Condition and Progress of the East Africa Protectorate from its Establishment to the: 20th July, 1897.
Africa, No. 6 (1898).
Correspondence respecting the abolition of the Legal Status of Slavery in Zanzibar and Pemba.
Africa.

Diplomatic and Consular Reports. Reports on the Island of Pemba for the year 1900.

Germany.

Diplomatic and Consular Report. Report on German East Africa for the year 1900.

Diplomatic and Consular Reports. Report on German Colonies for the year 1900-01

Africa, No. 7 (1904

Report by His Majesty's Special Commissioner on the Protectorate of Uganda.

Africa, No. 9 (1901).

Report by His Majesty's Commissioner on the East Africa Protectorate.

Zanzibar.

Diplomatic and Consular Reports. Trade of Zanzibar for the year 1902.

Africa, No. 6 (1903).

Report by His Majesty's Commissioner on the East Africa Protectorate.

Africa, No. 10 (1904).

Memorandum on the State of the African Protectorates administered under the Foreign Office.

The Persian Gulf. Bombay Selection, No. 24, 1856.

Report on the Zanzibar Dominions, Bombay Selections No. LIX. New Series, 1861. LIEUT.-COLONEL C. P. RIGBY.

Precis of Information concerning the British East Africa Protectorate and Zanzibar. Revised in the Intelligence Divisions, War Office, December, 1900.

The Map of Africa by Treaty. HERTSLET.

Narrative of Voyages to explore the Shores of Africa, Arabia, and Madagascar; performed in H.M. Ships *Leven* and *Barracouta*, under the direction of Captain W. F. W. OWEN, R.N., by command of the Lords Commissioners of the Admiralty. 1833.

Imams and Seyyids of Oman. BADGER.

Missionary Labours in Eastern Africa. KRAPF.

Zanzibar. BURTON.

Memoirs of an Arabian Princess.

Dhow Chasing. SULIVAN.

Rise of our East African Empire. LUGARD.

The Foundation of British East Africa. J. W. GREGORY.

The Partition of Africa. J. S. KELTIE.
The Mission to Uganda. PORTAL.
Letters of Bishop Tozer, 1863-873. Edited by GERTRUDE WARD.
A Memoir of Bishop Steere. R. M. HEANLEY.
Life of Bishop Smythies.
The History of the Universities' Mission to Central Africa, 1859-98.
Banani. The Transition from Slavery to Freedom in Zanzibar and Pemba. H. S. NEWMAN.
The Universities' Mission to Central Africa Atlas.
Die Portugiesenzeit von Deutsch und Englisch-Ostafrika.